PROFESSIONALIZATION AND PARTICIPATION IN CHILD AND YOUTH CARE

Professionalization and Participation in Child and Youth Care
Challenging understandings in theory and practice

Edited by

E.J. KNORTH
Leiden University

P.M. VAN DEN BERGH
Leiden University

F. VERHEIJ
Erasmus University Rotterdam

LONDON AND NEW YORK

First published 2002 by Ashgate Publishing

Reissued 2018 by Routledge
2 Park Square, Milton Park, Abingdon, Oxon OX14 4RN
711 Third Avenue, New York, NY 10017, USA

Routledge is an imprint of the Taylor & Francis Group, an informa business

Copyright © E.J. Knorth, P.M. Van den Bergh and F. Verheij 2002

Erik J. Knorth, Peter M. Van den Bergh and Fop Verheij have asserted their right under the Copyright, Designs and Patents Act, 1988, to be identified as the Authors of this work.

All rights reserved. No part of this book may be reprinted or reproduced or utilised in any form or by any electronic, mechanical, or other means, now known or hereafter invented, including photocopying and recording, or in any information storage or retrieval system, without permission in writing from the publishers.

Notice:
Product or corporate names may be trademarks or registered trademarks, and are used only for identification and explanation without intent to infringe.

Publisher's Note
The publisher has gone to great lengths to ensure the quality of this reprint but points out that some imperfections in the original copies may be apparent.

Disclaimer
The publisher has made every effort to trace copyright holders and welcomes correspondence from those they have been unable to contact.

A Library of Congress record exists under LC control number: 2002019413

ISBN 13: 978-1-138-72824-0 (hbk)
ISBN 13: 978-1-138-72822-6 (pbk)
ISBN 13: 978-1-315-19004-4 (ebk)

Contents

List of Contributors   *ix*
Foreword   *xiii*
Acknowledgements   *xv*

1   Professionalization and Participation in Child and Youth Care: Two Sides of One Coin?
  Erik J. Knorth, Peter M. Van den Bergh and Fop Verheij   1

PART I: HISTORICAL PERSPECTIVES

2   Demystification in the Century of the Child: The Conflict between Romanticism and Disenchantment in (Residential) Youth Care from the 1830s to 2000
  Jeroen J.H. Dekker   27

3   The Century of the Participating Child
  Micha De Winter   49

PART II: PROFESSIONALIZATION

4   Child and Youth Care Work at the Cross-Roads of the Century: From a Recognized Profession Back to an Amateur Humanitarian Mission?
  Emmanuel Grupper   65

5   Building a Professional Identity: The Challenge for Residential Child and Youth Care
  Margaret Lindsay   75

6   Knowing a Way toward Professional Child and Youth Care: The Therapeutic Home Parent Model
  Craig N. Shealy   87

7 The Role of Residential Child and Youth Care
   Workers in Care Planning: An Exploratory Study
   Erik J. Knorth and Monika Smit   107

8 Professionalization and Institutional Abuse in
   the United Kingdom
   Matthew J. Colton   121

9 Cultural Factors Related to Burnout in Child and
   Youth Care Workers in Thirteen Cultures
   Victor Savicki   135

10 Workload and Prevention of Burnout in Special
   Child and Youth Care Services: A System Analysis
   Jef Breda and Elke Verlinden   159

PART III: PARTICIPATION

11 The Involvement of Families in Planning and
   Delivering Care
   Mona Sandbæk   179

12 Participation by Children in Care Planning:
   Research and Experiences in the United Kingdom
   Ruth Sinclair   191

13 Early Residential Foster Care: Parental Experiences
   Concerning Their Co-operation with Professional
   Workers
   Marie-Pierre Mackiewicz   201

14 Listen to the Client. (Foster) Children about
   'Difficult' Parents: How to Handle Conflicts
   with Them
   Elly Singer, Jeannette Doornenbal and Krista Okma   213

15 Listen to the Client. Battered and Abusing Women
   Speak of Their Early Victimization in Out of Home
   Placement
   June Price   229

PART IV: EPILOGUE

16 The Challenge in Child and Youth Care Research and Practice:
   Professionalization *and* Participation
   Erik J. Knorth, Peter M. Van den Bergh and Fop Verheij   241

Index   249

List of Contributors

Editors

Dr. Erik J. Knorth, Associate Professor Child and Youth Care. Leiden University, Department of Education, Centre for Special Education and Child Care (Leiden, The Netherlands).

Dr. Peter M. Van den Bergh, Assistant Professor Child and Youth Care. Leiden University, Department of Education, Centre for Special Education and Child Care (Leiden, The Netherlands).

Dr. Fop Verheij, Professor Child and Adolescent Psychiatry. Erasmus University Rotterdam, Sophia Children's Hospital – Department of Child and Adolescent Psychiatry (Rotterdam, The Netherlands).

Other Contributors

Dr. Jef Breda, Professor Sociology and Social Policy. University of Antwerp, Department of Sociology and Social Policy (Antwerp, Belgium).

Dr. Matthew J. Colton, Professor Applied Social Studies. University of Wales Swansea, School for Social Sciences and International Development (Swansea, United Kingdom). Professor at the Department of Child and Adolescent Psychiatry, Norwegian University of Science and Technology (Trondheim, Norway).

Dr. Jeroen J.H. Dekker, Professor of History and Theory of Education. University of Groningen, Department of Education (Groningen, The Netherlands).

Dr. Micha De Winter, Professor Social Education. Utrecht University, Department of Child and Adolescent Studies (Utrecht, The Netherlands).

Dr. Jeannette Doornenbal, Assistant Professor Education. University of Groningen, Department of Education (Groningen, The Netherlands).

Dr. Emmanuel Grupper, Head of Department for Training of Youth Workers School of Education, Beit Berl College. Director of Residential Education and Care Division, Ministry of Education (Beit Berl/Tel Aviv, Israel).

Margaret Lindsay, OBE MA MSc, Independent Consultant in Child and Youth Care, Glasgow (Glasgow, Scotland).

Dr. Marie-Pierre Mackiewicz, Assistant Professor Education and Training. University of Lille, Department of Education, Teachers' Training Centre (Lille, France).

Krista Okma, MA, PhD student, Utrecht University, Department of Developmental Psychology (Utrecht, The Netherlands).

Dr. June Price, Assistant Professor Nursing and Allied Health. Fairleigh University, Department of Nursing and Allied Health (Teaneck [New Jersey], United States of America).

Mona Sandbæk, Senior Researcher. NOVA, Norwegian Social Research Institute (Oslo, Norway).

Dr. Victor Savicki, Professor of Psychology. Western Oregon University, Division of Psychology (Monmouth [Oregon], United States of America).

Dr. Craig N. Shealy, Associate Professor Clinical Psychology. James Madison University, Department of Psychology (Harrisonburg [Virginia], United States of America).

Dr. Ruth Sinclair, Director of Research, National Children's Bureau (London, England).

Dr. Elly Singer, Associate Professor Developmental Psychology. Utrecht University/University of Amsterdam, Department of Psychology (Utrecht/Amsterdam, The Netherlands).

Dr. Monika Smit, Assistant Professor Child and Youth Care. Leiden University, Department of Education, Centre for Special Education and Child Care (Leiden, The Netherlands).

Dr. Elke Verlinden, Researcher Sociology and Social Policy. University of Antwerp, Department of Sociology and Social Policy (Antwerp, Belgium).

Foreword

Child and youth care in most Western European countries or regions has seen more changes in a span of barely twenty years than in past centuries. One of the more important developments in child and youth care is that care personnel, clients and society have become more critical about the need for out-of-home placement of children and young people in general and placement in residential care in particular. A combination of factors for example, changes in target group (the target group is no longer orphans but children who are living in problem situations); studies that point out residential care's limited positive short and long term effects; the oversimplified presentation to the general public of these results; the breakthrough of the systemic approach in care; the high cost of residential care have reduced residential care to 'pariah-care'. By this term Fritz Mayer refers to both the marginalization and the stigmatization of young people who have been placed in care, and of the residential facilities that were designed to meet their needs.

In some countries this has resulted in a drastic expansion of foster care, and in others in the extension of alternative forms of care, such as day care and treatment programmes or family preservation programmes. 'Family preservation' was sometimes given priority over 'child protection'. It turned out, in practice as well as in research, that none of these forms of care offered a solution to all the problems of families and children and that new forms of child and youth care were not always as effective as existing forms. The recent history of child care has taught us that the problems we are facing now cannot be solved by just one form of care. Discussions on priorities or of one form of care being superior to the other have not optimized the quality of care. Clients need a continuum of care, from family support to residential care, i.e. 'needs-driven' care. Needs-driven care means that the offered help is in proportion to the problems that arise and is adapted to the client system's needs. This means that it takes into account the parents' perspective and expectations and the children's rights. The nature, intensity and duration of support is geared adequately and in a flexible way to each family's specific needs and potentialities. Needs-driven care requires a very flexible way of tackling the specific needs and potentialities of each family. It demands also a very differentiated and flexible network of easily accessible services, facilities and establishments.

In order to deliver services of high-quality, all forms of child and youth care that belong to this continuum must pay attention to 'professionalization' and 'participation', which are the central themes of this interesting and important book, and which are preceded by an exciting historical perspective.

Bruno Bettelheim was right, at least in this matter, when as early as the mid-fifties he chose to name one of his works 'love is not enough'. Themes he raised in his work such as how to build a professional identity, how to find a way to a professional child and youth care, what causes malfunctioning (abuse, burnout) of child and youth care professionals and how can it be prevented or taken care of, are questions that are raised again in this book by today's experts.

Luckily in recent years there has been an increasing recognition of the need for professionalization in child and youth care. This has not been the case to the same degree for the participation of children and their parents in the care process. Too often in practice child and youth care professionals still forget that the main objective of any form of child and youth care should always be to improve the 'fit' between the child and the social environment. This means that the parents and child or young people are involved as full 'partners' in the care process. 'Listening' to parents and children remains for many youth and child care workers a difficult task. What 'listening' in the full sense of the word actually means in child and youth care, and how children and their families can be involved in care is thoroughly discussed in this book.

This volume takes a unique place in the many publications on child and youth care because it is not only solidly underpinned from a scientific point of view but also relevant to practice. It is furthermore exceptional that a group of experts from eight different countries succeed in compiling such a coherent book. It is no coincidence that the editors come from the research group of Orthopedagogics of Leiden University and from the research group of Child and Adolescent Psychiatry of the Erasmus University Rotterdam.

We hope that the knowledge disseminated in this book will result in improved policies and practices and will further stimulate international and interdisciplinary scientific co-operation in these domains.

Prof. Dr. W. Hellinckx
President European Scientific Association on Residential and Foster Care for children and adolescents (EUSARF)
Head Section of Orthopedagogics, Catholic University of Leuven, Belgium

Acknowledgements

The publication of this book is made possible through the co-operation of many. The Board of the Stichting Congress 2000 of the Dutch section of FICE (Fédération Internationale des Communautés Éducatives) made the production of this book possible. We are grateful to: Aad Vroon from FICE who delivered an important contribution in realizing this project; the Leiden University for the subsidy we received for this project; Matthew Colton, who put us in touch with the publisher Ashgate and its representative Katherine Hodkinson; and Susan Rhodes and Hans Kok, who helped us in translating texts. We are greatly indebted to all these people and organizations.

E.J. Knorth
P.M. Van den Bergh
F. Verheij

Chapter 1

Professionalization and Participation in Child and Youth Care: Two Sides of One Coin?

Erik J. Knorth, Peter M. Van den Bergh and Fop Verheij

Introduction

The number of children and youth with severe emotional and behavioural problems that make use of provisions for child and youth care (short: cyc) is sizeable. In looking at the forms of care in which youth are (temporarily) placed – it mainly concerns foster or residential care – research by Maza (1996; see Pecora, et al., 2000) shows that in the USA in 1994 more than half a million children and youth stayed in residential or family foster care.[1] One year earlier Colton and Hellinckx (1993) published a study with data on the number of minors in care in the (then 12) member states of the EU; this number amounted to over 400,000.[2] After adding the number of children and young people that are placed out of home in Australia (± 15,000)[3] and Canada (± 75,000),[4] it turns out that more than a million children and youth in the rich western world is (temporarily) entrusted to the care of cyc-workers and their supervisors. Furthermore, when we consider the number of families of all these young clients, it can be seen that the number of people asking for support is similar in size to the total population of Ireland.[5] On a global scale the numbers are even much higher, but there is a lack of reliable figures covering Central and Eastern Europe,[6] and especially Asia and South-America.

Child and youth care is under pressure, not only because of the high numbers of users (children, youth and parents) – Pecora et al. state that because of high usage the child and youth care system '... in many areas of the country [USA] remains *stressed*' [Pecora, et al., 2000, p. 1] – but also because of the demands that are increasingly placed on the quality of care provisions by society and the various professional groups. Child and youth care is no longer judged on its good intentions, but more and more on its quality and achievements (Donker, 1987; Else et al., 1992).

By taking *professionalization* and *participation* as guiding concepts for analysis it is possible to reflect on the quality of care. With the first concept the role of workers is discussed, and with the second, the role of clients. Professionalization and participation may not be the alpha and omega of the question about quality in child and youth care, but they do refer to two fundamental dimensions in this, what Arieli (1996) called, 'people processing' sector.

This introductory chapter begins with a conceptual and pragmatic examination of what the notions 'professionalization' (of workers) and 'participation' (of clients) mean in the debate about quality in child and youth care. Because it is sometimes suggested that these processes are antagonisms (see for instance Bisschops, 2001; Lochhead, 2001), attention is also given to how the two processes relate to each other. Finally, this chapter introduces the various contributions to this book.

Quality and Professionalization

In addressing the question about the quality of care it is not unusual to distinguish three categories for description: input, process (or throughput), and output (cf. Colton, Hellinckx, Van den Bruel & Williams, 1994; Van IJzendoorn, 1997; see also Chapter 10 in this book).

- The category *input* refers on the one hand to the characteristics and problems of the clients: children and families in need of care, and on the other hand to the means in terms of financial possibilities, characteristics of the staff and organizational conditions (for instance in-service training, and how the consultation and decision-making processes are conducted) that are available to shape the care process.
- The category *process* refers to the actual implementation of care; the activities and interventions that are carried out with members of the client system (primary process), and the activities deployed by supervising staff to support this primary process.
- The category *output* refers to all that results from the process of care. It concerns the (changed) functioning of clients in terms of behaviour, perceptions and attitudes. Output can also refer to the costs of care, and the opinion of staff, of partner organizations and of the general public about what has been accomplished.

To be able to evaluate or promote the quality of care a *standard* is needed: a norm which indicates what, assuming upon a certain set of problems as starting point (input), should be done ideally (process) to achieve the chosen result (output). Or in a less abstract way: what should be done to reduce the behavioural problems of ten year old Johnny Johnson (aggression, running away from home), for his parents to be able to take him back into their home and support his development into adulthood?

This standard could be derived, at least for a part, from the *professional knowledge and insight* that are available in the domain of child and youth care. Quality and professionalization in the field of care are notions that are closely connected (Eisikovits & Beker, 1983; Kroneman, 2000; Lochhead, 2001).[7] Professionalization refers primarily to the extent to which practitioners and institutions are guided by sound knowledge and insight (into the nature, background and approach of the problems presented by clients), and express this by skillful and respectful treatment at the individual and at the organizational level. The foundation of this knowledge lies in systematized 'practice wisdom' and research-based data and theories (Anglin, 1992).

It is not illogical in this context that the concept of professionalization of care is often associated with the *level of education* of the workers and the extent to which an organization pays attention to (and makes means available for) education in the form of extra schooling, training and in-service-training (Beker, 1997; Edens, 1992). An example of this association is a discussion by Trede (1999), who, in comparing the level of professionalization ('Professionalisierungsgrad') of residential cyc-workers in a few European countries, without any further explanation, connects this concept to the level of education of workers in residential youth care.[8]

This concept of professionalization not only points to a level of expertise, but also to the fact that the use of this expertise has its price. A salary, and appropriate *working conditions* (including the caseload size) form the tangible expression of society's recognition of the profession of a child and youth care worker – a recognition which, however, is quite limited, especially when viewed from the point of view of financial reward (Lochhead, 2001).[9] Trede (1999) asks whether this limited societal recognition could be the 'aftermath' of the long cherished belief that every 'respectable citizen is capable of raising his children, even children with special needs'. In this context Trede refers to the concept of 'Un-Berufe' from classical sociology, by which was meant that social fields like youth care do not require any additional qualifications of a person than 'everybody's qualifications' ('Jedermanns-qualifikationen', p. 803). In other words, these are knowledge and skills that are present in every adult who is interested in his fellow human being. However, apart from a few exceptions (see for instance Chapter 8), the image of child and youth care as 'Un Berufe' is largely history. In the western world, anno 2002, working with children whose developments are disturbed, and working with their parents, is generally seen as a profession that needs a good professional education, appropriate support and 'on-the-job' training.

More and more, professional groups and public bodies draw up requirements for the way in which care workers conduct their work, which suggests that professional actions can be accounted for. This accountability of professionals is becoming an increasingly important feature of professionalization (Pecora et al., 2000). In this *professional ethical standards and protocols* play a prominent role (see for instance the work of Mattingly [1995] in the USA, and that of FICE [1998] in Europe).

In summary, the various sources of professionalization in the field of child and youth care can be presented as follows (see Figure 1.1):

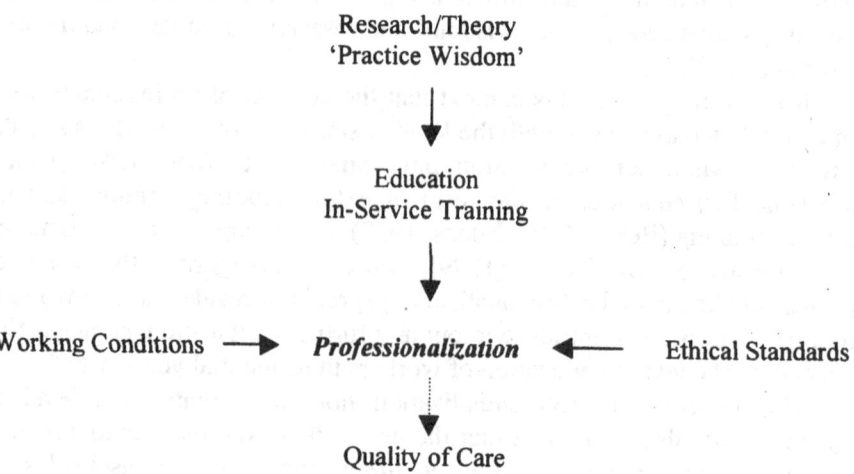

Figure 1.1   Sources of Professionalization

Professionalization, a Closer Consideration

It has been stated that valid knowledge and skills, generated by scientific research and systematized experiences from practice, deliver a crucial contribution to a professional child and youth care. These knowledge and skills distinguish child and youth care from well meant charity or – in the words of Grupper (Chapter 4) – from merely a 'humanitarian mission'. However, to achieve the central goal – reducing the psychosocial needs of a child and its parents – more is needed than just the instrumental use of knowledge and skills as if it were the utilization of a technology.

Clients' problems are generally so complicated that the practitioner who starts to look for evidence-based 'if-then' knowledge ('if this is the problem, then this intervention should applied [to solve the problem]') runs into at least two barriers (Rispens, 1983):

- in closer analysis this type of (social-)technological knowledge is not or hardly available;[10] and
- if this knowledge is available, the question is whether it can be applied in the individual case of this particular child or young person.[11]

Professional care for individual children or youth and their parents – say the Johnson's – implies the repeated construction of an 'N=1 theory': using general knowledge and insight the nature and background of the problems of Johnny Johnson and his family are specified, and what needs to happen to reduce or solve their problems is also specified. Actually an 'ideographic theory' is formulated (cf. Westmeyer, 1976), which – if it is right – results in a treatment plan that is attuned to the individual case (Klomp, Van den Bergh & Harinck, 1997; Verheij, 1999).

One could also formulate it differently: to realize *needs-led* care the metaphor of consulting a 'cookery book with recipes' is inadequate. Initiating, implementing and evaluating youth care are rather to be regarded as a *selection or decision process* (Van der Ploeg & Van den Bergh, 1987), in which professionals *and* clients determine the particular 'care arrangement' that will be offered, on the basis of an exchange of information and opinion. The choices that are to be made rest, on the one hand, on professional knowledge and insight (as explained above), and on the other, on information, considerations and feelings of the client (Knorth, Van den Bergh & Smit, 1997). This introduces the role of those central to child and youth care: the children, youth and their families.

Quality and Participation

There are all sorts of reasons why it is desirable that clients (children, youth and their parents) fulfil an *active role* in the process of care. Thoburn, Lewis and Shemmings (1996) name the following four reasons.

Knowledge It is the youth and the parents themselves who in the end know best what precisely is happening in the family and what has already been tried in the past to resolve the problems (input). They also know best the (potential) strengths of the family. Further it is the family that can point to what the process of care should achieve (the aim), what it produces for them once the care has started (process), and what they see as the results (output). Referring to this last point one sees that procedures for systematically collecting *client feedback* have taken an important place in modern quality policies (see, for instance, Fletcher, 1993; Jumelet, De Ruyter & Kayser, 1999).[12]

Rights Parents and children have the right (or should have the right) to be informed about what is said about them, and they have (or should have) a say in important decisions that concern them. In several countries this right for information and the right to have a say is laid down by law (Van Unen, 1995). However that does not mean that concerning this point in practice the participation of parents and youth is always completely realized or can be realized (Thomas & O'Kane, 1999; Verheij, 1997; see also Chapter 11 and 12).

Empowerment Being involved as a partner in care may help parents, children and young people feel less powerless and function more competently. The empowerment philosophy, with its emphasis on strengths of people in care instead of on their deficits, forms, in a growing number of countries, the cornerstone of the policies and clinical practice in the care for both youth and adults (cf. Hodges & Pecora, 2000; Jumelet & Haarsma, 1998; Katz, 1995; Saleebey, 1997). A rather radical implementation of this philosophy in the form of the so-called Family Group Conferences model (Connolly & McKenzie, 1999; Lupton & Nixon, 1999), is now being adopted on a large scale.[13]

Effectiveness A more co-operative, participatory working relationship is likely to lead to an improved progress in the care process. To support this participatory relationship, Thoburn et al. refer to a review of Lewis (1992) which concerns the field of protection. Recently Scholte et al. (1999) reported about a comparative study involving 243 self-referred clients of (non-governmental) services for child and family welfare in the Netherlands, The UK (Wales) and Spain (Catalonia). One of their findings is that the more social workers discussed their decisions about service provision with users the higher the reported levels of satisfactory involvement in services in all three countries (p. 386).

Intermezzo

Active involvement and participation of clients is increasingly considered to be a crucial standard for the evaluation and improvement of the quality of child and youth care. Sometimes even young clients are actively involved in the *development* of quality criteria in care. A nice example in The Netherlands can be found in a publication by Van Beek, Hameetman and Meerdink (1999).[14] These authors examined, via open interviews with more than 500 children and youth from 8 to 18 years in children's homes and day-care centres, what according to these children and youth are important issues in the care and support that they receive. The remarks were classified in three clusters: the process of care, the workers, and the organization. Regarding the first cluster: the process of care, Table 1.1 presents as an illustration the *children's quality criteria* (as they should be named according the authors).

Table 1.1 Children's quality criteria with respect to the process of care in a (semi)residential setting

What children and youth find important is:
- that I know why I am here
- that I receive information about the care
- that they involve me in decisions
- that at the start I am not left on my own
- that I am allowed to adjust
- that I am allowed to live a life that is as normal as possible
- that I can do things together with other children in the group
- that my group is peaceful
- that I am safe in the group
- that I have enough freedom
- that important others can be there for me
- that I understand my life story
- that I can leave in a good manner.

Source: Van Beek, Hameetman & Meerdink (1999, p. 9).

Each of the criteria in Table 1.1 has been elaborated further and completed with countless examples and quotations, and each is suitable as a norm for testing in practice. It is striking that the first three criteria request information about and involvement in choices. As the following paragraphs will show, these are important conditions for participation.

Participation, a Closer Consideration

To specify the concept of participation, at least two approaches are useful: a) the nature of the activities aimed at participation that the clients experience; and b) the level of participation that is under discussion.

Nature Within the process of providing care for clients a wide range of activities and processes can be distinguished, in which children or young people and parents already participate more or less actively. Participation can, as a start, be connected to the *personal treatment*. Examples are that clients:

- actively co-decide about the design of their own treatment plan;
- make use of a regulation for complaints;
- negotiate earned credits for 'desired behaviour';
- complete an inventory about client satisfaction;
- be present at so called review meetings;
- et cetera.

Participation can also reach further than being involved in the design or in judging the personal treatment, by encouraging involvement in work in the life group, the institution or youth care *in general*. Examples are:

- taking care and informing fellow clients;
- participating in a clients' council;
- discussing the house rules with the staff;
- producing a youth newspaper together with others;
- being involved in the selection process of new personnel;
- et cetera.

That the active participation of children, youth and parents does not come about as a matter of course will become clear in Part III of this book. In cases where care involves an out of home placement of the child or youth, parents in particular easily become sidelined. Nonetheless, increasing attention is evident in literature regarding actively involving parents in the care of their son or daughter (Dekker & Van den Bergh, 2002; Knorth & Smit, 1997; Verheij, 1997).

Level Research on the participation of children, youth and parents in child and youth care often relates back to the so-called 'participation ladder'. This ladder, originally developed by Arnstein (1969) to determine the level of participation in the community by civilians, was used by Hart (1992) in the context of UNICEF reports to characterize children's participation projects (see also De Winter, 1997).[15] Later the 'ladder' was adapted for use in youth care (Thoburn, Lewis & Shemmings, 1995), and has been used in various research projects (e.g. Thoburn et al., 1995; Sinclair & Grimshaw, 1997). The latest version identifies the following increasing levels of participation (from bottom upwards):

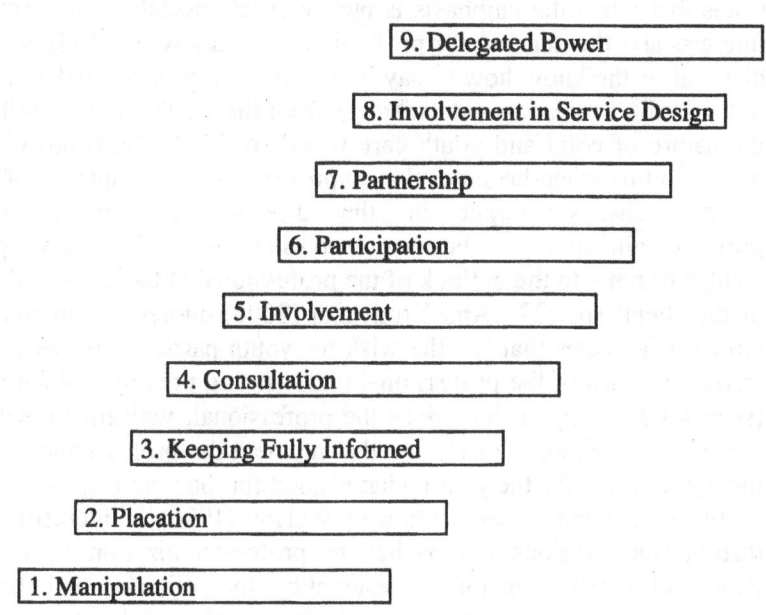

Figure 1.2 Participation ladder, adapted by Thoburn et al. (1995)

In research by Sinclair and Grimshaw (1998) on young people's participation in review meetings only levels 3 to 7 were found. In a recent publication by Shier (2001) five levels (covering the range between the levels 3 to 9 as mentioned above) have been elaborated for their implications on the behaviour of adults towards children. The 'lowest' level (level 3 in Figure 1.2) Shier characterizes as: *Children are listened to*. In his opinion listening to a client is a basic hallmark of any form of participatory practice, and a conditio sine qua non for all 'higher' forms of participation.

Professionalization and Participation: Antagonisms?

Now that the concepts 'professionalization' and 'participation' in youth care have been clarified, and their importance to the quality of the cyc-work has been outlined, the question arises how professionalization and participation relate to each other – or more precisely – whether they impede each other. Several authors mention this. Lochhead (2001), for instance, states that when the emphasis is put on strict specialization, protection of interests and the demand for professional autonomy ('... only we have the disposal of the know how to say how it is ...'), professionalization carries the risk of '... creating a detachment from the clients that is antithetical to the nature of child and youth care work' (p. 75).[16] Bisschops (2001) also mentions this when he states that improvements in the quality of the work is not always sought in the direction of specialization and professionalization, '... because that often urges us to give priority – wanted or not – to the outlook of the professional at the costs of the outlook of the client' (p. 127). And Kroneman (2000) quotes a pronouncement of Groen, who states that '... the wish for youth participation puts the whole *traditional* idea of the professional under strong pressure. When a youth is (seen as) a co-expert, how does the professional, with his knowledge and experience, position himself? At that moment the professional is no longer the expert who tells the youth what is good for the youth' (p. 31).

In this context a contribution of Welsby (1996) is interesting. Welsby distinguishes various approaches to professionalization in (residential) child and youth care: the 'bureaucratic', the 'clinical' and the 'values-based' approach. Concentrating on decision-making meetings in child care, he sees as characteristic of the *bureaucratic approach*:

- that (too) much time is spent establishing the correct procedures rather than on child's needs;
- form filling;
- deferring issues to senior staff or committees;
- gearing meetings to the agency's needs, not the child's;
- focusing on the agency's policy.

According to Welsby the *clinical approach*, in our view better described as the '*expert approach*', is characterized by matters as:

- the child is the object (rather than subject) of concern;
- referral to experts;
- discussion among professionals often takes place in private;

- application of theory and decisions are left to those best qualified (and best paid).

The *values-based approach* of professionalization, in favour of which Welsby pleads, is characterized by:

- procedures that vary from individual to individual;
- unnecessary forms will not be completed;
- open discussions of all relevant issues can take place;
- professionals, non-professionals (e.g. parents) and young people plan together;
- meetings will be held as much at the convenience of young people as adults.

It is clear that, according to this last approach, the use of professional knowledge and skills very much asks for attunement, in the sense that a started care arrangement is the result and the expression of a relationship of dialogue between youth, parents and professionals.[17] With reference to Klomp and Van den Bergh (1999) this is specified as the *participatory approach of professionalization*. In this approach professional expertise should be offered as a service in which the professional treats clients with respect: the concept of 'sensitive professionalization' (Anglin, 1992) could also be used here. The professional must be constantly alert not to feed the iatrogenic feelings of incompetence and impotence in children, young people and parents; a danger that in practice is always lurking, especially in a medically-oriented treatment setting (Oppenoorth & Spaander, 2002).

From this point of view professionalization (of workers) and participation (of clients) do not need to form an antithesis. On the contrary, the 'emancipation' of both partners in the care process, provided this occurs in a good balance, will bring the quality of child and youth care to a higher level and can increase its effectivity (see also Groen, 2001).

Against the background of this view, presented in Figure 1.3, the different contributions to this book will be introduced.

Part I: A Historical Perspective

The first two contributions use a historical perspective. *Dekker* begins his argument, in Chapter 2, with a critical analysis of the work of Ellen Key. Her famous and influential publication from 1900, *Das Jahrhundert des*

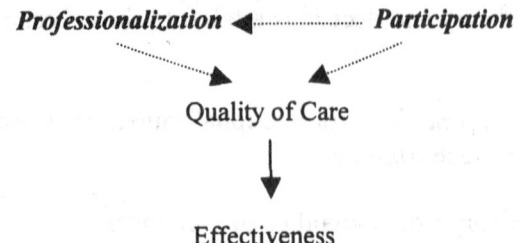

Figure 1.3 Professionalization and Participation related to Quality of Care

Kindes (The Century of the Child), was and is generally interpreted as a warm plea to create space in upbringing for the natural development of the child, and to grant children the right to live in their own safe world within the context of family life.

However, according to Dekker, this 'icon' for professional educators must be seen in a wider context, namely as a reflection on the (pedagogical) conditions for an adequate reproduction and progression of the human race. Dekker questions to what extent Key's utopia, strongly coloured by Romanticism, has become reality in the 20th century. He concludes that the development in thinking and practice regarding the upbringing and care that a child needs, and especially a child at risk, has meant a disenchantment of Key's romantic image of childhood. Rationalization ('Entzauberung') of the social order (amongst other things), leading to legislation that sanctioned re-education of neglected and 'difficult' children, to the immense growth of scientific knowledge of the (disturbed) development of children and to the relative professionalization of (residential) child and youth care, means that according to Dekker and in retrospect 'The Century of the Child' could be better characterized as a child-*oriented* than as a child-*centred* epoch.

Where Dekker describes a part of the background of the tendency for professionalization in the 20th century, *De Winter* questions, in Chapter 3, the status of children's participation in questions of policy and upbringing that have governed their path of life. Apart from the thoughts and practices of a handful pedagogues like John Dewey, Anton Makarenko, Janusz Korczak and Kees Boeke, who were very sympathetic towards 'youth participation', the prevailing practice in the western world was one of – in the words of Dasberg (1975) – 'grootbrengen door kleinhouden' (bringing them up by keeping them small). However at the end of the 20th century De Winter remarks on a rediscovery of children and young people as active participants in their own upbringing and education. According to De Winter both idealistic and strategic reasons underlie this rediscovery. The implication for child and youth care is, according to De Winter, that a dialogue should always be started with youth to enable cyc-workers to attune to the own relevant ideas and thoughts of clients, no matter how damaged they might be and no matter how dependent they might be from the answers that professionals can offer. A *participatory pedagogy* will help children and young people develop a feeling of connection with and responsibility towards others, and will – in a wider context – promote social cohesion in the community.

Part II: On Professionalization

In the first contribution in the section on professionalization in child and youth care (Chapter 4), *Grupper* addresses a factor which has great significance for the level of professionalization: the *economic factor*. Grupper discusses the impact that this has for working conditions, including aspects like personnel size, payment, caseload, facilities, etcetera (see the left side of Figure 1.1). He states that the field of child and youth care, and especially in the expensive forms (i.e. the residential sector), is confronted with two paradoxes. Firstly, the institutions for child and youth care are better equipped than ever to do qualitatively good work, while the (mostly negative) public attention for the sector evokes the image of nothing being changed or improved. Secondly, in many countries the need for intensive (expensive) care is higher than ever, while the last decades show a picture of a quantitative reduction of institutions offering this kind of care. Grupper signals the danger that this can lead to a movement back to non-professional working models. As someone who does not want to close his eyes to the budget reductions he opts for a different route; he pleads for intensifying professional co-operation and differentiation in professional qualifications of staff.

In Chapter 5 *Lindsay* discusses the professional identity of the (residential) child and youth care worker and what is needed to strengthen it. Next to improvements in the public image of youth care she distinguishes three aspects that are relevant for this professional identity: education and training of the cyc-worker, the attitude of the worker in ethical and normative matters, and the status and responsibilities that are granted to workers within the organization (compare the three sources in Figure 1.1). At all three levels Lindsay expects improvement to be both possible and necessary, and she offers a number of grounded suggestions. For instance, in relation to the first point (education) she describes in a *learning pyramid*, the subjects and areas that should be dealt with in a curriculum for child and youth care workers.

The contribution of *Shealy* (Chapter 6) closely connects with this. On the basis of various sources and his own research, he arrives at a detailed competence profile of the child and youth care worker, called the *Therapeutic Home Parent (THP) model*. Starting from the premise that youth care in the USA relies too much on 'doing' and 'being' and not enough on 'knowing' Shealy researches what is known in the research literature about the behaviours and characteristics of 'effective' therapists/counsellors. Next to it he reviews research in the domain of developmental psychopathology, looking for behaviours and characteristics of parents that are associated with 'poor' emotional, behavioural and mental outcomes of offspring. A comparison of these data sets with the judgment of a group of experienced child and youth care workers, who were asked to point out what is typical for 'good' and 'bad' practitioners, shows remarkable parallels. A list, derived from this, of 'Personal Characteristics (PCs)', completed with a list of 'Work Behaviours (WBs)' and 'Knowledge, Skills and Abilities' (KSAs) derived also through the panel, is finally examined, starting from the question what are the absolute *necessary* and most *wanted* PCs, WBs and KSAs for the profession of child and youth care worker. The result forms the heart of the THP model.[18]

One of the WBs in the model of Shealy is the development and evaluation of treatment plans. In many countries the validity of such plans is seen as an important indicator for the quality of professional conduct within an institution. Research in The Netherlands by *Knorth* and *Smit* (Chapter 7) concludes that on this point great differences exist, which is demonstrated by the variety of described problems, goals and means in treatment plans. Further in this research, group workers speak about what it means to work with treatment plans. From their responses it is apparent that workers would like to play a role in treatment planning. They are most keen to have an active part in determining the *means* that are being used to counter the problems of youth, as well as in the *evaluation* and adjustment (when necessary) of the treatment plan. In other words they especially wish to participate in areas where they can bring forward their own experiences and expertise. The research further produces suggestions that can enhance the validity and practical usefulness of treatment plans.

In Chapter 8 *Colton* investigates what must be done to improve the quality of residential youth care, especially in the United Kingdom, and the potential role of a more professionally equipped staff. The strongly reduced residential sector in the UK has in the last two decades been concerned by the uncovering of a number of negative practices (such as sexual abuse of pupils and irresponsible disciplinary actions). The author argues that in his country the professional identity of the residential child care worker is weak, and that unqualified personnel is not the exception. According to Colton this surely has played a role in the named practices, but it is not the complete story. Explanations for these practices should also be sought in social attitudes (such as inequality of persons and groups) and the handling of moral codes (contempt for children's rights), as well as in the organizational design of care (bureaucracy, hierarchic relations, lack of openness, and the large size of institutions) – matters that refer to both the right and the left side in Figure 1.1.

That the profession of cyc-worker is a demanding one, is sufficiently known. It is therefore not that surprising that in this profession a high turn over exists and quite a number of people leave the profession, permanently or temporarily, with signs of *burnout* (Fleischer, 1985). The two last contributions in this section are about this subject.

In Chapter 9 *Savicki* reports on an international comparative research. Within the concept of burnout three dimensions are distinguished: emotional exhaustion, depersonalization, and (insufficient) personal accomplishment. From his study it appears that at a personal level the coping style of the worker is decisive for the chances that burnout develops. Factors in the working environment that prove to be of importance include: perceived work pressure, the extent to which innovation is emphasized, support by management, friendliness and support perceived in co-workers, and a good work planning. At the organizational level, two cultural aspects prove to be relevant in particular: the extent to which one tries to avoid insecurity by rules and procedures, and the extent to which personal actions and responsibility are appreciated. Finally, on a national level, it is of particular importance whether a nation adheres much interest to career success. Savicki rounds off with five implications.

In Chapter 10 *Breda* and *Verlinden* report on a study conducted in Belgium (Flanders). On the basis of time registration and log entries they examined what activities actually were happening within two types of child and youth care agency: one aimed at delivering voluntary help (Special Youth Assistance Committee), and the other aimed at help in a judicial framework (Social Service of Juvenile Court). Amongst other things, the research demonstrated that the workload is high and that staff perform overtime on a regular basis. Connecting the workload-scores to a measure for burnout, it became apparent that there was hardly any connection between the two. The authors conclude that, for the prevention of burnout, workload-reduction is opportune, but that more is needed. They elaborate on this from three angles: the reduction of non-case related activities, the modernization of administrative support of the primary process, and the attention for psychological factors that contribute to work satisfaction.

Part III: On Participation

The third part of this book, on participation, starts with a contribution from *Sandbæk* (Chapter 11). Central to this contribution is the involvement of *parents* in the planning and delivery of care. Sandbæk concludes that, within youth care, there is often a one-sided focus on parental shortcomings. In focusing in this way workers often misunderstand how many efforts parents have usually already undertaken to find solutions and to help their children. Research from the author shows that in most cases the parents are the ones that look for contact with child welfare and protective services. In addition, when several social workers are involved in a case, the parents are often the connecting link between them. When a child leaves an institution, be it prematurely or not, parents again prove to be the ones that help a child to re-establish roots in society. Sandbæk makes a plea to take the knowledge and insight that parents have seriously, to involve them as real partners in decision-making processes, and to value much more their capacity as an 'agency' for their child.

The contribution of *Sinclair* (Chapter 12) is complementary to that of Sandbæk in the sense that the participation of *children and youth* in the process of care planning is questioned. The author reports about research in England and Wales which examines what happened with the principle – laid down in the Children Act 1989 – to really involve children and youth in review meetings that concern them. The results show that young clients are seldom well-informed about the planning process. In two out of three cases, they were consulted before the review meetings and in more than half of the cases, they attended a meeting. Consultation and attendance are more frequent when older children are involved. The interviews with youth show on the one hand how much importance they attribute to their attendance at review meetings, while on the other hand they experience the meetings as uncomfortable and often meaningless. Many do not feel they are listened to or have their views taken into account. Sinclair gives a number of ideas as to how this can be improved.

In Chapter 13, written by *Mackiewicz*, the role of parents of children that are placed out of home is again pictured, now based on experiences gained in France. An analysis of how parents and professionals relate once a child is placed – shows a number of antagonisms that make co-operation difficult (Mackiewicz' contribution is concerned with very young children).

On the basis of the work of Elias the author distinguishes four angles from which the role of parents and professionals can be legitimized. Depending on how this question of legitimization is handled and how the tasks with respect to the care for the child are perceived, three ways are distinguished in which parents handle the respite foster care relationship: opposition, delegation and collaboration or co-operation. Research conducted by the author demonstrates that, at the start of a placement, most parents use a delegation-strategy. Yet with most parents co-operation can be achieved. In the second part of his contribution the author addresses a number of factors that hinder or promote such co-operation.

A basic condition for participation of parents and children in care is that they are *listened to* seriously. This is not only about the clinical practice (as is explained above), but also about the research practice. In the intermezzo an example was already discussed. The two last contributions in this book are based on this staring point of listening to clients.

In Chapter 14 *Singer, Doornenbal* and *Okma* give a report of a comparative research into the way children – it concerns 8-13 year old foster children and 'own children' – cope with everyday conflicts with their parents or foster parents. The conflict that they deal with in this chapter results from a parental ban on joining an attractive activity (here: watching television) in which other children are allowed to participate. Singer et al. used both imaginary situations ('imagine now that you ...') and real-life examples ('have you ever experienced such a thing ...'; 'what did you do then ...', et cetera). Research shows that most children try to get their own way, mostly by asking why and showing their emotions, especially their anger. In this context the authors speak of an *emotion culture*. An important difference between foster children and 'own' children is that the foster children do not go as far in 'playing on the emotions of the foster parents'. They are less secure about their relation with foster parents, and they are more liable to withdraw to express their emotions on their own, or to seek distraction. The research further shows: that the same external behaviour of children (as demonstrated with two cases) can hide a completely different inner experience; that behaviour and experience are strongly context related; and that one cannot simply draw conclusions for real-life situations from the answers that children give to imaginary situations.

In Chapter 15 *Price* shows how women, who as young children had been a victim of physical and/or sexual abuse, look back on their life and on the help they received, and which strategies they used (and still use) to carry on. All the women interviewed have a history of out of home placements, and it soon becomes clear how disastrous these experiences of abuse are. A sense of belonging does not develop. The women develop such survival strategies as dissociation, avoidance of relationships, and substance abuse. Price notes that a placement in a foster home or a children's home meant that the women, once more, were exposed to victimization. Some recreate the scenario of their own traumas in their current relationship with partners and children. The story of these women once more underlines the necessity of giving a structural character to the feedback of (previous) cyc-clients and to confront continuously the institutions and their workers with this information. One can assume that such continuous feedback on the basis of the participation principle would also contribute to the professional level of child and youth care.

Part IV: Epilogue

An epilogue follows in Chapter 16. Building on the various contributions to the book *Knorth, Van den Bergh* and *Verheij* consider the new questions and tasks that will confront child and youth care at the beginning of the 21st century. They conclude that more attention should be given to the *process* of working with children, youth and families, both in practice and in scientific research. The authors present a draft of how this can be realized.

Notes

1. There were 501,611 children (Pecora et al., 2000, p. 2).
2. There were 414,121 children (Knorth, 1998, p. 117). About some Western-European, *not*-EU member states we find in Gottesman (1994) additional data with regard to the numbers of youth placed in residential or family foster care at the beginning of the 1990s, namely for Austria (3,000 children); Finland (9,000 children); and Sweden (12,000 children).
3. Bath (1998) reports that in 1996 in Australia 14,677 children were placed out of home.
4. Anglin (1991) reports that in 1978 in Canada 75,497 children were placed out of home.
5. A few years ago Ireland had a population of 3.6 million inhabitants (Ruxton, 1996).
6. In two readers edited by Gottesman data can be found for some Eastern-European countries with regard to the numbers of youth placed in residential or family foster care at the beginning of the 1990s, namely in Gottesman (1991) for Croatia (4,400 children), and more recently in Gottesman (1994) for Hungary (27,000 children); Poland (15,000 children in residential care institutions; 14,000 children in assessment centres; number of children in foster care not mentioned); Slovakia (6,000 children); and Slovenia (2,300 children). According to us the given numbers – and that also holds for the earlier mentioned numbers – must be taken as the best documented estimates.
7. Sometimes professionalism and quality of care seem almost identical, such as in the next description of Twijnstra (1989, pp. 44-45): 'Professionalism ... refers to the quality of the care programmes on offer, which means the extent in which the performance of

the social workers ... meets the expectations that can be formulated for its effectiveness. [For this purpose] the social worker must have sufficient expertise, built on knowledge, skills and attitude. For this he also must be supported by organizational conditions'.

8. He states in this context amongst others that the degree of education in (West) Germany is relatively favourable: at the end of 1994 more than 80 percent of the child care workers finished more than one relevant education. In contrast he reports with a referral to Madge (1994) that in the UK 41 percent of heads of homes, and 80 percent of the other staff in local authority homes had no relevant qualifications at all (see also Ruxton, 1996).
9. However, the salary of child and youth care workers strongly varies; in the 1990s within Europe, Denmark beat everyone with a salary level that for instance was twice as high as the level in Italy (Madge, 1994, p. 98).
10. In the German speaking regions this 'deficit' is specified as the 'Technologiedefizit' (Lühmann & Schorr, 1979).
11. Veerman and Ten Brink (2001) conclude for instance on the basis of a high number of follow-up studies and reviews of international literature on the treatment of children with emotional and behavioural problems that '... after a period of child and youth care improvements can be observed yet it is difficult to predict the children that will benefit' (p. 216). Moreover the authors state that the chances for continuation of the problems, in spite of treatment, '... are more than two and a half times as great as compared to the chance of improvement' (p. 215).
12. These authors name amongst others the following methods for obtaining client feedback: written questionnaires, individual interviews, group interviews and panels, observation, an inviting attitude, therapy contact, right to complain, clients' council, a clients' trust person, treatment plan, and evaluation meeting.
13. Central to this way of working is that the family that is in great psychosocial need, and the social network surrounding the family are involved in a collective conference to thoroughly recognize the problems (for instance maltreatment of a child by the father), propose solutions, design a plan to execute the proposals and come to concrete agreements. The role of professionals at these conferences is limited: for instance they bring up relevant information about treatment possibilities, but they play no leading role at the conference (and are not present for an important part of the meeting). The first research results, for instance, in terms of adequacy of the plans made and satisfaction of the involved participants, are positive (cf. Lupton & Stevens, 1998).
14. See for other examples Fletcher (1993), Langsted (1994), and Thomas (2000).
15. The 'ladder of participation' adapted by Roger Hart (1992) consisted of the following levels: 1. Manipulation; 2. Decoration; 3. Tokenism; 4. Assigned but informed; 5. Consulted and informed; 6. Adult-initiated, shared decisions with children; 7. Child-initiated and directed; 8. Child-initiated shared decisions with adults.
16. These refer to what Hutschemaekers and Neijmeijer (1999, p. 60), observed from a classical sociological angle, count as the *power approach* of professionalization.
17. This forms the core of the approach that De Winter and Noom (2001) support with regard to professional work with homeless youth. They speak about a *dialogue-driven approach*.
18. Shealy has received a lot of remarks in the USA on his model (see: *Child and Youth Care Forum*, 25, n.5 (1996), with contributions of Arieli, Baizerman, Beker, Christiansen, Goocher, Magnuson and VanderVen).

References

Anglin, J.P. (1991). Residential care for children and youth in Canada. In M. Gottesman (Ed.), *Residential child care: An international reader* (pp. 48-62). London: Whiting & Birch.

Anglin, J.P. (1992). Review of 'Knowledge Utilization in Residential Child and Youth Care Practice', edited by Jerome Beker and Zwi Eisikovits. Washington, DC: CWLA Press, 1991. *Child and Youth Care Forum, 21*, (4), 287-290.

Arieli, M. (1996). Do Alabama and New-Moab belong to the same child care universe? A response to Shealy. *Child and Youth Care Forum, 25*, (5), 289-291.

Arnstein, S. (1969). Eight rungs on the ladder of citizen participation. *Journal of the American Institute of Planners, 35*, (4), 216-224.

Beker, J. (1997). Training and professional development in child care. In J.K. Whittaker, *Caring for troubled children: Residential treatment in a community context* (pp. 205-230). Hawthorne (NY): Aldine De Gruyter.

Bisschops, L. (2001). Beheerszucht en betrokkenheid in de jeugdzorg: De paradox van twee dominante trends. *Nederlands Tijdschrift voor Jeugdzorg, 5*, (3), 124-130.

Colton, M.J., & Hellinckx, W. (Eds.) (1993). *Child care in the EC: A country-specific guide to foster and residential care*. Aldershot: Ashgate.

Colton, M.J., Hellinckx, W., Van den Bruel, B., & Williams, M. (1994). Assessing quality in residential child care. *Social Work and Social Sciences Review, 5*, (3), 219-235.

Connolly, M., with McKenzie, M. (1999). *Effective participatory practice: Family Group Conferencing in child protection*. Hawthorne, NY: Aldine De Gruyter.

Dasberg, L. (1975). *Grootbrengen door kleinhouden als historisch verschijnsel*. Meppel: Boom.

Dekker, M.T.M., & Van den Bergh, P.M. (2002). *Ouderparticipatie in Medisch Kleuterdagverblijven* (working title). Amsterdam: SWP Publishers (forthcoming).

De Winter, M. (1997). *Children as fellow citizens: Participation and committment*. Oxford: Radcliffe.

De Winter, M., & Noom, M. (2001). Iemand die je gewoon als mens behandelt... Thuisloze jongeren over het verbeteren van de hulpverlening. *Pedagogiek, 21*, 4, 296-309.

Donker, M.C.H. (1987). *De toets der goede bedoelingen*. Utrecht: NcGv.

Edens, F.M. (1992). The enhancement of professionality of residential child care workers. In J.D. Van der Ploeg, P.M. Van den Bergh, M. Klomp, E.J. Knorth, & M. Smit (Eds.), *Vulnerable youth in residential care: Part II* (pp. 177-186). Leuven: Garant Publishers.

Eisikovits, Z., & Beker, J. (1983). Beyond professionalism: The child and youth care worker as craftsman. *Child Care Quarterly, 12*, (2), 93-112.

Else, J.F., Groze, V., Hornby, H., Mirr, R.K., & Wheelock, J. (1992). Performance-based contracting: The case of residential foster care. *Child Welfare, 71*, 513-526.

FICE – Fédération Internationale des Communautés Educatives (1998). FICE Bulletin, 14 (Summer). Available: http://www.cyc-net.org/fice-curr.html.

Fleischer, B.M. (1985). Identification of strategies to reduce turnover among child care workers. *Child Care Quarterly, 14*, 130-139.

Fletcher, B. (1993). *Not just a name: The views of young people in foster and residential care*. London: National Consumer Council (in co-operation with the Who Cares? Trust).

Gottesman, M. (Ed.) (1991). *Residential child care: An international reader*. London: Whiting & Birch.

Gottesman, M. (Ed.) (1994). *Recent changes and new trends in extrafamilial child care: An international perspective.* London: Whiting & Birch.
Groen, A. (2001). Professionele kwaliteit in de jeugdzorg. *SPH Tijdschrift voor Sociaal Pedagogische Hulpverlening,* nr. 41, 60-65.
Hart, R.A. (1992). *Children's participation: From tokenism to citizenship.* Innocenti Essays, no. 4. Florence: UNICEF.
Hodges, V.G., & Pecora, P.J. (2000). What is strengths-based service planning? In H. Dubowitz, & D. DePanfilis (Eds.), *The handbook for child protection practice* (pp. 379-383). Newbury Park, CA: Sage.
Hutschemaekers, G., & Neijmeijer, L. (1999). *Beroepen in beweging: Professionalisering en grenzen van een multidisciplinaire GGZ.* Houten: Bohn Stafleu Van Loghum.
Jumelet, H., De Ruyter, D., & Kayser, T. (1999). *Gebruikmaken van cliëntenfeedback in de jeugdzorg.* Utrecht: NIZW Publishers.
Jumelet, H., & Haarsma, L. (1998). Empowerment in de jeugdzorg: Cliënten als participanten. In Th. Royers, L. De Ree, & G. Verbeek (Eds.), *Empowerment: Eigenmachtig worden in de hulpverlening* (pp. 57-67). Utrecht: NIZW Publishers.
Katz, I. (1995). Approaches to empowerment and participation in child protection. In C. Cloke, & M. Davies (Eds.), *Participation and empowerment in child protection* (pp. 154-169). London: Pitman.
Key, E. (1900). *Das Jahrhundert des Kindes.* Berlin: Fisher.
Klomp, M., & Van den Bergh, P.M. (1999). Werkbare hulpverleningsplanning in de (semi-) residentiële jeugdhulpverlening. In E.J. Knorth, & M. Smit (Eds.), *Planmatig handelen in de jeugdhulpverlening* (pp. 251-269). Leuven/Apeldoorn: Garant.
Klomp, M., Van den Bergh, P.M., & Harinck, F.J.H. (1997). Treatment planning in residential institutions. *Child and Youth Care Forum, 26,* (5), 343-355.
Knorth, E.J. (1998). You can't always get what you want... A selective review of studies on child placement and decision-making. *International Journal of Child and Family Welfare, 3,* (2), 115-134.
Knorth, E.J., & Smit, M. (1997). Elterliche Partizipation bei Heimbetreuung in den Niederlanden. *Praxis der Kinderpsychologie und Kinderpsychiatrie, 46,* 696-708.
Knorth, E.J., Van den Bergh, P.M., & Smit, M. (1997). A method for supporting intake decisions in residential child and youth care. *Child and Youth Care Forum, 26,* (5), 323-342.
Kroneman, M. (2000). Professionalisering. *0 / 25 Tijdschrift over Jeugd, 5,* (7), 30-31.
Langsted, O. (1994). Quality in child care; from the child's perspective. In P. Moss, & A. Pence (Eds.), *Valuing quality in early childhood* (pp. 28-42). London: Paul Chapman Publishing Ltd.
Lewis, A. (1992). An overview of research. In J. Thoburn (Ed.), *Participation in practice: A reader.* Norwich: University of East Anglia Press.
Lühmann, N., & Schorr, K.E. (1979). Technologiedefizit der Erziehung und die Pädagogik. *Zeitschrift für Pädagogik, 25,* 345-365.
Lupton, C., & Nixon, P. (1999). *Empowering practice? A critical appraisal of the family group conference approach.* Bristol: The Policy Press.
Lupton, C., & Stevens, M. (1998). Planning in partnership? An assessment of process and outcome in UK Family Group Conferences. *International Journal of Child and Family Welfare, 3,* 135-148.
Madge, N. (1994). *Children and residential care in Europe.* London: National Children's Bureau.

Mattingly, M. (1995). Developing professional ethics for child and youth care work: Assuming responsibility for the quality of care. *Child and Youth Care Forum, 24,* (6), 378-391.

Oppenoorth, W. H., & Spaander, M. (2002). Disempowerment of parents as an effect of residential child and adolescent psychiatry. In P.M. Van den Bergh, E.J. Knorth, F. Verheij, & D.C. Lane (Eds.), *Changing care: Enhancing professional quality and client involvement in child and youth care services.* Amsterdam: SWP Publishers (forthcoming).

Pecora, P.J., Whittaker, J.K., Maluccio, A.N., & Barth, R.P., with Plotnick, R.D. (2000). *The child welfare challenge: Policy, practice and research. Second edition.* Hawthorne (NY): Aldine De Gruyter.

Rispens, J. (1983). *De theorie van de kundige ingreep: Over de theoretische fundering van klinisch en orthopedagogisch handelen.* Assen: Van Gorcum.

Ruxton, S. (1996). *Children in Europe.* London: NCH Action for Children.

Saleebey, D. (Ed.) (1997). *The strengths perspective in social work practice. Second edition.* New York: Longman.

Scholte, E.M., Colton, M.J., Casas, F., Drakeford, M., Roberts, S., & Williams, M. (1999). Perceptions of stigma and user involvement in child welfare services. *British Journal of Social Work, 29,* 373-391.

Shier, H. (2001). Pathways to participation: Openings, opportunities and obligations. A new model for enhancing children's participation in decision-making, in line with Article 12.1 of the UN Convention on the Rights of the Child. *Children and Society, 15,* 107-117.

Sinclair, R., & Grimshaw, R. (1997). Partnership with parents in planning the care of their children. *Children and Society, 11,* 231-241.

Thoburn, J., Lewis, A., & Shemmings, D. (1995). *Paternalism or partnership? Family involvement in the child protection process.* London: HMSO.

Thoburn, J., Lewis, A., & Shemmings, D. (1996). Partnership-based practice in child protection work. In M. Hill, & J. Aldgate (Eds.), *Child welfare services: Developments in law, policy, practice and research* (pp. 132-143). London: Jessica Kingsley Publishers.

Thomas, N. (2000). Giving children a voice. In G. Van den Berg (Ed.), *Lost and found* (pp. 53-56). Utrecht: SJN.

Thomas, N., & O'Kane, C. (1999). Experiences of decision-making in middle childhood. The example of children 'looked after' by local authorities. *Childhood, 6,* (3), 369-387.

Trede, W. (1999). Heimerziehung als Beruf: Die Situation in Europa. In H.E. Colla, Th. Gabriel, S. Millham, S. Müller-Teusler, & M. Winkler (Eds.), *Handbuch Heimerziehung und Pflegekinderwesen in Europa – Handbook residential and foster care in Europe* (pp. 801-806). Neuwied/Kriftel: Luchterhand.

Twijnstra, M.H. (1989). Kwaliteit en professionaliteit in de jeugdhulpverlening. *Tijdschrift voor Jeugdhulpverlening en Jeugdwerk, 1,* (3), 44-51.

Van Beek, F., Hameetman, M., & Meerdink, J. (1999). *Dat ik niet alleen hun werk ben. Trends in 'kinderkwaliteitscriteria' over de (semi)residentiële jeugdhulpverlening.* Utrecht: SWP Publishers.

Van der Ploeg, J.D., & Van den Bergh, P.M. (Eds.) (1987). *Besluitvorming en jeugdhulpverlening.* Leuven/Apeldoorn: Acco.

Van IJzendoorn, M. (1997). *Kwaliteit zonder kapsones: Een denkkader voor kwaliteitszorg in de welzijnssector.* Utrecht: NIZW Publishers (4th ed.).

Van Unen, A. (1995). *New legislation on care for children and young people in England, Germany and the Netherlands.* Amsterdam: Defence for Children International (DCI).

Veerman, J.W., & Ten Brink, L.T. (2001). Lessen uit follow-up onderzoek. In H. Van Leeuwen, W. Slot, & M. Uijterwijk (Eds.), *Antisociaal gedrag bij jeugdigen: Determinanten en interventies* (pp. 207-224). Lisse: Swets & Zeitlinger.

Verheij, F. (1997). Het samenwerken met ouders en gezin als een kind of jeugdige in intensieve zorg of behandeling is. *Tijdschrift voor Orthopedagogiek, Kinderpsychiatrie en Klinische Kinderpsychologie, 33*, 102-109.

Verheij, F. (1999). Behandelingsplanning met oog voor de ontwikkelings- en levensdomeinen van kinderen en adolescenten. In E.J. Knorth, & M. Smit (Eds.), *Planmatig handelen in de jeugdhulpverlening* (pp. 235-250). Leuven/Apeldoorn: Garant.

Welsby, J. (1996). A voice in their own lives. In W. De Boer, M. Geldmacher, L. Haarsma, L.E.E. Ligthart, & S. Meuwese (Eds.), *Children's rights and residential care in international perspective* (pp. 137-145). Amsterdam: Defence for Children International (DCI).

Westmeyer, H. (1976). Grundlagenprobleme psychologischer Diagnostik. In K. Pawlik (Hrsg.), *Diagnose der Diagnostik* (pp. 71-101). Stuttgart: Klett Verlag.

PART I

HISTORICAL PERSPECTIVES

Chapter 2

Demystification in the Century of the Child: The Conflict between Romanticism and Disenchantment in (Residential) Youth Care from the 1830s to 2000

Jeroen J.H. Dekker

Introduction

'This book will be returned to time and again during this just starting Century, it will be quoted and refuted' (Rilke & Key, 1902, p. 249).[1] With this sentence, the German poet Rainer Maria Rilke (1875-1926) opened his review of *Das Jahrhundert des Kindes* by the Swedish pedagogue, feminist, and socialist Ellen Key (1849-1926). Her book was published in 1900, was translated into German in 1902, and became a best-seller. Even today, every pedagogue knows at least the title of her book. In the same year of his review, Rilke started a correspondence with Key, which continued for twenty years. Key, then 52 years old, remained unmarried and, not having children of her own, looked on Rilke, then 26 years old, and his wife Clara, as if they were her own children. 'You and your wife have become like children for Ellen Key', so wrote Key to Rilke in a letter written between 29th January and 5th February 1903 (Rilke & Key, 1902, p. 7; cf. Andresen & Baader, 1998; Dräbing, 1990; 't Hart, 1948).[2] In his letters to Key, Rilke often called himself her child or her son, and, from his first letter involved her in his domestic affairs. After informing Key that he was impressed by the German translation of her book, and stating that he would send his review to her, he involved her with the young couple's problem of finding a baby-sitter, no doubt a problem familiar for many such couples. His daughter Ruth was nine months old, and her mother Clara intended to go to Paris to skill herself even better as a sculptress under the guidance of the famous French sculptor Auguste Rodin (1840-1917). Who should be Ruth's baby-sitter when her father was writing poems and her mother was making sculptures? 'Have you a solution? Do you, with so many acquaintances, know someone who could be of use for my beloved wife?' so asked Rilke in his first letter of 6 September 1902 to Key (Rilke & Key, 1902, p. 5).[3]

The end of that story is something for the history of babysitting and day nursery. The important issue now is Rilke's opinion on Key's *Das Jahrhundert des Kindes*. He enthusiastically considered Key as 'the child's advocate and apostle'. The future was central, however, for Key, according to Rilke, and children are a means to realise that future. Key was 'unsatisfied with the present circumstances and she places all her hope in the child, which is the future [...] The Children are progress itself'. Until now, so argued Rilke children have been slaves, especially when attending a school which was organized along Herbartian ideas, from the famous German pedagogue and philosopher Johann Friedrich Herbart (1776-1841). Such a school system worked like a 'systematic fight against personality', and that fight should end as soon as possible. The similarities which Key observed between child and artist pleased the young poet very much. In his experience, the academy of arts often influenced the young artist as negatively as the school influenced the young child: as a 'systematic fight against personality' (Rilke & Key, 1902, pp. 250, 252-254).[4]

When Ellen Key published her book in 1900 and proclaimed the 20th century to be the Century of the Child, she demonstrated a talent for the propaganda of her own ideas. She travelled around the world, gave many presentations, and saw her book translated into more than ten languages, including Japanese. The Century of the Child became a notion, famous all over the world. It borrows Key's idea of progress. The beginning of the 20th century is, according to adherents of Key, the start of child-centred upbringing, the century as a whole characterized by carrying out Key's programme. Indeed, she proclaims a new Century, namely that of the Child, and she tells the educators that good education makes the future. She is generally considered a modern thinker because she writes in a very effective and rhetorical way about the future. In emphasizing the best interests of the child, and the importance of educators, she became popular, until today, amongst an overwhelming majority of pedagogues and social workers.

And yet, arguing that Key's book is the true start of child-centred upbringing, that her educational ideas are modern, and that she is an outspoken herald of the Century of the Child, raises at least three questions. Firstly, there is no evidence for her argument that child-centred upbringing should start only from 1900. Such a view makes all history of education before that magic year no more than pedagogical pre-history, history before the origins of childhood, education and child-centred upbringing. On the contrary, many studies argue convincingly that child rearing should be considered as a structural element of human behaviour, this notwithstanding variations in time and place. However, child rearing, it is argued in the modern history of childhood, is not a phenomenon that was invented in a particular period of history (Becchi & Julia, 1996; Bedaux, 2000; Dekker, 1996a; Dekker & Groenendijk, 1991; Dekker, Groenendijk & Verberckmoes, 2000; Pollock, 1983; Pollock 1987; Shahar, 1990; Wilson, 1980).

Secondly, although Key is speaking in a very suggestive way about the future, that does not make her ideas automatically modern. Key worked very eclectically and made use of rather different sources in developing her own ideas, from Spinoza's pantheism to Galtung's eugenics, from Montaigne's ideas on savoir-vivre to Nietzsche's 'neue Mensch', and from Rousseau's radical ideas on childhood to Darwin's evolutionism (Andresen & Baader, 1998; Dräbing, 1990). She borrowed her basic ideas on childhood and education, namely about the natural development of the child and the central position of the mother in child rearing, directly from Jean-Jacques Rousseau's famous *Émile*, published in 1762. Rousseau (1712-1778) was popular in the Key family. Her great-grandfather admired him, and the name 'Émile' was frequently used in the family: Ellen Key's father was called after him ('t Hart, 1948). Her image of childhood has also many similarities with romantic poets like William Blake (1757-1827), who wrote: 'And I wrote my happy songs / Every child may joy to hear', and William Wordsworth (1770-1850). Wordsworth, in his *Ode on Intimations of Immortality from Recollection of Early Childhood*, put the child on the throne of innocence. He considered childhood as the best part of life, and the child itself as a human being not far from God, as is clear from the following verse: 'Though inland far we be, / Our Souls have sight of that immortal sea / Which brought us hither, / Can in a moment travel thither, / And see the Children sport upon the shore'. This was typical for romantic ideas on childhood (Baader, 1996; Cunningham, 1995). Key wrote on the concept of holiness of the child, which was central for her pedagogy, in her main book: 'The age of the holiness of the child will arrive' (Key, 1903, p. 42).[5] Such ideas on the holiness of the child were also developed by Johann Gottfried Herder (1744-1803), Rousseau (1712-1778), Johann Wolfgang Goethe (1749-1832), Johann Christoph Friedrich Von Schiller (1759-1805), the brothers August Wilhelm (1767-1845) and Friedrich Schlegel (1772-1829), Novalis alias Friedrich von Hardenberg (1772-1801), Friedrich Schleiermacher (1768-1834) and Friedrich Wilhelm August Fröbel (1782-1852) (Andresen & Baader, 1998; Rosenblum, 1988).

Motherhood was also holy, according to Key, in contrast with the earthly fatherhood (Andresen & Baader, 1998). According to Key, women should be content with minor intellectual performance, because maternal obligations exhausted the forces and so diminished the space for intellectual performance (Key, 1903).[6] Central in Key's pedagogical utopia – for indeed she was a utopian thinker – was the relationship between generations, in particular between mother and child, in contrast to Rousseau, whose pedagogical utopia was centred in the world of the child (Andresen & Baader, 1998). Summing up, Key's basic ideas about childhood and education were not so much modern, as well as borrowed from Romanticism (Depaepe, 1998; Van Crombrugge, 1995).

Lastly, the image of Key as the herald of the Century of the Child is not a matter of fact. Key, who hardly attended school and learned her basics mainly by private teaching and self-study (Dräbing, 1990), has become famous among pedagogues for attacking the Herbartian school system, in one of the chapters of *The Century of the Child*. No doubt that was the main reason why so many adherents of the *Reform Pädagogik*, or Progressive Education, such as the Dutch Jan Ligthart (1859-1916), whose school in The Hague was visited by Key, were so enthusiastic about Key's ideas (De Jong, 1996). For the rest, *Reform Pädagogik* was very heterogeneous indeed (Andresen & Baader, 1998; Depaepe, 1998; Oelkers, 1989, 1995). Pedagogues like Ligthart, Maria Montessori (1870-1952), Jean-Ovide Decroly (1871-1932), and Key, amongst others, had in common their criticism of the Herbartian school system, but differed from each other in many respects regarding their educational systems.

Key was different in another way too. It is the thesis in this chapter that the central topic of her book on the Century of the Child is not about the best interests of the child, but on progress, evolutionism, and eugenics, summarizing on the realization of a new human being. I would suggest that with another title, for example 'The Century of Progress', 'The Century of the Supreme Human Being', or 'The Century of the Adequate Reproduction of the Human Race', Key's book would never have become so popular among progressive educational circles. Yet, the first sixty pages of chapter one contain a eugenic message, i.e. the pursuit of the adequate reproduction of the human race. In his enthusiastic report from 1902 Rilke was not referring to this message. She propagates a new age with a superior human being and a new morality, from the point of view of the 'holiness of the generation' (Key, 1900, pp. 2, 52).[7] In her utopia, the *via educationis* is not the goal, but the main means (Andresen & Baader, 1998). In quoting extensively the main evolutionists of her time like Darwin, Galton, and Spencer, and relying on Nietzsche, she emphasizes the risks of degeneration (Key, 1900), the necessity of euthanasia on children with a psychologically and physically incurable disease or handicap (cf. Andresen & Baader), and the risks for a marriage between people with inadequate hereditary material (Key, 1900).[8] According to Key, the first right of a child should be the right to choose its parents (Key, 1900).[9] Society should act in name of the not yet begetted child, and in a eugenic way: 'Society should prevent marriages in particular in such cases where heredic diseases are clear' (Key, 1900, p. 58).[10]

This way of arguing was not unique in Key's time. On the contrary, writing about eugenics was in vogue, in contrast to its practise, which, at least in Europe probably only occurred on a broad scale in Nazi-Germany, and, until the 1970s in Sweden (Andresen & Baader, 1998). Although the contents of her eugenic message were not special, the effective and rhetorical presentation of it was. Key made children the most important pawn in the pursuit of progress and the supreme human being, her idealistic and romantic ideas of the holiness of child and of motherhood being part of her eugenic utopia. In a social Darwinist way, Key made eugenics the foundation for new relationships between generations and sexes, according to Andresen and Baader (1998). By good marketing, Key's book became the standard bearer of the *Reform Pädagogik* movement. Its title became an icon for many pedagogues who were concerned about 'the best interests of the child'.

In the Century of the Child, apart from the neo-romantic enchantment of the child by Key and her adherents, child and education were influenced by a development from the 16th century which started with science and theology, and named by Max Weber *Entzauberung*, i.e. disenchantment. First we go briefly into the meaning of this development for the history of pedagogical youth care. Then, residential pedagogical youth care before the start of the Century of the Child is looked at. A true story about the end of romanticism and the start of Disenchantment will be given, and the acceleration of the disenchantment process around 1900 by the introduction of Child Acts and the emergence of Child Science will be examined. It will be concluded that the 20th century should not be coined as the Century of the Child, but rather as the Child-Oriented Century.

The Concept of *Entzauberung*

A contemporary of Ellen Key, Max Weber (1864-1920), great sociologist, social-economic historian and jurist, presented his idea of 'Wissenschaft als

Beruf' [science as a profession] on 7th November 1917, in a lecture for students at the University of München. The German philosopher Karl Löwith (1897-1973), who attended Weber's lecture as a student, was impressed by his pointed questions and his words, in which his life-long experience and knowledge was condensed.[11] Weber criticized the irrational movements of his time and he characterized science as the most important aspect of the process of intellectualization or rationalization in the modern world. Rationalization started with the emergence of the great religions, through which the magic worldview was pushed back. From the Renaissance, science started to play a role in further pushing back irrational ways of thinking (Dassen, 1999). He called this process 'intellectual rationalisation by science and scientifically oriented technology'.[12]

Weber is not meaning by this rationalization that modern man has more insight in the conditions of life [die Lebensbedingungen]. For example, in our time, many modern citizens can drive a car, use a computer, send an email, surf on the Internet, and communicate by mobile telephone. However, very few of them will have any knowledge of what exactly is going on when driving, emailing, internetting, or using the mobile telephone. In primitive cultures, much more practical knowledge of these conditions of life is present, for these are much less complex. Rationalization according to Weber is something else: 'There are in principle no mysterious incalculable powers that play a role. Rather we can master by calculation everything. But that means: *the disenchantment of the world* [italics JD]. No longer must we – like the savage for whom such power existed – grasp at magical means to master or implore the spirits. But technical means and calculations accomplish that' (Weber, 1919, p. 594; English translation by Mitzman, 1969, p. 226).[13] Weber did not invent the concept of *Entzauberung*. It was born in the German Romantic period and is to be found in the works of Schiller, Novalis, and Johann Christian Friedrich Hölderlin (1770-1843). Weber, however, who mentioned the concept in 1913 for the first time in his work, made it famous. Only he was sustaining his analysis of rationalization to the end, including religion and science as phases in the process of *Entzauberung* (Dassen, 1999; Wax, 1991).

Entzauberung does have two important consequences for child rearing and education. Firstly, a belief was born in the possibility of getting knowledge of the children's world *in toto*. At the end of the 19th century, child science flourished, as Depaepe (1993) showed. All secrets of the young human being, including the so-called magic world of the child, should and could be approached scientifically. The same was true with the effects of parental behaviour. We know about Freud's trying to trace almost any serious psychological problems to the traumatic effects of parenting and in traumatic experiences of the young child, using rational methods to invade the unconsciousness. This rationalization of the child and education, including its magic aspects, was incompatible with the romantic and enchanting image of childhood, developed by Rousseau and the romantic poets, and adopted by Key and the *Vom Kinde aus* movement.

The second consequence hits the heart of pedagogics, in particular utopian focused pedagogics as formulated by Key. For, according to Weber, rationalization also means that eventually the world does not have meaning and sense. In his own words: 'It is the destiny of our time that the last and most sublime values are drawn back from the publicity' (Weber, 1982, p. 612).[14] In other words, *Entzauberung* also meant a world without illusions and this idea is incompatible with mainstream pedagogics. What would remain of educational goals in a senseless world with illusions put aside? Orientation on goals has always been important in classic pedagogics, as shown by, amongst others, Langeveld and Nohl (Hintjes, 1981). In the next section it will be shown that, in the educational domain in the 19th century, the conflict between romanticism and *Entzauberung* became explicit in the world of care and re-education of children at risk already.

Residential Youth Care before the Century of the Child

Perhaps, the *Entzauberung* of child rearing can be found for the first time in the history of schooling. Philippe Ariès emphasized in 1960, fifteen years before Michel Foucault, discipline as mean force in the history of schooling from the 16th century (Dekker & Lechner, 1999). Discipline is part of the *Entzauberung* process in so far as it is embedded in the process of transformation of the individual, based on the belief of knowing the inner emotions of that individual. *Entzauberung* grows in importance in 19th century care and re-education of criminal children and children at-risk. First, a brief overview will be given of the images of childhood upon which this care and re-education were based. Then, the birth of residential re-education will be described. Finally, the deadlock of the romantic image of childhood and the beginnings of *Entzauberung* will be shown by a true story that happened in a re-education home.

Three Images of Childhood in Residential Youth Care

Three images of childhood are dominating education at the beginning of the 19th century. Most radical was Rousseau's image of childhood, a very child-oriented view, developed in his *Émile* from 1762. He asserted the right of a child to be a child, to be happy as an innocent being, and to be brought up in a natural way, preferably by his or her mother. As we saw above, many romantic writers, poets and artists followed him in this way of thinking about the image of childhood, including Ellen Key (Cunningham, 1995; Hwang et al., 1996).

A second image of childhood, present before Rousseau, was John Locke's idea of the child as a *tabula rasa*, developed in his *Some Thoughts Concerning Education* from 1693. In fact, Locke did not believe in the idea of a child to be 'considered only as white Paper, [...] to be moulded and fashioned as one pleases'. He limited his *tabula rasa* concept to ideas only, not to abilities or temperaments (Cuningham, 1995, pp. 62-63). However, the vulgarized and popular version of his concept proved to be the more influential one. According to that version, focused on the child as a whole, including its abilities and temperaments, the child was not an innocent being, as was argued by Rousseau, but an empty one, to be filled by the educators. This concept originated in Humanistic and Reformation Europe, as can be seen in texts by Erasmus and J. Cats (Cunningham, 1995; Dekker, Groenendijk & Verberckmoes, 2000).

The third image of childhood was the idea of the child marked by the Original Sin. This image is rather neglected in the history of education of the 19th century. However, it was the central image of childhood behind many activities in the field of children-at risk, undertaken by adherents of the Réveil movement and by British Evangelicals, as for example the Dutch Otto Gerhard Heldring, the German Johan-Hinrich Wichern, and the British Lord Shaftesbury. The Original Sin has always been important in Christian pedagogical thinking, but the acceptance of this belief did not prevent Christian pedagogues and moralists, in particular protestant ones, from having a rather optimistic pedagogical vision, from the Renaissance. It is true that the 19th century Réveil adherents of the Original Sin were rather pessimistic (Dekker, Groenendijk & Verberckmoes, 2000; Hendrick, 1990; Hilton, 1991; Innes, 1998, p. 32). Yet, this pessimistic attitude did not prevent them from becoming, after ca. 1830, very active in the field of care for children at-risk, for the burden of the Original Sin stimulated educational activism.

The Birth of Residential Re-education

At the beginning of the 19th century, the marginal position of children became the subject of special reconsideration, in particular by philanthropists. Specific interventions for marginal, at-risk children, became acceptable (Bec, 1994; Cunningham & Innes 1998; Dekker, 1990; Farge, 1986a, 1986b). Many methods of intervention were proposed and introduced, including improvement of schooling, and family patronage systems (Tétard, 1994). All these methods kept the children at home, with their families. However, for certain categories of children such methods were believed to be insufficient. Risks had gone too far for the criminal and seriously deprived children, for whom a future of vagrancy or adult criminality seemed unavoidable. For these children, a radical solution was necessary, so was the opinion of the majority of European philanthropists, among them Charles Lucas and Frédéric-Auguste Demetz from France, Édouard Ducpétiaux from Belgium, Mary Carpenter, Matthew Davenport Hill and the Reverend Sydney Parker from England, Willem Suringar from the Netherlands, and Johann-Hinrich Wichern from Germany. Only by taking the children out of the dangerous big towns and into residential homes in the isolated and sane countryside, a healing process was possible. In the 1830s, residential care for criminal and at-risk children was born with the foundation of famous homes like the Rauhe Haus near Hamburg in Germany in 1833, the Dutch Boy's prison in Rotterdam (1833), the French Mettray (1839), Red Hill (1849) in England, and in 1851 Ruysselede in Belgium and Mettray in the Netherlands (Dekker, 1998; Dupont-Bouchat & Pierre, 2001; Leonards, 1995; Lindmeier, 1998). Orphanages were founded much earlier, in the late middle ages in Italy, with the famous example of the Florentine *Ospedale degli Innocenti* in Florence, and in the Netherlands, with early examples in Leiden and Utrecht (Gavitt, 1990; Groenveld, Dekker & Willemse, 1997). At the end of the century, thousands of children's homes were founded.

Images of childhood were behind these activities. Orthodox protestant pioneers like Shaftesbury and Heldring, representatives of Christian philanthropy, built their pedagogy on the concept of childhood marked by Original Sin. Founders of homes like Mettray, in France and in the Netherlands, representatives of the modern Enlightenment philanthropy, built their pedagogics on a mix of Enlightenment and Romantic ideas. In this world of re-education of children at-risk, the romantic image of childhood reached a deadlock. One example of this process will be given, at the Dutch home for re-education of children-at-risk *Nederlandsch*

Mettray. This particular process, however, can be traced in re-education homes all over Europe in the 1870s and 80s.

Children-At-Risk at Dinner: Romanticism in a Deadlock, Entzauberung in the Lift

Willem Suringar (1790-1872) was the most important 19th century Dutch philanthropist. He belonged to the international philanthropic elite and was the author of books on prisons and on poor relief. Member of the board of the first national Dutch philanthropic society, the *Maatschappij tot Nut van 't Algemeen* [The Society for the General Good], he was also co-founder, in 1823, of the *Genootschap tot Zedelijke Verbetering der Gevangenen* [Dutch Society for the Moral Amelioration of Prisoners]. In 1845, like so many philanthropists of his time, he visited Mettray, the French colony for criminal boys (Dekker, 2001; Dekker & Lechner, 1999; Wines, 1880). He was so impressed by the re-education at Mettray that he decided to start such a home in the Netherlands too. In *My visit to Mettray*, also published in Dutch, French and German, he wrote down his impressions of his visit to Mettray. He was impressed as much by the moral atmosphere and the pedagogical character as by the system of rewards and punishments. This system was a mixture of Enlightenment and Romantic pedagogical ideas. In his *Nederlandsch Mettray*, founded in 1851, deprived boys were admitted.

Not long after his death in 1872, in the years 1873-1884, the life on Suringar's love-baby *Nederlandsch Mettray*, where he was also buried, was destabilised. Two rivalling parties, the Head and his opponents, produced contradictory reports about the boys, and there was a fundamental difference of opinion about the way in which the orders should be implemented. The Head was Andries Meeter (1817-1889), former Director of the Reformatory of Alkmaar, and an adherent of the romantic image of childhood (Leonards, 1995). One particular incident, described elsewhere in detail (Dekker, 1994)[15] is taken as an example of the long chain of incidents between rivalling factions during those years 1873-1884.

On Monday the fifteenth of January 1883, a large number of boys refused to appear at the review prior to lunch. They didn't want to eat. The newly appointed Deputy-Head had decided that the existing orders on what should be served at mealtimes should be strictly adhered to. The menu stated that the boys should be given pea soup with bacon on Mondays. In practice they were given not only soup with bacon but they also got an extra piece of bacon or bone of meat as well. Before proceeding the new Deputy consulted his superior, the Head, about what should be done, and the latter replied that soup should be served without bacon in it, and that the boys should also get a piece of bacon apart from this. The Deputy proceeded believing he had the backing of his superior. The boys petitioned against having to eat soup without bacon in it. The Head told them that this was according to the orders for the day, but on this day the boys simply were not taking it. The boys, who had to be cured first and foremost of disobedience as the worst childhood fault, revolted. The situation escalated. The boys disobeyed a fundamental rule of the colony – obeying orders. Moreover, the Head added oil to the fire: 'Now boys, if it turns out that not serving bacon in the soup was based on a misunderstanding then this will be changed, in consultation with the gentleman in question [the Deputy Head]'. This, as the boys were well aware, made the position of the Deputy untenable. They heckled him and threw mud and pieces of wood at him. He disappeared prematurely from the scene.

Confidential documents contain extensive reports on the behaviour of the boys and their Head. One of these documents was written by a member of the Board W.O.F. Schas. His letter was discussed in the meeting of the Board on 29 January 1883. Schas lived in Gorssel, near *Nederlandsch Mettray*, and he could, as it were, hear the boys bellowing whenever he took a walk in his garden. Only some days after the boys refused to eat, he took up his pen and wrote down his accusations on paper. He produced an account covering ten folio pages with the title 'a concise history of what we have been through with Mr. Meeter in the last 3 years', in which the following judgement of the Head was given. 'Mr. Meeter is not a weak person in human terms, as he has been portrayed, but he is weak out of principle, because he can not see any other way of conducting affairs. The boys are encouraged by his constant giving in, and therefore will not accept any discipline from anyone else, and it is, I believe, impossible to keep a crew of wicked lads from the lowest social classes in order without discipline'. Schas had characterized him perfectly, namely as an adherent of the romantic image of childhood.

However, hardly any trace of the crisis found its way into the public documents. Even the dismissal of the Head, a decision which brought the crisis to an end, was reported in a way that only insiders would understand. The members of the local departments, in cities like Amsterdam, Rotterdam, and the Hague, read the annual report, which did not mention the problems at all, and the annual reports of their own departments, in which the situation in the colony was presented in extremely rosy terms. The Head compiled these reports, which included information on the behaviour and progress of each boy who had been sent by the department. He used his power over the flow of information as a weapon in the fight with the Board, and was convinced that his interpretation of the behaviour of the boys was the only right one. In reading the reports of the department of The Hague, the impression exists that one is reading about quite different children from the ones described in such negative terms in other sources, as for example the report by Schas. The Head used almost exclusively superlatives when publicizing the progress of 'his' boys. 'Extremely good', 'Excellent behaviour', 'A pleasant, well-mannered boy who promises to become the jewel in the colony's crown', etc. Were these the same boys who rioted, refused to eat, fought with the police, heckled the deputy, threw mud and wood and generally vandalized the place? They were.

After the crisis had been resolved, peace returned and the orders were again in force and discipline was strengthened. The family homes, part of the romantic way of re-education, were rebuilt to barracks, so that even in the architecture, the belief in the romantic image of childhood of these children-at-risk, so loved by their Head, Meeter, was over. Thus, almost twenty years before Key published her book on the Century of the Child, founded on a romantic image of childhood, the romantic child-oriented treatment of children-at-risk, present in this residential re-education home, reached a deadlock. The childhood of these at risk children was disenchanted.

Child Science, Children Acts, and the *Entzauberung* of Childhood around 1900

Two phenomena accelerated the *Entzauberung* of childhood and children at-risk around 1900, namely the birth of Child Science and the introduction of Children Acts. Toward the end of the nineteenth century, medical concepts were introduced into the existing pedagogical theories, which developed from merely philosophical and moral systems to empirical ones. The Leipzig professor Adolf Heinrich Ludwig Von Strümpell (1812-1899) published in 1890 his several times reprinted book *Die Pädagogische Pathologie oder die Lehre von den Fehlern der Kinder* [Pedagogical Pathology, or, the science of Child Deficiencies]. With his approach, he stood at the centre of the international development of pedagogy of his time (Depaepe, 1993). In his view, pedagogical pathology and therapy were far more complex than medical pathology, for two reasons. Firstly, pedagogical pathology stressed prevention, contrary to medical pathology. Secondly, only one hundred medical child diseases were known, whilst more than three hundred pedagogical and moral child deficiencies could be mentioned! Such a complex discipline as pedagogical pathology had therefore to be propagated and at the same time developed further, especially for those residential institutions for deprived and criminal children, which then could only play a prophylactic or even only a philanthropic role (Von Strümpell, 1890, p. 97).

Von Strümpell was not alone in his opinions. On the contrary, a new paradigm developed, in the Netherlands, in Belgium, Germany, France, and the Anglo-American world, under the names of pedagogical pathology, child-study, pedology, and experimental pedagogics. In 1894, for instance, a London Child Study group, inspired by G.S. Hall, the American child psychologist, was formed (Hendrick, 1992). Eventually, the Edinburgh psychiatrist Sir Thomas Clouston became one of the leading figures of the British child-study-movement. Although looking to child-science from a medical point of view, for example in his *Morals and Brain* (1912), education was very important indeed for Clouston. Education was necessary for the realization of practical moral conduct and for the regulating of, in his words, 'impulse and desire, passion and temptation', as was an 'active role for teachers, parents, youth workers, and social administrators' (Hendrick, 1990, p. 110; see also Depaepe, 1993; Hurt, 1998; Pritchard, 1963; Rose, 1985). Examples of contemporary French studies are Descoedres, Ley, and Philippe. The founding fathers of Dutch pedagogical pathology, Jan Klootsema, K. Andriesse and A.J. Schreuder, were originally schoolmasters (Andriesse, 1905; Schreuder, 1905). Like Von Strümpell, they were deeply concerned about the demarcation of pedagogical pathology *vis-à-vis* medical pathology. Their goal was the foundation of an independent pedagogical pathology. Klootsema (1867-1926) was the author of the first handbook on pedagogical pathology written in Dutch, entitled *Deprived Children. Introduction into Pedagogical Pathology and Therapy*. He defined child deficiencies from a pedagogical point of view as deficiencies which, although complicating child education, can be eliminated by pedagogical means. He was aware of the academic standing of the medical sciences in his country – a recently acquired standing – and therefore he was not opposed to co-operation between psychiatrists and pedagogues. The medical nomenclature could be of especial use to the pedagogues (Klootsema, 1904). Klootsema based his ideas on practical experience, starting his educational career as a schoolmaster, being, between 1898 and 1901, head of the School for Speech Defective and Retarded Children in Amsterdam, and then (Deputy)-Director of State Reformatories in Alkmaar and Doetinchem (Willemse, 1993).

The second phenomenon in stimulating the *Entzauberung* of the child was the introduction of Children Acts. Until ca. 1900, the balance between professional and parental educational power was sustained by moral and social limits, not by legal ones. The success of residential re-education in this pre-Children Act years was dependent on the efforts of philanthropists and pedagogues to have the parents believe in their ideas on children's deficiencies, for parental participation concerning children's protection could not be forced by law. In other words, the balance of educational power requested an amount of persuasion on the part of the pedagogues, and of participation on the part of the parents. This did stimulate the growth of residential re-education, but also caused huge frustration to planned educational change, so strongly desired by professionals and pedagogues. Therefore, the need for legal force, resulting in a shift of the balance of educational power to the advantage of the pedagogues (backed by the State and by private initiative, in particular Christian institutions) and to the disadvantage of the parents, grew in the last decades of the 19th century. Then, re-education received protection by law through the introduction of children's acts, starting in France in 1889 and then subsequently established in all European countries around the turn of the century. In the same years, re-education received justification by the above sketched new child science. The Children Acts shifted the pedagogical power in the direction of the state and the professional pedagogues at the same time as Ellen Key announced the Century of the Child (Neuenhaus, 1993).

Conclusion: From the Century of the Child to the Child-Oriented Century

In the 20th century, children received more special rights than ever before in history. Also the economy, in particular since the 70s, became child-focused as never before. Science became focused on children's behaviour in a historically unprecedented way, with great influence on educational practice and child and youth care. This orientation on children was stimulated by romantic ideas about childhood and education by Key and other idealists in school experiments under the umbrella of *Reform Pädagogik*. At the same time, however, many aspects of children's life were disenchanted: a conflict between Romanticism and Disenchantment emerged in education and child rearing.

Firstly, the development of child-oriented rights started in the 19th century with the Factory Acts, the Children Acts and the Compulsory Education Acts. This process culminated in the *1989 United Nations Convention on the Rights of the Child*. This Convention contains all sorts of rights for the protection of children, including the right to be heard in any decision that may affect her or his life. With this Convention being a treaty, not only a declaration, there exists a juridical obligation for all States subscribing and ratifying it to protect children. Only a few states, including the USA, did not subscribe. Secondly, the Western economy has, in three specific areas, demonstrated an historically unprecedented child-oriented character in recent decades. Firstly, in the last decades of the 20th century, at least in the Western world, children's labour has again become very important. It was necessary for many children to contribute to the family's income until far in the 19th century, when this phenomenon was pushed back by the introduction of Factory Acts. Now, children's labour serves not as a contribution to the family's income, but as a source of income for the children themselves. Important parts of western economy, for example retail, catering, food, and, in the Netherlands, the distribution of newspapers, cannot run without children's labour. Secondly, children are important consumers, the clothes industry and clothes retail, computers, games, cafés, discos, earning enormous amounts out of children. Thirdly, although parents' investments in their children is not a new phenomenon, its scale became unprecedented in the last decades. According to Cunningham, in the 90s a child in Britain cost over £100,000, which seems to be normal in all Western countries (Cunningham, 1995).

Probably, there is no evidence for the argument that child-oriented violence happened more often in the Century of the Child than before. However, the reversal, namely that it diminished, has no evidence either. A new phenomenon is the growing concern for violence against children, child abuse, child prostitution, and child pornography, distributed widely by the new media, including the Internet. The media are worried about violence against children – everybody knows the name and the face of Marc Dutroux – just as police and justice, child and youth care institutions, and social scientists. This can be seen, apart from the huge amount of books and articles published, including Kempe's classic article on the Battered Child Syndrome (Kempe, 1962), in the emergence in 1977 and 1992 of *Child Abuse and Neglect* and *Child Abuse Review*, specialized journals on child abuse. More certainty exists about violence that is not specifically child-oriented in the Century of the Child. That kind of violence has turned out to be dramatically effective in killing children, namely the massacre of innocents during the great wars and ideological conflicts of the century. The conservatively estimated overall numbers of victims are incomparable with wars and conflicts before this century. Figures are for the Second World War 50 million, for the Mao Zedong Terror 40 million, for the Stalin Terror 20 million and for the First World War 15 million victims approximately (Dockrill, 1991; Shafritz, 1993). This was the result of the changing character of wars, hitting purposefully the civil population, including its children, more than before, and, of course, the ideology driven massacre, intending to eliminate ethnic groups or sometimes even a race as a whole, including its children. The Nazi Holocaust was responsible for a huge number of young victims, the reason why perhaps the best-known icon of youth in the 20th century is the Jewish girl Anne Frank, who wrote her diary in Amsterdam, and was killed in Bergen-Belsen.

The disenchantment of child and youth is perhaps most evident by the development of the educational sciences and of developmental psychology, with its effects on the practice of child and youth care. By using diagnostic methods, new therapy techniques, and by introducing planned change models for the individual child as well as for the care system, child and youth care contributed substantially to the *Entzauberung* of child and youth. One of its consequences was that considering it as a profession *all* child rearing got more support. Child rearing should and could be learned, by professional educators as well as by parents themselves. This idea was disseminated by the successful genre of child rearing advice literature, consisting of books, periodicals, TV-programmes, and recently CD-Roms, out of which one example became the bible of child rearing, namely Dr. Spock's famous advice book (Bakker, 1995; Wubs, 2000). Many parents were apparently not lonely because they could fall back on Dr. Spock. At the end of the century, also courses in parenting were developed, and university chairs were established in the discipline of parental support (Janssens, 1998).

Child rearing as a profession, to be learned systematically: this is *Entzauberung* of child-rearing *in extremis*. The self-evident act of parenting, practised by many generations in using motherly, sometimes also fatherly, intuition, and parental instincts, should be learned systematically. For a specific group of parents, adoptive parents, their parental potentiality has to be assessed by Governmental Child Protection Offices, before the adoption of the child and the parenting of the parents is approved of. Recently, an instrument was developed in which the assessment of pedagogical capital is central (Vinke, 1999). Lastly, the conflict between Romanticism and *Entzauberung* in education is shown symbolically by the development of the child-oriented Ritalin drug against Attention Deficit Hyperactivity Disorder, ADHD. Eventually, the wild and turbulent child of Romanticism, to be educated according to his of her natural development, could and should be domesticated now, being too active for its 20th century environment (DSM-IV; Greenhill, 1991; Prins, 1999; Van der Ploeg & Scholte, 1999; Weiss, 1993).

Summarizing: to observe the majority of Century of the Child parents and educators working hard in the best interests of their children and pupils was not special at all. This has been normal behaviour for most parents long before the emergence of the Century of the Child. Specific for this century was the huge scale on which the Western society became child-oriented, as to rights, economy, science, and care. It was not so much a Century of the Child, focused on the best interests of the child, as well as a Child-oriented Century, no doubt focused on the child, but for the benefit of a series of, potentially conflicting interests, including that of the child. In making the child the pawn in her ideas about the pursuit of progress with her 'höheren Typus Mensch', Ellen Key contributed to a Child Oriented-Century, not to a Century of the Child. During that century, her idea of the Century of the Child, icon among many professional educators, turned out to become disenchanted.

Notes

1. The complete text in German reads: 'Man wird im Verlaufe dieses begonnenen Jahrhunderts immer wieder auf dieses Buch zurückkommen, man wird es zitieren und widerlegen, sich darauf stützen und sich dagegen wehren [...] Ja, ich glaube sogar nicht zuviel zu sagen, wenn ich behaupte, daß es Menschen hervorrufen wird, die danach leben werden; denn es ist von lauter Wirklichkeiten erfüllt, und Wirklichkeiten – mögen sie auch überraschend sein – drängen immer danach, gelebt zu werden.' Parts of this paper were published in an abridged form as 'The Century of the Child revisited' in *The International Journal of Children's Rights* 8 (2000), 133-150.
2. In German: 'Sie und Ihre Frau sind Ellen Key so ein bischen als Kinder geworden seit Herbst'.
3. In German: 'Können sie sich einen Ausweg denken? Wissen sie, da sie so viele Menschen kennen, einen, der meiner lieben Frau irgendwie nützen könnte..?'.
4. In German: 'Sie ist unzufrieden mit der Gegenwart und hofft auf das Kind, welches die Zukunft ist. Sie will diese Zukunft groß und glücklich, und darin begegnet sie sich mit denjenigen, welche an einer Umformung der Gesellschaft arbeiten. [...] Die Kinder sind der Fortschritt selbst'. And further: 'ein systematischer Kampf gegen die Persönlichkeit'.
5. In German: 'Die Zeit wird kommen, in der das Kind als heilig angesehen werden wird'.
6. In Key's words: 'die Frau [verbraucht] durch ihre mütterlichen Funktionen so viel physische und psychische Lebenskraft [...], dass sie auf dem Gebiete der geistigen Produktion minderwertig bleiben muss'.
7. In Key's words: 'höheren Typus Mensch', 'neue Sittlichkeit', 'Heiligkeit der Generation'.
8. In Key's words: 'In erster Linie muss dies dadurch geschehen, dass der Verbrechertypus [...] verhindert wird, sich fortzupflanzen, damit seine Eigenschaften sich nicht auf seine Nachkommenschaft vererbern. [...] In zweiter Linie kommt dann die Förderung, dass die mit erblichen physischen oder psychischen Krankheiten Belasteten diese nicht einer Nachkommenschaft vererben'.
9. In Key's words: 'das erste Recht des Kindes das ist, seine Eltern zu wählen'.
10. In Key's words: 'Besonders in Bezug auf Krankheiten, von deren Erblichkeit man absolut überzeugt ist, muss die Gesellschaft ehehindernd eingreifen'.

11. In his autobiography, Löwith wrote down his impressions as follows: 'In seinen Sätzen war die Erfahrung und das Wissen eines ganzen Lebens verdichtet, [...]. Der Schärfe der Fragestellung entsprach der Verzicht auf billige Lösung. Er zerriss alle Schleier der Wünschbarkeiten [...]', quoted by Dassen (1999, p. 203).
12. In the original text: 'intellektualistische Rationalisierung durch Wissenschaft und wissenschaftlich orientierte Technik', scientific progress being 'ein Bruchteil, und zwar der wichtigste Bruchteil, jenes Intellektualisierungsprozesses, dem wir seit Jahrtausenden unterliegen' (Weber, 1919, p. 593).
13. Weber's original reads as follows: 'daß man, wenn man nur wollte, es jederzeit erfahren könnte, daß es also prinzipiell keine geheimnisvollen unberechenbaren Mächte gebe die da hineinspielen, daß man vielmehr alle Dinge – im Prinzip – durch Berechnen beherrschen könne. Das aber bedeutet: die *Entzauberung der Welt* [my italics]. Nicht mehr, wie der Wilde, für den es solche Mächte gab, muß man zu magischen Mitteln greifen, um die Geister zu beherrschen oder zu erbitten. Sondern technische Mittel und Berechnung leisten das. Dies vor allem bedeutet die Intellektualisierung als solchen'.
14. Weber's original text: 'Es ist das Schicksal unserer Zeit [...] daß gerade die letzten und sublimsten Werte zurückgetreten sind aus der Öffentlichkeit'.
15. The description of the incident is based on a series of documents (confidential letters and annual reports of departments of the 'Nederlandsch Mettray' from the Municipal Archives of Zutphen, *Archives of 'Nederlandsch Mettray'* [abbreviated as ANM]. Used are: Minutes of the Board of Governors for 1869-1884 (ANM 77); Documents submitted to the Commission over 1883-1884 (ANM 84); Letter, dated 26 January 1883 (ANM 87); Letter by W.O.F. Schas (ANM 115); Reports on the State of Pupils Placed by the 's-Gravenhage Department, 1852-1904 (ANM 611), referred to extensively in Dekker (1994), and Dekker (2001).

References

Andresen, S., & Baader, M.S. (1998). *Wege aus dem Jahrhundert des Kindes. Tradition und Utopie bei Ellen Key.* Neuwied/Kriftel/Berlin: Luchterhand.

Andriesse, K. (1905). Kindergebreken. In C.F.A. Zernike (Ed.), *Paedagogisch Woordenboek* (pp. 597-612). Groningen: Wolters.

Ariès, Ph. (1973 [or. 1960]). *L'enfant et la vie familiale sous l'ancien régime.* Paris: Seuil.

Baader M.S. (1996). *Die romantische Idee des Kindes und der Kindheit. Auf der Suche nach der verloren Unschuld.* Neuwied/Kriftel/Berlin: Luchterhand.

Bakker, N. (1995). *Kind en karakter. Nederlandse pedagogen over opvoeding in het gezin 1845-1925.* Amsterdam: Het Spinhuis.

Bec, C., Duprat, C., Luc, J.N., & Petit, J-P. (Eds.) (1994). *Philanthropies et politiques sociales en Europe (XVIIIe-XXe siècles).* Paris: Anthropos.

Becchi, E., & Julia, D. (Eds.) (1996). *Storia dell'infanzia I. Dall'antichità al seicento.* Roma/Bari: Gius. Laterza & Figli.

Bedaux, J.B. (2000). Introduction. In J.B. Bedaux, & R.E.O. Ekkart (Eds.), *Pride and Joy. Children's portraits in the Netherlands 1500-1700* (pp. 11-31). Gent/Amsterdam/New York: Ludion and Abrams.

Brieler, U. (1998). Foucaults Geschichte. *Geschichte und Gesellschaft, 24,* 248-282.

Carlier, C. (1994). *La prison aux champs. Les colonies d'enfants délinquants du nord de la France au XIXe siècle.* Paris: Les Éditions de l'Atelier.

Carpenter, M. (1851). *Reformatory Schools for the Children of Perishing and Dangerous Classes and for Juvenile Offenders*. London: Gilpin.
Child Abuse & Neglect. The International Journal. (1977-...). New York: Pergamon.
Child Abuse Review. Journal of the British Association for the Study and Prevention of Child Abuse and Neglect (1992-...). Chichester: John Wiley.
Cunningham, H. (1995). *Children and Childhood in Western Society since 1500*. London/ New York: Longman.
Cunningham, H., & Innes, I. (Eds.) (1998). *Charity, Philanthropy and Reform. From the 1690s to 1850*. New York: St. Martin.
Dassen, P. (1999). *De onttovering van de wereld. Max Weber en het probleem van de moderniteit in Duitsland 1890-1920*. Amsterdam: Van Oorschot.
De Groot, R., & Van der Ploeg, J.D. (Eds.) (1999). *Het kind van de eeuw: het kind van de rekening?* Houten: Bohn Stafleu Van Loghum [Special Issue *Tijdschrift voor Orthopedagogiek, 38* (12)].
De Jong, B.C. (1996). *Jan Ligthart (1859-1916). Een schoolmeester-pedagoog uit de Schilderswijk*. Groningen: Wolters-Noordhoff.
Dekker, J.J.H. (1990). The Fragile Relation between Normality and Marginality. Marginalization and Institutionalization in the History of Education. *Paedagogica Historica, XXVI* (2), 13-29.
Dekker, J.J.H. (1994). Rituals and reeducation in the nineteenth century: ritual and moral education in a Dutch children's home. *Continuity and Change, 9*, 121-144.
Dekker, J.J.H. (1996a). An Educational Regime: Medical doctors, schoolmasters, jurists and the education of retarded and deprived children in the Netherlands around 1900. *History of Education, 25* (3), 255-268.
Dekker, J.J.H. (1996b). Messaggio e realtà. Il significato pedagogico e morale dell'iconografia sull'educazione dei bambini nella pittura olandese di genere del XVII secolo. In E. Becchi, & D. Julia (Eds.), *Storia dell'infanzia I. Dall'antichità al seicento* (pp. 312-337). Roma/Bari: Gius. Laterza & Figli.
Dekker, J.J.H. (1998). Transforming the Nation and the Child: Philanthropy in the Netherlands, Belgium, France and England, c.1780-c.1850. In H. Cunningham & J. Innes (Eds.), *Charity, Philanthropy and Reform. From the 1690s to 1850* (pp. 130-147). Basingstoke: Macmillan/New York: St. Martin.
Dekker, J.J.H. (2001). *The Will to Change the Child. Re-education Homes for Children at Risk in Nineteenth Century Western Europe*. Frankfurt am Main: Peter Lang.
Dekker, J.J.H., & Groenendijk, L.F. (1991). The Republic of God or the Republic of Children? Childhood and Childrearing After the Reformation: an appraisal of Simon Schama's thesis about the uniqueness of the Dutch case. *Oxford Review of Education, 17* (3), 317-335.
Dekker, J.J.H., Groenendijk, L.F. & Verberckmoes, J. (2000). Proudly raising vulnerable youngsters. The scope for education in the Netherlands. In J.B. Bedaux, & R.E.O. Ekkart (Eds.), *Pride and Joy. Children's portraits in the Netherlands 1500-1700* (pp. 43-60). Gent/Amsterdam/New York: Ludion & Abrams.
Dekker, J.J.H., & Lechner, D.M. (1999). Discipline and Pedagogics in History. Foucault, Ariès, and the History of Panoptical Education. *The European Legacy, 4* (5), 37-49.
Depaepe, M. (1993). *Zum Wohl des Kindes? Pädologie, pädagogische Psychologie und experimentelle Pädagogik in Europa und den USA, 1890-1940*. Weinheim: Deutscher Studien Verlag.
Depaepe, M. (1998). *De pedagogisering achterna. Aanzet tot een genealogie van de pedagogische mentaliteit in de voorbije 250 jaar*. Leuven/Amersfoort: Acco.
Descoedres, A. (1916). *L'Éducation des enfants anormaux. Observations psychologiques et indication pratiques. Suivis d'un résumé des texts de Binet et Simon*. Paris/Neuchâtel.

Diagnostic and Statistical Manual of Mental Disorders (DSM-IV). (1994). Washington, DC: American Psychiatric Association.

Dockrill, M. (1991). *Collins Atlas of Twentieth Century World History.* Glasgow: Harper & Collins.

Dräbing, R. (1990). *Der Traum vom 'Jahrhundert des Kindes'. Geistige Grundlagen, soziale Implikationen und reformpädagogische Relevanz der Erziehungslehre Ellen Keys.* Frankfurt am Main: Peter Lang.

Dupont-Bouchat, M-S. (1996). *De la prison à l'école. Les pénitenciers pour enfants en Belgique au XIXe siècle (1840-1914).* Kortrijk-Heule: UGA.

Dupont-Bouchat, M.-S., Pierre, E., Fecteau, J.M., Trepanier, J., Petit, J.G., Schnapper, B., & Dekker, J.J.H. (2001). *Enfance et justice au XIXe siècle. Essais d'histoire comparée de la protection de l'enfance 1829-1914, France, Belgique, Pays-Bas, Canada.* Paris: Presses Universitaires de France.

Farge, A. (1986a). Marginaux. In A. Burguière (Ed), *Dictionnaire des Sciences Historiques* (pp. 436-438). Paris: Presses Universitaires de France.

Farge, A. (1986b). *La vie fragile. Violence, pouvoirs et solidarités à Paris au XVIIIe siècle.* Paris: Hachette.

Foucault, M. (1975). *Surveiller et punir. Naissance de la prison.* Paris: Éditions Gallimard [*Discipline and punish.* Middlesex: Penguin Books, 1977].

Gaillac, H. (1994 [or. 1971]). *Les maisons de correction 1830-1945.* Paris: Éditions Cujas.

Gavitt, P. (1990). *Charity and Children in Renaissance Florence. The Ospedale degli Innocenti 1450-1536.* Ann Arbor: The University of Michigan Press.

Geremek, B. (1989). Le marginal. In J. Le Goff (Ed.), *L'homme médiéval* (pp. 381-413). Paris: Seuil.

Greenhill, L.L., & Osman, B.B. (Eds) (1991). *Ritalin. Theory and Patient Management.* New York: Mary Ann Liebert.

Groenveld, S., Dekker, J.J.H., & Willemse, Th.R.M. (1997). *Wezen en boefjes. Zes eeuwen zorg in wees- en kinderhuizen.* Hilversum: Verloren.

Hart, 't, W.A. (1948). *Ellen Key.* [Ph.D Thesis]. Leiden: Rijks Universiteit Leiden.

Hendrick, H. (1990). *Images of Youth. Age, Class, and the Male Youth Problem, 1880-1920.* Oxford: Clarendon Press.

Hendrick, H. (1992). Child labour, medical capital, and the school medical service. In R. Cooter (Ed.), *In the Name of the Child. Wealth and Welfare, 1880-1940.* London: Routledge.

Hilton, B. (1991 [or. 1988]). *The Age of Atonement. The Influence of Evangelicalism on Social and Economic Thought, 1785-1865.* Oxford: Clarendon Press.

Hintjes, J. (1981). *Geesteswetenschappelijke pedagogiek.* Amsterdam/Meppel: Boom.

Hurt, J.S. (1988). *Outside the Mainstream. A history of special education.* London: B.T. Batsford.

Hwang, P.C., Lamb, M.E., & Sigel, I.E., (Eds.) (1996). *Images of Childhood.* Mahwah (New Jersey): Lawrence Erlbaum.

Innes, J. (1998). Church and Voluntarism. In H. Cunningham, & I. Innes (Eds), *Charity, Philanthropy and Reform. From the 1690s to 1850* (pp. 15-65). New York: St. Martin.

Janssens, J.M.A.M. (1998). *Opvoedingshulp: doel, methoden en effecten.* [Inaugural lecture for Chair in Child-rearing and Family Support]. Nijmegen: Nijmegen University.

Kempe, C.H., Silverman, F.N., Steele, B.F., Drögemuller, W., & Silver, H.K. (1962). The Battered-Child Syndrome. *Journal of the American Medical Association 181*, 105-112.

Key, E. (1903 [or.1900]). *Das Jahrhundert des Kindes.* Berlin: S.Fischer.

Klootsema, J. (1904). *Misdeelde kinderen. Inleiding tot de paedagogische pathologie en therapie.* Groningen: Wolters-Noordhoff.

Leonards, Ch. (1995). *De ontdekking van het onschuldige criminele kind. Bestraffing en opvoeding van criminele kinderen in jeugdgevangenis en opvoedingsgesticht 1833-1886.* Hilversum: Verloren.

Ley, A. (1904). *L'arriération mentale. Contribution à l'étude de la pathologie infantile.* Bruxelles.

Lindmeier, B. (1998). *Die Pädagogik des Rauhen Hauses. Zu den Anfängen der Erziehung schwieriger Kinder bei Johann Hinrich Wichern.* Bad Heilbrunn: Julius Klinkhardt.

Mitzman, A. (1985 [or. 1969, New York: Knopf]. *The Iron Cage. An Historical Interpretation of Max Weber.* New Brunswick/Oxford: Transaction Books.

Neuenhaus, P. (1993). *Max Weber und Michel Foucault. Über Macht und Herrschaft in der Moderne.* Pfaffenweiler: Centaurus-Verlagsgesellschaft.

NRC Handelsblad (1999). Special Issue on War, 6 May 1999.

Oelkers, J. (1989). *Reformpädagogik: eine kritische Dogmengeschichte.* Weinheim: Juventa Verlag.

Oelkers, J. (1995). Break and continuity: Observations on the Modernization Effects and Traditionalization in International Reform Pedagogy. *Paedagogica Historica XXXI*, 675-713.

Owen, D. (1964). *English Philanthropy, 1660-1960.* Cambridge, Mass.: Belknapp Press.

Petit, J-G. (1990). *Ces peines obscures. La prison pénale en France 1780-1875.* Paris: Fayard.

Philippe, J., & Paul-Boncour, G. (1910). *L'Education des anormaux. Principes d'éducation physique, intellectuelle, morale.* Paris.

Pollock, L.A. (1983). *Forgotten Children. Parent-Child Relations from 1500 to 1900.* Cambridge: Cambridge University Press.

Pollock, L.A. (1987). *A Lasting Relationship Parents and Children over Three Centuries.* Hanover, HH: University Press of New England.

Prins, P. et al. (1999). *ADHD: een multimodale behandeling.* Houten: Bohn Stafleu Van Loghum.

Pritchard, D.G. (1963). *Education and the handicapped 1760-1960.* London: Routledge & Kegan Paul.

Rilke, R.M. (1993). *Briefwechsel mit Ellen Key* [edited by Theodore Fiedler]. Frankfurt a.M/Leipzig: Insel Verlag [including Anhang I, Rilke, Rezension von *Das Jahrhundert des Kindes*, or. published in *Bremer Tageblatt und General-Anzeiger*, Jg. VI, Nr. 132, 8.6.1902].

Rose, N. (1985). *The Psychological Complex. Psychology, Politics and Society in England, 1869-1939.* London: Routledge and Kegan Paul.

Rosenblum, R. (1988). *The Romantic Child from Runge to Sendak.* London: Thames and Hudson.

Rousseau, J-J. (1966 [or. 1762]). *Émile ou de l'éducation* [with *chronologie et introduction par Michel Launay*]. Paris: Garnier-Flammarion.

Schreuder, A.J. (1905). Achterlijke kinderen. In C.F.A. Zernike (Ed.), *Paedagogisch Woordenboek* (pp. 35-86). Groningen: Wolters.

Shafritz, J.M., et al. (1993). *The Dictionary of 20th-century World Politics.* New York: Holt.

Shahar, S. (1990). *Childhood in the Middle Ages.* London: Routledge.

Strümpell, A.H.L. von (1890). *Die Pädagogische Pathologie oder die Lehre von den Fehlern der Kinder. Versuch einer Grundlegung für gebildete Altern, Studierende der Pädagogik, Lehrer sowie für Schulbehörden und Kinderärzte.* Leipzig.

Suringar, W. s.d. [1847]. *My visit to Mettray.* Leeuwarden: G.T.N. Suringar.

Tétard, F. (1994). Fin d'un modèle philanthropique? Crise des patronages consacrés au sauvetage de l'enfance dans l'Entre-deux-guerres. In C. Bec, C. Duprat, J-N. Luc, & J-P. Petit (Eds), *Philanthropies et politiques sociales en Europe (XVIIIe-XXe siècles)* (pp. 199-212). Paris: Anthropos.

Van Crombrugge, H. (1995). Rousseau on Family and Education. *Paedagogica Historica XXXI*, 445-480.
Van der Ploeg, J., & Scholte, E. (1999). *ADHD in kort bestek*. Utrecht: SWP.
Vinke, A.J.G. (1999). *Geschikt voor het adoptiefouderschap? De ontwikkeling en het gebruik van een taxatie-instrument voor het gezinsfunctioneren met het oog op interlandelijke adoptie*. Delft: Eburon [with Appendix: Vragenlijst voor Aspirant Adoptie Ouders (VAAO)].
Wax, M.L. (1991). Magic, Rationality and Max Weber. In P. Hamilton (Ed.), *Max Weber: critical Assessments 2* (pp. 59-65). London/New York: Routlege [or: *Kansas Journal of Sociology, 1967 3*, 12-19].
Weber, M. (1982 [or. 1919]). Wissenschaft als Beruf. In J. Winckelmann, *Gesammelte Aufsätze zur Wissenschaftslehere* (pp. 582-613). Tübingen: J.C.B. Mohr (Paul Siebeck).
Weiss, G., & Trokenberg Hechtman, L. (1993 [or. 1986]). *Hyperactive children grown up. ADHD in Children, Adolescents, and Adults*. New York: The Guilford Press.
Willemse, Th.R.M. (1993). Jan Klootsema (1867-1926), architect van de residentiële orthopedagogiek. In R. De Groot, et al. (Eds.), *Handboek voor Orthopedagogiek* (no. 1026, pp. 1-32). Groningen: Wolters-Noordhoff.
Wilson, A. (1980). The Infancy of the History of Childhood: an appraisal of Philippe Ariès. *History and Theory 19*, 132-153.
Wines, E.C. (1880). *The State of Prisons and of Child-Saving Institutions in the Civilised World*. Cambridge: Cambridge University Press.
Wubs, J. (2000). Vaders gezin, moeders verantwoordelijkheid. Opvoedingsvoorlichting in Nederland over moeders en vaders, 1945-1995. *Pedagogiek. Wetenschappelijk Forum voor Opvoeding, Onderwijs en Vorming 20*, 33-44.

Chapter 3

The Century of the Participating Child

Micha De Winter

Introduction

Like their counterparts in many Western countries, Dutch citizens and politicians worry about the moral decay of children and youth, inspired by shocking – but scientifically disputable – measures of juvenile delinquency and nuisance appearing in the media. Many blame the family, concluding that parents have failed to impart moral education.

Recently the Dutch government wanted to know what young people might think good family policy should be. To develop an answer, an ethnically-diverse group of 24 vocational school pupils aged 14 and 15 was asked by a research group from Utrecht University, to interview ten classmates each about the subject, and to discuss the results. Their findings were astonishing. The children, mostly from underprivileged neighbourhoods, said that the problem was not so much inside the family, but in the whole of their 'educational' environment. Occasional family-problems were 'normal', they felt, but normal problems could get out of hand because of a 'social education gap' – a gap between the care that parents can provide and the invitations to adult responsibilities that young people seek from the rest of society. Neither in their neighbourhoods nor in the large, anonymous schools they attend do they find a sufficient number of adults who really care about them, see to their safety, and provide help and attractive activities. To the kids, the family and the outside world are connected. The absence of caring adults in their social world puts all the pressure on their families, an unfair burden that some parents cannot bear. The young people's principal advice to the Minister of Welfare therefore was: invest in caring, educating adults, not in installing video monitoring in the schools. Children's participation – in this particular case through research and policy making – uncovered insights that policy-making adults had missed. Both the participating youngsters and the adult researchers concluded that a serious dialogue between young people and adults is strongly beneficial to the quality of youth policies and youth care (De Winter et al., 1999).

Youthland

Why are children and youth so seldom asked for insights about their own lives and needs? Partly because Western children, as the Dutch educationalist Lea Dasberg wrote in 1975, have long been raised by keeping them 'little'. Ever since the Enlightenment, she claims, children have been increasingly confined to the hot house of a special Youthland. In this land – or pedagogical province – the child was free to express its distinct nature unhindered, and could find shelter from the perverting influences of the street, child labour, wars, and loose adult morals (Dasberg, 1975).

This lengthening and shielding of childhood has undoubtedly had its merits. Exploitative child labour has become an exception in the West; very young people are seldom sent to fight as soldiers, and numerous measures have been taken to protect the young from maltreatment, abuse, and neglect. Moreover the recognition of children's distinct nature has helped generate a great deal of knowledge on the upbringing, education, development, and health of young people. As a result, many a Western country has apparently turned into a child's paradise. Mean infant-mortality rates have dropped from 10 to 25% around the beginning of the century to less than 1% in the late nineties, mainly as the result of improved hygiene and nutrition, preventive health care, and the general spread of affluence (Corsini & Viazzo, 1997, p. 13).

Though an enormous professional infrastructure of provisions for the education, welfare and mental health of children has been created in the twentieth century this special world of children has also come under attack. Infantilization has been blamed for an ever widening gap between the lives of adults and children, a gap that seemed to undermine both child-development and society itself. The social isolation of children was attacked for causing alienation between generations, child-rearing problems, learning disabilities and adolescent psychological turmoil (Plessner, 1946; Van den Berg, 1958).

Historical Onsets of Participation

Different 20th century educationalists, such as John Dewey (1938), stated that the only way children could familiarize themselves with human culture and learn the cultural meaning of events and actions, was by active participation in social life. These educators often did not think of development as a natural process. Only through communication with other children and culturally-experienced adults would a child achieve the necessary experience to participate fully in society. Dewey envisioned the 'reconstruction of experience' as both the tool and aim of upbringing. School was to be a working social community where children as young scientists experimented with natural objects and production techniques. That way, students would experience the same development of knowledge that mankind more generally had experienced. Not until children themselves, working together, had experienced the evolution of knowledge and learned in stages how to apply it, would they adopt a positive, progress-oriented attitude toward learning and living. Dewey rejected authoritarian teacher/student relations as inimical to this social laboratory situation. A democratic, fast-changing society could function only when its members had learned to take initiative and adapt to new circumstances on their own. The essence of education, for Dewey, was to acquire the capability to freely, fully and creatively participate in the democratic, developing community. In this process children absolutely need adult guidance. Similar ideas were developed by other twentieth century pedagogical reformers, such as Anton Semyonovich Makarenko and Janusz Korczak. Both have experimented with various forms of self-government by children, although on the basis of very different ideologies and educational views. Makarenko (1980), worked with neglected and vagrant children in two Ukrainian communes between 1920 and 1935. Group responsibility here was seen as instrumental to the creation of collectivist ideas (Goodman, 1949). Korczak, working with Jewish orphans in 1920s Warsaw, developed a children's court, children's parliament and children's newspaper as components of an education based on equality and mutual respect between children and adults.

In the Netherlands, the Werkplaats Kindergemeenschap (Workshop Children's Community), founded in 1926 by Kees Boeke (1934), was a striking example of educational reform in which the pupils (workers) played an important part in the decision-making of the school. As with other progressive reform-schools, learning by doing, self-motivation and self-development of pupils as members of the school-community were at the centre of Boeke's educational philosophy and practice (Kuipers, 1992).

Dewey and other progressive reformers can be considered to be important 'founding-fathers' of a modern participatory pedagogy. By emphasizing how children grow in, through and for the community, these reformers resisted infantilization even while they embraced the emancipation of pedagogy from authority and tradition.

In contrast to progressive reform ideas, the current trend in educational sciences and schools toward limiting education to the transmission of existing 'objective' knowledge is only the most modern version of an old habit of alienating children from relevant social experiences and disregarding their creative cultural and social potential (Biesta, 1995, p. 32).

Children's and Youth's Participation

At present, children and young people are gradually – in the tradition of the reformers mentioned above – being rediscovered as active participants in their own upbringing and education. What could be the reason for the current revival? There is an idealistic and a cynical answer to this question.

The *first*, idealistic reason could be that increases in children's active participation represent a growing embrace of democratic ideals of citizenship. The United Nations Conventions on the Rights of the Child, ratified by most member nations since 1990, officially defined participation as a human right for children. Although in practice children's rights are still massively abused in many countries, the fact that most governments have recognized them at least in theory might indicate a gradual acceptance of egalitarian ideals.

The active involvement of children and young people in their own environment and decision-making is 'a basic right with beneficial effect' (De Winter, 1997). Participation has two principal categories of benefit. A society that requires certain attitudes and competencies of adult citizens has a fundamental obligation to teach the necessary skills to young people. In a modern plural democracy, citizens need, among other abilities, the capacity to negotiate, to form independent, critical opinions about social issues, to act in socially responsible ways, to respect other people with different backgrounds, opinions and interests, and to show solidarity and community spirit. Since democratic values and skills are not developed in theory but have to be learned in practice, all citizens, young and old, require practice and room to gain experience.

Participation, besides nourishing the skills of citizenship, also fosters children's psychological well-being. A society committed to children's participation will also maintain a developmental environment that satisfies basic human needs for social attachment and solidarity. By giving young people a chance to make their own contributions and treating them as valued members of society or of a community, in short, social as well as individual purposes are served.

A *second*, more cynical, reason for the rediscovery of children's participation emphasizes its disciplinary, or even stronger, its repressive potentials. Participation as a mainstream pedagogical device has emerged in the late twentieth century, just as Western societies have grown concerned about social cohesion. Burgeoning cultural, ethnic, religious and moral diversity strains the capacities of individualistic societies, producing an urge for self-discipline and social control. Self-control becomes the major vehicle for maintaining social order whenever social relations are egalitarian (Van Daalen & De Regt, 1997). Children's and young people's participation in this sense could be explained as a 'smart trick'. Assigning them the responsibility for their own behaviour and environment suggests that they are to be taken seriously, disciplining them in a more or less attractive way. Michel Foucault (1977) himself could not have invented anything cleverer!

Certainly idealistic and cynical pedagogical motives can and do exist side-by-side, particularly when adults deploy children's participation as an instrument of problem-solving. When Moroccan school-children in Amsterdam are trained to be peer-educators for friends at risk for criminal behaviour, or when New York City teenagers are asked to design a preventive strategy for truancy, both perspectives become visible (De Winter, 1977; Hart, 1992). The participants certainly are being highly validated, and they almost certainly learn a lot. At the same time, they are part of a carefully planned strategy of normalization: the organizers hope that peers might be able to achieve what adults alone cannot establish.

Participation in Youth Care

As fellow citizens, minors have a socially-embedded right to professional help when problems that they cannot handle on their own present themselves. This professional care should observe the elementary rules of democracy. The organization and implementation has to be subject to adequate social control, the legal position of clients has to be adequately provided for, and the views of the client must be heard and taken seriously. Since the nineties the Dutch government and institutions have been working on a client policy aimed at consolidation and formalization of these *civil rights*. All children and young people, and therefore, certainly also those requiring help because of psychosocial or family problems, need a stimulating social environment that helps them develop self-respect and social competence. Active commitment teaches them to get an increasingly better grip on their own lives, to assume responsibility for themselves and for their environment. In other words: also in youth care, that is the whole network of services concerned with the voluntary and involuntary care of young people and parents, participation is of the utmost importance. This sector is concerned with a combined educational and social aim, which is to enable young people who have problems to ultimately participate fully in social life. And so youth care is faced with a double challenge: problem-solving and education for citizenship. These two aspects are closely connected. Conditions which, in principle, are important for the development and education of all young people, and which can be summed up under the headings of participation and active commitment, appear to have a preventive and curative effect for young people with problems. On the basis of developmental psychological findings one could say that a lack of opportunities for gaining meaningful social experiences can in itself be seen as a source of psychosocial and behavioural problems in youngsters. Conversely, the increasing of opportunities for experience can reduce the risk to such problems (De Winter, 1997). Studies in the field of mental health, 'coping research' in particular, allow us to draw comparable conclusions. Traits that can form a buffer against negative influences of the environment and events, can considerably influence people's mental well-being. 'Hardy' individuals are characterized by, among other things, commitment and a sense of control over their own life situation. Ample opportunities for participation can positively influence the hardiness and coping style of young people. For this it is very important that the young person gets sufficient social support and has a meaningful social network. Treatment programmes that make use of 'learning by experience' confirm this. Treatment programmes that actively involve young clients in interventions and in their (residential) living environment have been proved to have a greater and more lasting effect than do programmes in which they are merely the passive object of treatment (Jagers & Slot, 1993).

Nevertheless, in current youth care practice, this insight is by no means always applied. The idea that young clients contribute to their own treatment and to the daily living situation (in the case of residential care) is not generally accepted, although terms such as 'activating' and 'encouraging self-help', are frequently used, particularly in policy documents. Despite the positive experiences, forms of (partial) self-government for young people with severe behaviour disorders, are fairly rare.

Where attempts at client participation have been made within youth care, so far with little success, this has taken the form of residents' committees or client organizations. One of the problems that one encounters in this type of approach is that young people are barely interested in the abstract themes that are brought forward. Moreover, as in education, the system of indirect representation does not really work, because it is difficult to motivate supporters. This is not very surprising when participation is not a habit on the 'day-to-day' level of the client community. While the frequently advocated intention to attribute to clients the role of consumers would strengthen the client's role in 'directing' his own treatment, this fails to appreciate the professional and educational responsibility of the social worker. Young people with problems are dependent on professionals who, if need be, can offer them answers. This is the essence of an educational relationship. But this is not to say that the views of the client himself should be ignored. On the contrary, these must be taken very seriously, and taking young people seriously means that response is sometimes necessary. Here again, education for citizenship and care can go hand in hand. Willingness to enter into a dialogue is an important condition for reinforcing self-respect and social competence. But, on the other hand, this dialogue takes place within a learning and development setting in which support, and sometimes leadership, by adults are indispensable. Client policy that is developed on behalf of young people, therefore, has to justify the educational character of the treatment situation. In the first instance, such policy has to create the conditions that are needed for a meaningful and just 'learning environment': a social climate in which young people can gain experience in relation to adults and their peers and consequently, perhaps for the first time in their lives, feel themselves to be wanted, valued and respected members of a community.

Strengthening the civil rights of young clients, in the vein of the UN Convention on the Rights of the Child, is a moral obligation of society (Veerman, 1992). Not 'regulated', but no less essential for their future well-being, is work on the development of commitment. Participation for young people with problems is not an extra burden. It is a justified social claim and, moreover, an educational necessity. And first and foremost, it is with this in mind that modern youth care must formulate its client policy.

Example: Participatory Action Research with Homeless Youth

One of the ways to enhance youth participation inside or outside the care system, is co-operative research. Our Utrecht research group is developing so called 'peer-research', in which young people from a certain target group act as co-researchers to investigate the quality of care and youth policies. Recently a study was carried out with homeless youngsters aged 15 to 24 years, boys and girls from different ethnic origins living in Amsterdam, Rotterdam and The Hague. The goal of the project was to identify the most important reasons why professional help for this group of vulnerable young people so often fails, and, even more important, to find solutions for this problem (Noom & De Winter, 2001).

Nineteen homeless youngsters agreed to participate as co-researchers. They received a two day training in a conference centre, in which the goals and methods of the project were discussed, a questionnaire was developed and interview-techniques were practised. After the training each co-researcher went out to interview about ten other homeless youngsters. For each written interview-report that met the criteria the interviewer was paid ten Dutch guilders (4.5 Euros). This way 190 interviews were carried out. The results were written down in a preliminary report that was discussed with the young interviewers. On the basis of the data, brainstorming-sessions were organized. The participants in these sessions were the interviewers and so called 'relevant adults': professionals working in the care system, managers of institutions for homeless youth and local policy makers. About half of the available time was used to identify the main factors that cause problems between the youngsters, professionals and the institutions, the other half was used to find the best possible solutions that could be agreed upon. Without going into detail here, the main problem was found to be the lack of communication between the young clients and their professional caretakers. Like all adolescents, homeless youngsters go for autonomy. They want to make their own decisions. Often they experience professional interference as intrusive, although they realize that strong support and guidance is necessary. One of them said: *I have a big mouth, but I am glad that my social worker often saves me from the mess I make of my life.* Professionals and institutions have trouble in handling this ambivalence. The balance between helping and intrusive interference is hard to find. A social worker characterized the qualifications for his job in a shelter for homeless youngsters as follows: *You should be a professional with considerable life-experience who works fifty hours a week for a very modest salary and at the same time you should be prepared to keep smiling while being called names.*

In the course of the sessions there appeared to be a consensus on the way the gap of communication could best be closed. Instead of 'top-down' solutions (as professionals often think of), and instead of 'bottom-up' solutions (as young clients seem to advocate), the participants agreed that 'dialogue' should be the guiding principle of the relationship between clients and professionals. A homeless young person has the task of defining what kind of professional help he or she needs and wants. The social worker assesses the possibilities and risks of a certain approach. Together they work out a plan to which they are prepared to commit themselves. At the level of institutions the dialogue should imply the introduction of a council that represents clients, social workers and managers. Particularly young people want to be involved in the process of designing the rules. They think rules in a home are often too strict, but on the other hand they admit that rules are necessary. Being actively involved in decision-making is expected to create a sense of connectedness: this is an institution that trusts and welcomes its clients by showing positive expectations. Rules that are mutually agreed upon have a better chance of being accepted. In such an atmosphere of dialogue both adults and young people expect clients to gain self-esteem and social competence.

Towards a Pedagogy of Participation

By engaging in serious dialogue with young people about the problems they experience, adults communicate positive respect, a far better message than the persistent demonization that young people hear from the 'man in the street', the press and the policy-makers.

However, children's participation matters for much more than prevention and behavioural management. Developed as a central concept of modern pedagogy, participation could avoid the historical, social and personal pitfalls of infantilization. Participation bridges the gap between 'Youthland' and the rest of society, while still respecting children's distinct individual and social needs.

Contemporary society seems to threaten childhood in a paradoxical way. Children can be held apart through sentimental infantilization (Zelizer, 1985). At the same time, the pressure-cooker of societal expectations hurries them prematurely into adulthood and consumerism (Elkind, 1981; Postman, 1982). And that may be the best case. At worst, considerable numbers of marginalized young people are left without any affirmative social bonds at all (De Winter et al., 1999).

Contemporary children and young people are growing up in a world of contradictory demands and expectations. They are urged to 'live their lives in their own individual way', and to 'take the interests of others into account'. They learn to revel in the pleasures of consumption, with the ethic of ecology in their other ear. Adults all around them search for unambiguous social norms and values while requiring openness and tolerance in a society of cultural differences. Child rearing and education thus inherently feature paradox. There should be an intermediate pedagogical activity, a kind of teaching that neither throws children unguided into the depths of adult contradictions, nor protects children falsely behind a veil of sentimental simplifications.

Participatory Pedagogy as a Triangular Relation

Participatory pedagogy is aimed at the triangular relation between a child, a responsible adult and the social world. After all, 'the social world' is not an alien, static entity for which children should be prepared in advance, but a dynamic system in which they themselves, together with adults, are important actors and agents of change. Therefore in a participatory pedagogy, while an adult mediates between the child and the social world, the social world itself – consisting of both children and adults – mediates the interactions of teacher and learner. For example, a participatory school would not view itself as a safe haven for children moving from a state of social incompetence toward the full demands of mature citizenship. Rather, it would be organized as a social training ground in which children's active involvement – both in their own learning process and as organizers of school-life – is both an instrument and a goal of education. The curriculum would not be mediated by educators dedicated to filling pupils with 'objective' knowledge and shared values. A participatory curriculum would provide children instead with the opportunity to experience and address everyday social dilemmas in a context rich in guidance and support. The key to participatory pedagogy thus is that people learn through interactive experience and communication. Social knowledge and values are not simply being transferred from an active educator to a passive recipient, but, in Dewey's terms, knowledge and values grow in a well co-ordinated joint action. Children are neither shielded from social reality, nor left to unguided exposure. 'The social world' is created jointly as children and adults interact as fully responsible subjects, in a context that considers such exchange as one of its main pedagogical tasks. Within the triangle of children, adults and social context, whether in schools, families, or neighbourhoods, adults are irreplaceable, not because they represent the outside social world *to* children in the classical sense, but because they are responsible for introducing children to the mutuality of social processes. Therefore the adult's task is to unpack and interpret the social dilemmas of everyday life, to help children to acquire the necessary communication skills, and to structure an effective process of mutual interaction and problem-solving.

Educators should take differences among children into account. Children grow up in rather different circumstances, that, by early childhood, have already created large differences in their participatory skills and attitudes. Denying those differences will only enlarge the social distance between children, and turn participation into another tool reserved for an already privileged elite.

Engaging children in social participation naturally requires a loving, caring and respectful pedagogical environment. By exhibiting and modelling these attitudes, adults can provide children with the sense of trust and safety necessary for the give and take of participation. Caring respect, however, is not the same as the kind of equality between children and adults sought by anti-authoritarian pedagogy. Pedagogical relationships between adults and children are, by definition unequal in knowledge, social experience and responsibility. This very inequality, however, could be the starting-point for participatory learning. Along similar lines as Habermas' more recent critical theory of communication (Habermas 1998), Dewey argued as much in his concept of 'reconstruction of experience'. The maturation of knowledge and values through joint action often requires the more experienced, coordinating, helping, and sometimes provoking hand of the educator.

Participation is Needed

Children's and youth's participation is an ambivalent concept. On the one hand the active social involvement of children and young people helps materially to connect them to the community. Durkheim (1984) had at the end of the nineteenth century already argued that connectedness, mutual dependency, and a sense of lasting, serious responsibility for others are essential to human well-being and happiness. In this sense a participatory pedagogy can counterbalance the excesses of post-modern individualism and challenge the presumption that, whatever the cost, self-interest should prevail over co-operation and solidarity.

On the other hand, children's and young people's participation is a kind of social gunpowder, a powerful vehicle susceptible to all sorts of social and political usages. Misused, a participatory pedagogy can become just a new, modern cover for the same old pedagogical process of imposing social standards and values on children and youth. The distinguishing criterion however is that participatory pedagogy practices the very democracy it preaches. By recognizing that, as developing fellow-citizens, children have the right to be actively engaged in shaping pedagogical goals and methods, teachers invite and instruct them to take joint responsibility for their own environments. The goals of democratic upbringing, actually reflected in pedagogical action, become real in children's experience.

It is almost self-evident that in extremely individualistic societies a participatory paradigm of education will elicit much resentment or anxiety. A culture consecrated to the interests of the individual will undoubtedly be inclined to suspect that by emphasizing the social nature of education, participation could be used to indoctrinate the children. Participatory pedagogy may find a warmer reception in democracies with a more social orientation. Like many other Western societies, such countries include increasing numbers of people with different interests, cultural backgrounds, economic resources, values, life-styles and ideologies. Within this context, participation might strengthen or maintain social cohesion, an issue of major political concern. Showing diversity to youngsters, instead of alienating them from it by adopting a false neutrality, could enable them to develop their own, autonomous social identity, and teach them to handle diversity in a socially responsible way. In a society committed to universal justice, youth participation is no longer just another visionary pedagogical scheme, but a serious attempt to align social education with the ideals of democratic citizenship.

Epilogue: Where Do We Go?

Most modern theories of child and adolescent development emphasise the role that young people play as co-constructors of their own environment. In its turn the social environment has a significant influence on the developmental process. A major pedagogical implication of this scientific consensus is that the concepts of culture and society can no longer be seen as static entities, to which young people should be prepared during their stay in the waiting room of a separated Youthland. In this context social education means that children and adolescents – with the support and monitoring of adults – gradually learn to shape their environment. It also means that the pedagogical quality of the social environment should be questioned: do schools, institutions and neighbourhoods provide young people with sufficient possibilities for social learning and the development of responsible citizenship? The peer-research that was referred to earlier in this chapter shows that we are still far away from a participatory revolution. Young people are still hardly ever asked what they think about their quality of life, only occasionally they are being involved in the process of decision-making with regard to their living conditions.

In different European countries and organizations (such as the Council of Europe), youth participation however is recently becoming a major political theme. As yet this new interest expresses itself mainly through the formation of children's and youth's councils at local, national or European levels, and through the participation of young people in conferences on themes that worry adults: alcohol, smoking, substance abuse and juvenile delinquency. Although the danger of tokenism is realistic, it is important to keep an eye on the positive effects of such developments: it could well be that the new generation succeeds to change the dominant pedagogical discourse in a constructive direction through the anxiety that youth brings about in politicians and society. Active involvement of children and young people this way is becoming a sine qua non to improve the quality of life in societies. The new generation needs it, so does a civilized society.

References

Biesta, G.J.J. (1995). Opvoeding en intersubjectiviteit. Over de structuur en identiteit van de pedagogiek van John Dewey. *Comenius*, 15, 21-36.
Boeke, K. (1934). *Kindergemeenschap: Ervaringen en perspectieven van 'De Werkplaats' in Bilthoven*. Utrecht: Bijleveld.
Corsini, C.A., & Viazzo, P.P. (1997). *The decline of infant and child mortality. The European experience: 1750-1990*. The Hague: Martinus Nijhoff Publishers/Unicef.
Dasberg, L. (1975). *Grootbrengen door kleinhouden als historisch verschijnsel*. Meppel: Boom.
Dewey, J. (1938). *Experience and education*. New York: Macmillan.
De Winter, M. (1997). *Children as fellow citizens. Participation and commitment*. Oxford: Radcliffe Medical Press.
De Winter, M., Kroneman, M., & Baerveldt, C. (1999). The social education gap. Report of a Dutch peer-consultation project on family policy. *British Journal of Social Work*, 29, 903-914.
Durkheim (1984). *The division of labor in Society*. New York: Free Press (first published in 1893).
Elkind, D. (1981). *The hurried child. Growing up too fast, too soon*. Reading, Mass.: Addison-Wesley.
Foucault, M. (1977). *The order of things: An archaeology of the human sciences*. London: Tavistock.

Goodman, W.L. (1949). *Anton Simeonovitch Makarenko. Russian Teacher.* London: Routledge & Kegan Paul Ltd.
Habermas, J. (1998). *On the pragmatics of communication.* Cambridge Mass.: MIT Press.
Hart, R.A. (1992). *Children's participation. From tokenism to citizenship.* Florence: Unicef Innocenti Essays nr. 4.
Jagers, J.D., & Slot, N.W. (1993). Competentievergroting door gedwongen residentiële behandeling. In S.J. Van Hekken, et al. (Eds.), *Paedologie: wetenschap en praktijk in discussie* (pp. 91-98). Amersfoort: College Uitgevers.
Korczak, J. (1920). *Jak Kochac Dzieco.* Dutch edition: *Hoe houd je van een kind.* Utrecht: Bijleveld, 1986.
Kuipers, H. J. (1992). *De wereld als werkplaats. Over de vorming van Kees Boeke en Beatrice Cadbury.* Amsterdam: IISG.
Makarenko, A.S. (1980). *Vorträge über Kindererziehung.* Berlin: Volk und Wissen.
Noom, M., & De Winter, M. (2001). *Op zoek naar verbondenheid. Zwerfjongeren aan het woord over de verbetering van de hulpverlening.* Utrecht: NPZ/Universiteit Utrecht.
Plessner, H. (1946). Over de infantiliserende invloed van de moderne maatschappij op de jeugd. *Paedagogische Studiën,* XXIII, 193-202.
Postman, N. (1982). *The disappearance of childhood.* New York: Delacorte Press.
Van Daalen, R., & De Regt, A. (1997). Participatie, zelfdiscipline en formele controle. *0/25 Tijdschrift over Jeugd, 2* (9), 10-13.
Van den Berg, J.H. (1958). *Metabletica of leer der veranderingen.* Nijkerk: Callenbach. English edition (1961): *The changing nature of man. Introduction to a historical Psychology (Metabletica).* New York: W.W. Norton & Company.
Veerman, Ph.E. (1992). *The rights of the child and the changing image of childhood.* Dordrecht: Martinus Nijhoff Publishers.
Zelizer, V.A. (1985). *Pricing the priceless child. The changing social value of children.* New York: Basic Books.

PART II

PROFESSIONALIZATION

Chapter 4

Child and Youth Care Work at the Cross-Roads of the Century: From a Recognized Profession Back to an Amateur Humanitarian Mission?

Emmanuel Grupper

Introduction

This chapter deals with a somehow 'forgotten' factor in the discussion about professionalization of the child and youth care field. It is a major and most influential component in every social reality – economic considerations. It is obvious that professionalization costs a lot of money, a fact that is creating strong opposition from various social partners. This factor has not always been taken into consideration, seriously enough, in the discussion about professionalization. Unfortunately, it might become a source for serious problems in the long run. Some examples are already known, like the reduction in the number of children in residential care in many countries. It is argued that instead of debating against or for professionalization of the field, innovative models have to be invented that look at professionalism as a continuum, with minimum and maximum boundaries. These new models have to implement differential levels of professionalism, in the planning of all services for children and youth in need of care, taking economic considerations into account.

Progress of the Child and Youth Care Profession

The child and youth care profession has made a great deal of progress in many countries since the end of the second world war (Jones, 1994). Although European countries are taking the lead, considerable progress has also been made in Canada, Australia, England, Ireland, Scotland, USA, Israel, South Africa and a few other places.

Many countries had opened highly sophisticated training programmes. France was the first to open 54 Training Centres after having voted in 1965 a law that gives legal status to the profession (Lambert, 1981). In the Netherlands, Germany, the Scandinavian countries, Spain, Italy, Switzerland, Belgium and Luxembourg, a large variety of training programmes had been developed; some of them in universities and others in specialized higher education colleges (for instance, the 'Fachhochschule' in Germany). Similar processes were also recognized in countries that were part of what used to be called 'Eastern Europe', like Poland, Yugoslavia, Czechoslovakia, Hungary and parts of the former Soviet Union (Amir & Lane, 1993; Gottesman, 1991; Tuggener, 1985).

The graduates being a large number of qualified social educators, developed a unique professional identity. These people implemented their professional know-how in a large variety of services both in community-based programs and in residential homes.

Parliaments voted laws that gave legal status to the profession. As mentioned above, the first was France that started this process in the early sixties. The most recent development was the decision of the Catalonian Parliament in Spain, in 1996, to hand over the responsibility of governing the social education profession to an independent *Collegium*, lead by representatives of the workers' professional association, in collaboration with representatives of the Catalonian universities (DOGC, 1996). This movement demonstrates the constant development of this rather young profession among the helping professions.

As part of this trend, Special Codes of Ethics had been implemented in many countries. In some of them they were developed by workers' organizations, like in France (Vidaud, 1996), Switzerland (cf. Ligthart, 1993) and the USA (Mattingly et al., 1995). In other countries like Belgium, a code of ethics had been imposed on the workers by legislation (Leblanc, 1999). In 1998, FICE (Fédération Internationale des Communautés Educatives) published a document entitled 'International Ethical Principles for People Working with Children and Young People', as a basic guideline for putting a National Code of Ethics together (Lane, 1998). The analysis of this document, and the work of others who are dealing with codes of ethics for youth workers (Mattingly et al., 1995), reveals that most of them are based on an attempt to define the workers' responsibility toward their various partners in care: the young clients and their families; the profession; the colleagues; the society at large; the agency they are working in; and – last but not least – themselves.

A comparative analysis, conducted by Gottesman (1994), presents 21 reports about changes occurring in countries which are members of FICE-

International. They demonstrate that the quality of services for children and youth with special needs, has considerably improved. It can be claimed that in countries where the profession developed, the basic rights of children and youth at risk are better fulfilled nowadays than ever before.

New Problems

However, new problems are appearing, caused by the professionalization process of the child and youth care field. Some of them are becoming of major concern lately.

First, professionalization has increased dramatically the costs of services for children and youth in need of special care. Youth workers with a professional identity tend to demand better working conditions for themselves and insist on high standards of care for their clients. This has brought about a significant reduction in the number of children in every group, either in residential care or in community-based programs. The direct consequence is an important increase in the number of people working in every programme (Grupper, 1992). The professional organizations of workers succeeded in achieving, in certain countries, a considerable reduction in the working hours for staff. The case of the 35 weekly hours in France these days is a demonstration of this phenomenon (Suzent, 2000). Increase in the workers' long-term training programmes, is another factor that imposes an important budgetary burden on public expenses. These factors contributed to a much higher cost of the services for children in need.

A comparative analysis of expenses per child in residential care, made by Gottesman (1990), demonstrates this discrepancy. The most expensive programme was found to be in Denmark where up to $30,000 were spent per child per month in a most sofisticated and beautifully designed residential program in Udby. At the opposite end of the scale, are the rather low budget programmes operated in Youth Villages in Israel, with para-professional direct care workers, maintaining an average cost of a child per month not exceeding $1,200.

Sadly enough, the increase in the cost of services has resulted in a meaningful reduction in the number of children and youth that can benefit from these specialized residential care programmes. The increase in costs has resulted in permanent pressure being placed on decision-makers and finance personnel to allow these services to be available only to a very small number of children, such as those with multiple-problems and emotional disturbances, homeless youth and refugee populations. For the others, like migrant youth living with their families, populations who have various types of family problems, school drop-outs and others, community-based programs are expected to be the proper answer.

The decision about every individual case is not always taken by pure professional considerations. Direct care workers who are doing intakes, are often limited in their professional decisions by administrative regulations. Many people join Knapp's (1979) statement that in many cases community-based solutions are just a formal 'cover' for not dealing seriously with the real problems of the populations at-risk. The outcome is therefore quite embarrassing: many children and youth whose problems are not considered to be 'serious' enough for being placed in residential care programmes, are not receiving any care whatsoever.

In Gottesman's review (1994), radical changes in residential care are reported. He claims that the greatly reduced number of children and youngsters in residential institutions and the closing down of a great number of institutions created a real transformation in the character and the structure of the child care system in many countries. Moreover, this raises two major paradoxical phenomena:

1. On the one hand residential children's homes and institutions in many countries (FICE member countries, for example) were never better prepared physically and more qualified professionally for their tasks than at the present time. Care workers are now better trained. Children's groups are much smaller. The caring process is more individualized, the adult-child ratio is higher. There are new laws and regulations regarding the care and protection of children. And the relations of the staff with the child's family are no longer perceived as a contradiction but rather play a complementary role. The paradox is that, on the other hand, the media continue to report mainly the failures and deficiencies, as if nothing has changed. The continuing antagonistic approach to temporarily separating deprived, underprivileged and handicapped children and young people from their dysfunctional families, is even more surprising when one observes the immense progress that these services went through.
2. The second paradox is that in spite of the significant progress in child care arrangements, many societies are trapped in a strange situation where children and young people desperately needing such assistance cannot benefit from it because of budget limitations. Paradoxically, advances in the quality of care gave birth to a quantitative regression in residential care. A systematic research done by Knorth and Van der Ploeg (1994) shows that in The Netherlands, for example, the number

of children in residential care dropped dramatically from 1970 to 1990 from 16,300 placements to 8,800 (a reduction of 46%). In Israel, while looking for budgetary savings, the government decided in 1997 (Grupper, 1999) on a reduction of 3,000 children in residential care, over a period of four years (750 less in each year).

Fulcher and Ainsworth (1985) claim that a new coalition is taking place composed of theoreticians in the social sciences who are against any form of extra-familial group care for needy children and youth, together with finance people whose main interest is the reduction of services' costs. One can add to it the argument presented in a book published by the American sociologists Krisberg and Austin, entitled *The children of Ishmael* (1978). Their main thesis is that because of the very limited political power of populations at-risk and in need of help, they are not powerful enough to put pressure on the decision-makers to invest the necessary amount of money in programmes that could improve their social and educational situation.

Knapp (1979) claims that the low degree of professionalism which is demonstrated by operating residential programmes with para-professional personnel, is very convenient for agencies who are running such programs. It enables them to keep the direct care worker in a low status, and accordingly, to reduce the ever growing expenses of such programmes. Krueger (1983) maintains that in the USA it sometimes amounts to real exploitation of workers. In a survey about status of various professional tasks he found the child care worker to be at the same level as the 'porter'. Linton, Fox and Forster (1986), add to these findings their statement that child and youth care workers in the USA can be considered as the 'proletarian' group of the child and youth care field.

The result of all this is a social reality that leave many populations at-risk without proper solutions of their problems. Many of them translate their frustration into violence. The outcomes are affecting the societies that are becoming hostile and dangerous in many different places and particularly at the big metropolis of our post-modern era.

Needs versus Resources

The discontent on both sides is constantly growing: the populations in need on the one hand, and on the other, the general public, political people, and the social educators. They feel frustrated because in spite of all their professional interventions and the considerable efforts displayed in the various programmes, the decision-makers do not give these problems a high priority. The budgets allocated are not sufficient to enable meaningful progress to be made. Let us look, as an example, at issues like drug addiction, teenage pregnancy and sexual abuse of children, to name only a few. In every one of these three items it can be seen that professional interventions alone cannot solve these problems. Without the total commitment of the community at large, significant improvement is hardly to be expected.

Voices are being raised lately, that question the overall benefit of maintaining highly professional and expensive socio-educational programmes if their impact is so limited. In the long run this may lead to decisions that could bring the child and youth care field back to its situation in Europe at the end of World War II, as described by Tuggener (1985). He claims that at this period, the special needs of children and youth at-risk were satisfied by the activities of non-professional people having humanitarian motives and good will, using as their their only competencies: empathy and love.

Although the message of Bettelheim's *Love is not enough* (1950) was largely accepted for many years, there are some voices at the moment, advocating going back to non-professional models. The dangerous implication could be the legitimation of this option as a future solution to the ever growing amount of social and educational problems in the multi-cultural societies of today, especially in the context of permanent budgetary cuts in the social services and the public sector.

A Look Forward

Kahan (1992) claims that with the implementation of 'free-market economy' concepts in social and educational policies and the introduction of 'cost-benefit' criteria in the field, there is a real danger for continuation of services to populations at risk. Hegstrup (1999) too, looking at this phenomenon from a Danish point of view, defines the 1980-1990 period as a depressing decade, that saw many public institutions closed because of the privatization of the public sector.

We maintain that there is a real danger that market-like professionalization 'without limits' will be auto-destructive for the child and youth care profession in general and to the professionalization process in particular. Unfortunately, it might become counter-productive and harm the huge professional development of the last fifty years. The challenge of the child and youth care field in the next century is to maintain professional and quality services for young people without exaggerating their costs.

It is argued that instead of debating against or for professionalization of the field, innovative models have to be invented that look at professionalism *as a continuum*, with minimum and maximum boundaries. These new models have to implement differential levels of professionalism in all planning of services for children and youth in need of care.

One possible direction could be to look for better links with other neighbouring professions and to create new collaborations among practitioners. The rigid boundaries between the various professions that are making interventions with the same child, results in a waste of money and in interventions that do not always serve the clients' interest. As an extreme case we can quote Waaldijk (1985) who mentioned eight different professional care workers who were dealing with the same child, without finding a way of helping him effectively. Eisikovits (1980) proposed looking at a residential institution as an idiosyncratic culture, and at the staff-resident interaction as a cultural 'scene'. According to this anthropological paradigm an *holistic perspective* of the child's needs is the best way to gain deep insights that will direct the workers to supply effective help. It can also be looked upon via the prism of an *ecological model* (Bronfenbrenner, 1979) that gives importance to every intervention done in the 'shared life space', using Fritz Redl's terms (Redl, 1966). Therefore, strong collaborations and shared responsibility of every member of staff, regardless of their specific training and their professional affiliations, are essential components in the future organization of the work in residential programmes. The application of these principles could result in a considerable reduction in the number of staff members, and thus reduce the programme's cost.

Some ideas for intermediate models, which implement the idea of differentiation in the level of professionalism among the staff can be presented from the reality of residential child and youth care in Israel.

One is a multi-dimensional training programme, through which non-professional group care workers are receiving four years of on-the-job two-fold professional training. One is group care in residential education and care institutions, the other is teaching in intermediate schools. It should enable them to convert, after several years of intensive work in residential care, to the teaching profession. After each year they receive a different diploma that changes their status in terms of salary. At the end of the four years they receive a university B.Ed diploma (Bachelor in Education), and they may convert to teaching in high school.

This model enables programmes to have workers at different level of professionalism: fully certified professionals, collaborating with workers who are still under on-going training and who accordingly receive a lower salary. This variety among staff can reduce the overall expenses of manpower, which is always the major component in the costs of a child and youth care programme. At the same time, it is creating new opportunities and future perspectives for people who have suffered from burnout effects. Every individual worker will have a different salary according to her/his credentials. Therefore, it will enable programmes to both maintain a workforce in which only a certain number of workers operate at a high professional level, and at the same time open new possibilities to reduce the overall costs of the programmes.

A second example from the Israeli scene is a model that seeks to professionalize only part of the child care staff. In a group home, for example, where 6-7 persons are working in shifts, only one or two persons will be trained as full professionals and the others will receive a lower and partial professional training. The professional staff member will be delegated the responsibility to lead the entire staff, but at the same time he or she supplies the staff with on-going professional supervision on a daily basis.

A third example is a differential allocation of funds for different types of residential care programmes, according to the severity of the clients' problems. Children and young people with serious and complex problems will receive higher professionalized services than those that suffer from less acute difficulties; they will be treated in larger groups with a higher ratio of children per staff. The whole network of residential education and care is classified to four degrees of funding:

1. Residential programmes which are mainly of the 'Education' type.
2. Residential programmes which are of the 'Rehabilitation' type.
3. Residential programmes which are of the 'Treatment orientation' type.

Lately, a fourth category is being introduced: children who are being placed in residential care after psychiatric hospitalization.

The categories of funding are related to the professional diagnosis of the individual child's situation, but the programme should adapt itself to give her/him the services needed, as part of the contract between the placing agency and the particular residential care programme. In this way, a child with multi-problems diagnosed as one in need of a placement in a category 2 programme, could be placed in a more heterogeneous category 1 setting. However, in that case the programme should be able to receive for him a much higher monthly payment from the placing agency, in order to secure this particular child with the extra individual services that should help him to integrate in a more open and normative environment.

These were just three examples of the kind of thinking that takes economic factors into consideration, in the overall planning of residential child and youth care. The main idea is to leave the 'either-or' thinking while dealing with professional services for at-risk populations, and to look for new and additional models of practice in between. These new models also should take into consideration the economic paradigm without losing the focus on the clients' needs for quality professional services.

References

Amir, E., & Lane, D. (1993). *Training of residential child and youth care staff.* Neurim: Youth Aliyah Publications (in collaboration with Fice).
Bettelheim, B. (1950). *Love is not enough.* New York: Free Press.
Bronfenbrenner, U. (1979). *The ecology of human development.* Cambridge: Harvard University Press.
D.O.G.C. (1996). *The law 15/96 of creation of the Colegium.* Barcelona: Diary Official de la Generalitat de Catalunya.
Eisikovits, R.A. (1980). The Cultural Scene of a juvenile treatment center for girls: Another look. *Child Care Quarterly, 12* (1), 36-45.
Fulcher, L., & Ainsworth, F. (Eds.) (1985). *Group care practice with children.* London/ New York: Tavistock Publications.
Gottesman, M. (1990). *Comparative survey about maintenance fees of children in residential care* (Hebrew). Tel Aviv: Israeli Residential Care Association (Internal Document).
Gottesman, M. (Ed.) (1991). *Residential child care: An international reader.* London: Whiting & Birch.
Gottesman, M. (Ed.) (1994). *Recent changes and new trends in extrafamilial child care: An international perspective.* London: Whiting & Birch.
Grupper, E. (1992). *Becoming a residential child care worker. An ethnographic study of the professional socialization process of new workers* (Hebrew). Unpublished Ph.D. Dissertation. Haifa: Haifa University, School of Education.
Grupper, E. (1999). The desired versus the actual model of residential child and youth care workers in Israel (Hebrew). *Mifgash, 9,* no. 12/13, 11-27.
Hegstrup, S. (1999). Ludvig Beck – pioneren der uddannede borneforsorgen I DK. *Tidsskrift for Socialpaedagogiske, 4.*
Jones, H.D. (1994). The social pedagogue in Western Europe. Some implications for European interprofessional care. *Journal of Interprofessional Care, 8,* (1), 19-29.
Kahan, B. (1992, December). *The residential scene in Britain.* Paper presented at Tel Aviv University, Tel Aviv, 14th December 1992.
Knapp, M.R.J. (1979). Planning child care services from an economic perspective. *Residential and Community Child Care Administration, 1,* (3), 229-248.
Knorth, E.J., & Van der Ploeg, J.D. (1994). Residential care in The Netherlands and Flanders: Characteristics of admitted children and their family. *International Journal of Comparative Family and Marriage, 1,* 17-27.
Krisberg, B., & Austin, J. (1978). *The children of Ishmael.* Palo-Alto: Mayfield.
Krueger, M.A. (1983). *Intervention techniques for child and youth care workers.* Dousman (Wisconsin): Tall.

Lambert, T. (1981). *Les éducateurs specialisés*. Paris: Les Publications du C.T.N.E.R.H.I.

Lane, D. (1998). A code of ethics for people working with children and young people. *Fice Bulletin, Special Issue, 14*.

Leblanc, J. (1999, October). *Les éducateurs sociaux: 'Auteurs' de leurs deontologie*. Paper presented at the AIEJI International Seminar in Israel 'Multi-cultural societies and their alienating effect on adolescents: Risks and challenges for social-educators and youth'. Jerusalem (Israel), 4-7 October 1999.

Ligthart, L.E.E. (1993). Care, its effects and limits. In E. Amir, & D. Lane (Eds.), *Training of residential child and youth care staff* (pp. 25-42). Neurim: Youth Aliyah Publications (in collaboration with FICE).

Linton, T.E., Fox, L., & Forster, M. (1986). The child and youth care workers: Marginal employee or professional team member? *Residential Group Care and Treatment, 3*, (4), 39-55.

Mattingly, M.A, Landau, J., Murphy, G., Tompkins-Rosenblat, P., & Griffin, S. (1995). *Code of ethics for practice of North American child and youth care professionals*. Pittsburg: International Leadership Coalition of Professional Child and Youth Care, c/o University of Pittsburg, Program in Child Development and Child Care.

Redl, F. (1966). *When we deal with children*. London: Collier & Macmillan.

Suzent, F. (2000). Editorial. *Mouv'Ance, 12*, nr. 11 (November), 1-2.

Tuggener, H. (1985). Social pedagogics as a profession: A historical survey. In H.D. Jones, M. Courtioux, J. Kalcher, W. Steinhauser, H. Tuggener, & K. Waaldijk (Eds.), *The socialpedagogue in Europe: Living with others as a profession*. Zürich: FICE International Publications.

Tutt, N. (1981). Foreword. In F. Ainsworth, & L. Fulcher (Eds.), *Group care for children* (pp. 1-5). London/New York: Tavistock Publications.

Vidaud, D. (1996). Professions du social: Mettre en place une deontologie commune. *Mouv'Ance, 10*, nr. 41, 1-2.

Waaldijk, K. (1985). Problems, conflicts and opportunities. In H.D. Jones, et al. (Eds.), *The socialpedagogue in Europe. Living with others as a profession* (pp. 109-137). Zürich: FICE International Publications.

Chapter 5

Building a Professional Identity: The Challenge for Residential Child and Youth Care

Margaret Lindsay

Introduction

For those interested in the welfare of children and young people living in residential care, the main challenge in the 21st century will be to redefine the role of the staff who work with them. To improve the care our children and young people receive in our residential services, this must be the key priority. For any group of workers, this is a crucial task. How workers understand their role, how they define what it is that they do at work, the values that are espoused as they work – all these will in turn dictate how they are perceived by other people – their colleagues, their managers, the young people themselves, and society in general. And how these groups perceive these workers will affect how well they are able to do their work.

The last century has seen huge movement and change in society. These changes have affected how children are perceived, and how the family functions. That in turn has defined how, in all the many and various cultures, the task of bringing up children is approached. In the case of children and young people who cannot be brought up within their own families, society's ideas about what is good parenting have inevitably been transferred onto the role of the residential worker.

Thus, as society's view of what makes for the good upbringing of children changes, so must the practice of those society employs to carry out this task for those children who cannot, for whatever reason, be cared for within their own homes. But if residential care is to lead rather than to follow that trend, those concerned with it and for it, must take an active role in thinking through what it is that residential workers do, and in building an identity which will enable and empower the staff caring for these children. Does the work done in residential child care have a 'professional identity'? Do those concerned with it want it to have a 'professional identity'? If it should have such an identity, how can one be created? What are the elements of professionalism that should be aspired to? These are crucial questions, worthy of considerable debate.

This chapter will address this theme from a number of angles. Firstly, it will discuss what are the key aspects of professionalism. Secondly, it will consider whether residential staff can be considered to be professionals according to these criteria, and, thirdly, it will address why this is such an important issue. Fourthly, it will consider how residential workers are seen today in the circles of influence within which they operate. Lastly, it will evaluate what all this may mean in terms of the challenge that faces the field of those interested in and involved in work with young people. What challenges does it pose, and how can they be addressed?

Aspects of 'Professionalism'

In preparation for this contribution, as well as reading around the issue, the author discussed the issue of professionalism with a few people from the general public. These people were deliberately chosen because they were not connected with social care and residential care. The idea was to find out how the general public defined 'a professional'. A range of answers were received, most of which were surprisingly consistent. The answers were tabulated, and it was found that they naturally broke down into four clear categories.

Learning It was felt that a 'professional' was someone who had specific education to equip them with the skills and knowledge for a job which was recognised as being complex and specialist. Statements such as *qualifications – you wouldn't go to a doctor without any!* and *degree of complexity – implies that you need knowledge, understanding, skill* demonstrated this. There was an expectation that training would be long, and demanding, and would require the hard work necessary to develop the expertise required.

Attitude It seemed that as well as knowledge, a certain attitude toward one's work was seen as a necessary attribute of the 'professional'. The word was seen to denote an attitude of mind which *goes beyond simply a job; it implies someone who has some kind of a calling; more than just money*. Other words used took this idea further – *serious, focused*; and there was a concept of a *moral code* – notions perhaps drawn from the example of the Hippocratic Oath in the case of medicine. Interestingly, a professional was also seen as someone who would take an active role in defining and redefining their professional role in the light of changing circumstances – they were not seen as passive or reactive, but as autonomous and proactive.

Responsibility and autonomy This concept seemed to follow from the earlier one, and was almost seen as a result of it. 'Professionals' were seen as having responsibility for what they did, and of being accountable for their work. They were also seen as being autonomous enough to carry out those responsibilities. They were felt to be have the *ability to make judgements and decisions which carry weight,* and as *someone who has to exercise judgement and has a certain amount of autonomy to exercise it.*

Public image Lastly, there was a clear element of awe and respect – even mystique – which went with being a 'professional'. Status was a key element. A sense of *I couldn't do that – most people couldn't do that* seemed to be important. This also led to a bestowing of trust – people were prepared to trust the judgement of the professional about issues that they knew they did not fully understand.

Thus these four elements seemed to typify how this small sample of the general public defined the concept of professionalism. In the light of these elements of a 'professional identity' then, can one consider residential workers to be 'professionals'? In order to determine this, each element will now be considered in turn in order to assess how far they seem to match up with residential child care as it is today.

Residential Workers: Are they Professionals?

Learning

Do residential workers have extensive and detailed education for their role? Over the last century, most countries have moved towards specifying in legislation what the necessary training for the key professional groups must be – teachers, lawyers, doctors et cetera have a nationally recognized system of education that must be completed successfully before entry, and usually some form of registration obtained. To date there does not, as far as the author is aware, seem to be any national registration system, underpinned by legislation, which requires residential staff to have specified training before entering their career. This is about to be the case in Scotland, where legislation will be enacted in 2001 which will require an approved qualification to be obtained before a worker can commence their career. What that qualification will be, is not yet known. However, a complex set of training opportunities are now being put in place, covering induction, vocational, professional and post qualifying training, which will allow the Scottish Social Services Commission, when established, to specify the approved training required for registration. This is a huge step forward for Scotland, and will put in place one of the most comprehensive approaches to the education of residential workers anywhere. But however that may be for the future, at present, it is still possible and indeed common for residential staff in Scotland to start work without any qualification of any sort whatsoever.

The pattern of preparation for the role of residential child care worker varies hugely from country to country. In the countries of the UK, residential care has grown out of social work, and as a result, most of the training is linked to or identical with the training given to field social workers. In Spain the roots seem to be more in education, as in some of the other countries on mainland Europe. In Canada and the US, much of the training is connected with youth and community work. In Romania, residential care for younger children is firmly placed within the health sector, and training likewise. Thus it is the case that training for residential child care workers is generally a subset of other training for other professional groups. This means that the skills which are considered appropriate and thus the content of courses is decided according to models which are not drawn from the field in which these staff will work when trained. It also means that the training is often offered by non-residential workers. Few other professional groups would expect most or all of those who educate new entrants to the profession to have no professional expertise themselves.

Some countries do deliver specialist training for residential work, and the concept of the pedagogue fits into this context. But, in the countries of the UK at least, and also in other countries, this is still a hotly debated issue. That specific training and education for their role is not seen as necessary by a significant section of the people directly concerned with making decisions about residential care, demonstrates that it is certainly not universally seen as a profession in its own right.

Whatever education and training is provided, if it is to make a difference, it must genuinely relate to the realities of the residential task. Often the training given in many countries is not a practical preparation for the realities of residential work. In Ireland recently, where specialist training for residential work has been well developed, there is considerable concern over the relevance of it for the complexity and practical issues that are faced in this most difficult job. The accusation that training is 'too theoretical' is a common one, which most of us will have heard at one time or another.

So what sort of training would prepare staff for their careers? Over the life of The Centre for Residential Child Care, some thought was given to deciding what a residential worker actually needs to know. Listed below are those aspects necessary to *the sort of knowledge and skill build up* that is required (also compare the contribution of Shealy in this volume).

1. Detailed knowledge and understanding of normal child and adolescent development – psychological, physical, emotional.
2. Skills in caring – nutrition, cooking, recreation, health, education, et cetera, taking into account culture, ethnicity, spirituality, et cetera.
3. Knowledge of children and families in difficulty, poverty, family stress, disability, et cetera.
4. The care system – history, legislation, settings.
5. Issues in practice.

These can be shown in the form of a pyramid (Figure 5.1). At all stages in this, there is a need to make the links between all the aspects of the learning, and to tie them firmly to the context of residential child care, and the actual practical tasks that will be faced within it on a daily basis.

So in summary, one can conclude that currently, residential work does not generally have training that would be considered parallel to most other professional groups, in either the length, content or specificity, nor in the legislative requirement for such training.

Attitude

There are some key – and difficult – questions that must be answered honestly in connection with this issue. Is the attitude residential staff adopt towards their work one which *goes beyond simply a job; it implies someone who has some kind of a calling; more than just money.* Are they serious and focussed? Do they take responsibility for their own professional development? It has to be admitted that over the years, this has not been an approach that is universally evident throughout residential child care. Partly because training is not mandatory before entry, residential staff have picked up the culture and values of the particular service in which they work. The history of abuse inquiries, of degrading care in large institutions, of children whose complaints are not heard, and of parents whose relationship

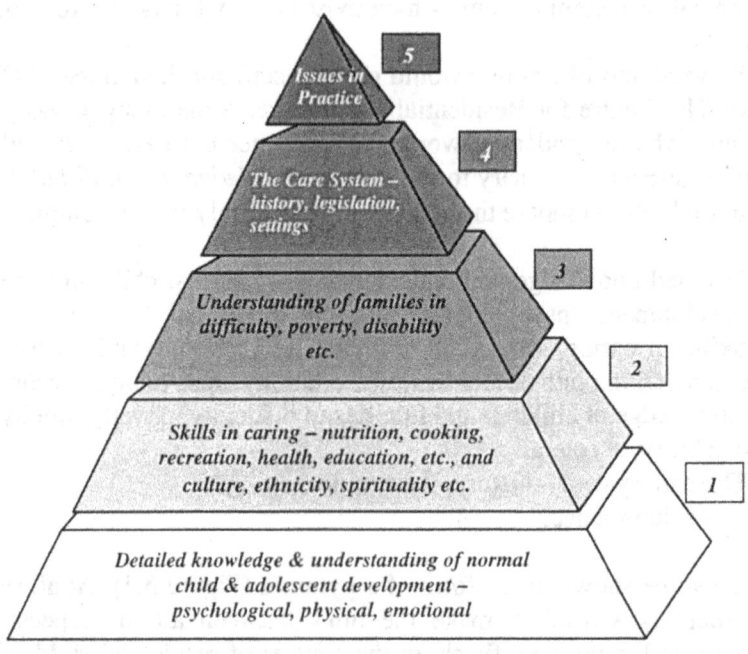

Figure 5.1 The Pyramid of Learning

with their children is stifled – all of these demonstrate that we have had difficulty in creating a strong sense of ethics and a proud adherence to key values about children's rights across the generality of our services.

But against that must be set the constant experience of finding staff, often working for low wages, and enjoying low status, yet believing passionately in the value of the youngsters with whom they work. Residential staff are often the last remaining advocates some of these very difficult young people have. They work for them, argue for them, fight for them long after most of the other professionals involved have long since despaired of them. It can be an embattled sense, sometimes with a slightly arrogant touch to it – *we know best, and no-one else understands this child the way we do*. But none the less, it is a vitally important sense of calling and commitment, which needs to be shaped, nurtured and encouraged, as it forms the seeds of professionalism. It is from this that the constructive culture, so essential to the good residential unit, can grow. This sense of values is inherent in the work – without it, few services would be able to function. When The Centre for Residential Child Care ran its international conference in 1996 (cf. Macquarrie, 1996), it was decided to use the occasion to celebrate these values, and this was done by trying 'to use the heart as well as the head'. Residential care will never be a totally cerebral exercise – it involves the whole person, emotions as much as intellect. Hence the conference used a poetry wall, and invited people to write poems on it, which was later published (Lindsay, 1997). Sentiments were expressed such as *Our job is to deal with things that are real, and still dream of how else it might be; and not to loose hope as we strive to cope with the anger and pain that we see* ... and *You mentioned the forbidden word Love. I can now challenge the procedures, well-meaning though they are. I can reach out to the child and do what I know best* ... There is a core of vision and values which underpins more of residential care than the mass media often portrays. That is the professional heart of residential child care.

Responsibility and Autonomy

In 1998 a research study was conducted into residential services in Finland, Ireland, Scotland and Spain (EUROARRCC, 1998). Two hundred Child Behavior Checklists (Achenbach, 1991) were completed on children in residential care across the four countries, eighty young people were interviewed, and the views of a range of staff and managers were sought.

One of the findings was the common experience of residential workers having low status, and not being treated as professionals by their colleagues. The report concludes 'It was noted that in the four countries, despite an increasing level of professionalism, care workers still have a poor status relative to the other caring professions' (EUROARRCC, 1998, p. 132). As one Irish worker noted: 'Residential care workers no longer see themselves as part of an inter-disciplinary team in which their role is valued. But often it is the care workers who feel that they are not fully appreciated within the team of professionals involved in caring for the child' (ibid., p. 123).

This will be a sentiment familiar to many here. Residential workers may care for the child for more hours than any one else apart from a parent, may become intimately involved with all areas of their lives, and yet be excluded from some of the key planning for that child's life and future.

Public Image

The public image of residential work has already been referred to. Negative publicity has such a huge effect on the various aspects of this work. It affects how staff feel about their work, how safe children feel in their care, and the esteem – or lack of it – in which both the staff and young people are held by the society within which they live their lives.

The negative public image of residential child care is surely one of the most serious challenges facing this work for the 21st century, as will be discussed below.

In summary then, it appears that as far as learning goes, and the acquisition of recognized skills, residential work has some way to go before it can be considered as a profession. In terms of attitude and value basis, there is solid ground to build upon. Autonomy and responsibility is craved by residential staff, who see it as necessary for them to be able to take their place among the team of helping professionals, but which they often feel is denied them. Public image is poor, and this does not make it easier to obtain the respect and status that should go with the conduct of such a difficult and important role.

Does it Matter if Residential Staff Are Considered to Be Professionals?

The lack of professional recognition for residential work has a negative effect on the service offered in three main ways:

- on *staff*, in terms of recruitment and retention, morale and self-image and identity;
- on *quality of care*, in terms of low expectations of what can be achieved, reduced safety, and a culture of failure; and
- on *young people*, in terms of poor role modelling, fear on entering care, and future discrimination on leaving care.

These are the central areas which determine how effective our services are for children. It is vitally important that these issues are addressed. To do so, attention has to be focussed on the key points at which we have to make an impact. Macbeath (2000) has defined these as *circles of influence*. It is in these areas that we must make the push for change.

Circles of Influence

Macbeath (2000) distinguishes five circles of influence: the 'self'; the children and young people; the organization; the system; and the general public (cf. Figure 5.2).

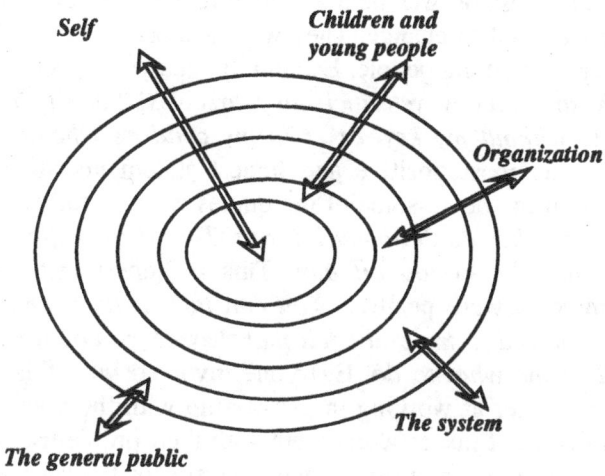

Figure 5.2 Circles of Influence

Self

Residential staff must be given a chance to work together to develop a professional consciousness, and to define what it means to be a residential worker. The isolation of residential work makes this difficult. The habit of negativity and self-criticism so prevalent among residential workers is worsened because they are often only brought together to discuss conditions of service and disputes with management. They need fora in which they can meet, discuss their practice, challenge each other and the outside world to define good residential practice. New technology can help with this – fora like the Child and Youth Care Net (CYCNet) have already proved their worth in getting residential workers and those with an interest in it working together world wide.

Children and Young People

Children are often positive and sensible about the value of the staff that work with them. The author spent a fascinating hour with two Irish young people who were living in a residential unit. They could define quite clearly what were the elements of a 'good residential worker'. At one conference, an open session was held at which residential staff gave their views about what needed to change. They were acutely self-critical about the care they offered to young people. Eventually, one young person – a girl – spoke up: *Why are you always criticising yourselves? I don't know what I would have done without my keyworker in my children's home.* Young people often have the most positive and honest statements about staff. In the study referred to above, some of the quotes were as follows: *They moan and are cranky. They don't do much for us. They drink coffee and tea all day; They tell us what to do all day.* This is honest criticism. But many other comments were positive: *You can talk to them and have a good laugh; They talked to me and I felt that they cared about me, because they were telling me what to do.* Everyone involved with this work has to become much better at working in partnership with the young people who use the services, not just to assist them with their problems, but also to enlist them in developing the professional expertise or the staff who work with them, and in defining their practice, as well as in addressing the issues of public image.

Organization

Too many organizations are not able to manage residential care properly because they do not understand it (Waterhouse, 2000). The logistics of residential care are complicated. Often any attempt to develop quality, therapeutic care is nullified by the difficulty in getting the right staff on the right shift with the right young people. Recent time spent reviewing services in one area with four homes, confirmed to the author the way in which endemic chaos reduces any quality that managers try to build into their residential care services. Endemic staff shortage, and the constant demand to 'find somebody to cover Saturday night's shift' means all too often that longer term issues are never addressed, because the immediate need is always so pressing. In turn, these various short term solutions to fill gaps in the rosta result in exhausted staff covering units they are not familiar with, and young people being cared for by an endless succession of staff who are strangers to them. As an inevitable result, behaviour problems escalate, and units spiral out of control. The focus then becomes care and control and 'firefighting', rather than the planned, therapeutic care that everyone really wants to deliver. It is essential for agencies which provide residential care to become much better at managing the day-to-day realities of residential child care, so that a stable and reliable environment can be created, in which a professional child care service can then develop.

The System

The wider system of child care is diminished because the professionalism of residential work is not recognised and developed. In all countries that the author has studied and where she has visited residential services, staff have consistently not been used to the full, and yet there was a huge need to value the skills of face-to-face work with children. Social work, education and health services in most countries do not often seem to value the key role and skill involved in this face-to-face work. They need a cohort of people who have a professional identity which encompasses these very special skills. Too often, the future of residential work is discussed and debated in the corridors of power with no residential worker present. A clearly defined role for residential care with a clear purpose and remit is acutely needed, within an overall national strategy, and this presupposes the existence of a respected group of practitioners to staff these units and work with these children.

The General Public

The media are no allies of residential child care. But it is essential to tackle them proactively, deliberately feeding positive accounts of life in residential care, so that they begin to understand and to portray the role of the residential worker more sympathetically. But to do this, the workers and managers concerned must become better at explaining what they do, and communicating the value system underpinning child care. These very people are often their own worst enemies when it comes to this. Some of the confusion in the eyes of the public about the role of residential work is worsened because the history of the different systems, which has meant that residential workers have been subsumed into different professional groups. For example, as mentioned above, in the countries of the UK, the role is often titled *Residential Social Worker*; in several European countries, it is *Social Educator*; in Romania, in homes for younger children staff are *Nurses*, and those for older children are *Educators*, in India, the term used is *Guards* – a term that speaks volumes about how these workers are perceived. In few countries is the role of the residential worker valued for itself, for its aspects of child rearing and nurturing, of upbringing and therapy. This is the message that must be clear before the general public can be expected to hear it.

In Conclusion: What is the Challenge?

The challenge is to build a professional identity based on knowledge, responsibility, values, and to actively improve the public image of residential child care. It is a challenge for all involved with these children and young people, in all the many different cultures and nations. Residential child care has been allowed to become a 'cinderella' – overlooked, undervalued and poorly understood, and hence its dynamic potential to change children's lives has been limited. Now is the time to unleash its power by creating a profession to be proud of.

References

Achenbach, T.M. (1991). *Manual for the Child Behavior Checklist/4-18 and 1991 profile.* Burlington (VT): University of Vermont, Department of Psychiatry.

European Association for Research into Residential Child Care [EUROARRCC] (1998). *Care to listen?* Glasgow: Centre for Residential Child Care (CRCC) Publication.

Lindsay, M. (Ed.) (1997). *Realities and dreams: The poetry of child care.* Glasgow: Centre for Residential Child Care (CRCC) Publication.

Macbeath, J. (2000, June). *Professionalism.* Plenary address to the Child Care Conference at the Centre for Residential Child Care, June 8, Glasgow, Scotland.

Macquarrie, A. (Ed.) (1996). *Realities and dreams. Plenary papers from the International Conference on Residential Child Care.* Glasgow: Centre for Residential Child Care (CRCC) Publication.

Shealy, C.N. (2002). Knowing a Way toward Professional Child and Youth Care: The Therapeutic Home Parent Model. In E.J. Knorth, P.M. Van den Bergh, & F. Verheij (Eds.), *Professionalization and Participation in Child and Youth Care* (pp. 87-108). Aldershot: Ashgate.

Waterhouse, R. (2000). *Lost in care. Report of the Tribunal of Inquiry into the abuse of children in care in the former county council areas of Gwynedd and Clwyd since 1974.* London: The Stationery Office.

Chapter 6

Knowing a Way toward Professional Child and Youth Care: The Therapeutic Home Parent Model[1]

Craig N. Shealy

Introduction

Child and youth care practitioners, scholars, advocates, and administrators from around the globe recognize that the field of child and youth care must derive a new paradigm and consensus vis-à-vis professionalization. At the same time the vexing question of how best to get there remains. Aside from lingering fears that professionalization will imperil the essential humanity of child and youth care practice (e.g., see Baizerman, 1996), legitimate questions remain about how exactly such status could and should be achieved. This chapter describes one path by which such status might be attained, and does so via a data- and theory-based process that culminated in a model of professional child and youth care called the *Therapeutic Home Parent (THP) model*.

At the outset, it is worth emphasizing that no claim has been or is made that such a model is the best or only way to conceptualize and actualize a profession of child and youth care (Shealy, 1996a, 1996b). However, the THP model does imply that professionalization will not be realized unless specific competencies are acquired and demonstrated, both prior and subsequent to assuming such roles and responsibilities in the real world. In this way, the THP model represents a qualitative departure from the prevailing ethic (at least in the United States) as to what matters most in child and youth care practice. Along these lines, and more specifically, the following statement is highly congruent with the thrust of the current chapter: 'As we begin the 21st century, the achievement of professional status and competency should be an – if not the – essential goal for the child and youth care field and its practitioners. But, this objective will not and cannot be achieved if the field continues to insist that personal experience, intuition, and the like are more important than the need for practitioners to know and demonstrate mastery of relevant data and theory'.[2]

As will become clear, from the perspective of the Therapeutic Home Parent model at least, there is little reason to question the essential tenet of this statement – that professionalization is essential for the field and its practitioners – since asking whether the field should 'professionalize' is akin to asking whether it is really a good idea to build safer airplanes or more fuel efficient cars. In the field, few child and youth care practitioners question whether professionalization is a good idea (cf. Shealy, 1996a, 1996b, 1997, 1999), especially if enhanced professionalization may lead to greater respect and better compensation. And so, the question of professionalization seems really to be about values and specifics – that is, whose vision of professionalization is best for the field and its practitioners, and whose devil is in which details. As such, the focus in this chapter is on values and specifics in the context of three basic points. First, the field of child and youth care has historically focused on what child and youth care practitioners should do or be in order to be competent professionals. Second, an unfortunate (perhaps unintentional) consequence of this focus has been a lamentable lack of emphasis on what must be known for competent, and thereby professional, practice. Third, what is needed in the larger field is a consensus framework or model for how the field can remain true to the best aspects of its caring and humane traditions, while acquiring and demonstrating that knowledge which is necessary and sufficient for a professional field of practice and inquiry in child and youth care.

The Doing and Being Schools

In the United States at least, the field of child and youth care has emphasized *doing* and especially *being* at the expense of what *must be known* to be competent professionally. Specifically, in arguing for what makes for 'quality' child and youth care, the Doing School tends to emphasize growth and development through activity, whereas the Being School points to experiential, intuitive, and relational capacities. Of course, many (perhaps most) scholars and practitioners recognize the synergy and interdependence among these Schools, but may still lean toward one tradition or another.

VanderVen, for example, might be considered a persuasive spokesperson (at least in the United States) for the Doing School, since her observation that the self develops and is organized through activity is a consistent theme in her writing (VanderVen, 1996, 1999). However, as VanderVen (1999) also observes, '... within the child and youth care field, the number of writings on activity programming as a function of the practitioner [what I would call the Doing School, CNS] are far fewer in number than those that focus on the relational aspects of child and youth care work [what I would call the Being School, CNS]' (p. 137).

The philosophy of the Being School is fundamentally phenomenological and humanistic, and is described by Krueger (1997) as follows: Child care practitioners '... focus on questions such as whether [they] can dance, play, have fun, and be with others ... They observe each other and comment on their sense of presence and rhythm ... as well as their strategies and techniques' (p. 414).

Because the core principle of the Being School is that 'child and youth care work is a process of self in action' (Krueger, 1997, p. 412), its adherents may be distressed by attempts to operationalize or prescribe what good child and youth care practitioners must be or do, much less what they must know (e.g., Baizerman, 1997; Shealy, 1997).

Knowing a Way toward Professional Status

The dominance, perhaps hegemony, of the Being School is not surprising, and could be seen as an historical artefact as much as a deliberate thrust. That is, the vast majority of child and youth care practitioners in the United States do not have their first exposure to 'the field' in any classroom or textbook, but rather on the job. So, it makes sense that a culture of being and doing rather than knowing would inevitably arise. Certainly, there are and have been formal programmes in the United States which educate and train practitioners prior to assumption of child and youth care responsibilities (cf. Shealy, 1996b, pp. 336-342), but the tradition and emphasis has been on developing skills in the 'real world' in part because legislative, regulatory, and funding systems have set relatively low knowledge and other inclusion and exclusion standards.

To be sure, experiential or field and practicum experiences in child and youth care are necessary, essential even. And in fact, all fields that train clinical service practitioners (e.g., counselling, psychiatry, psychology, social work) require experience in the real world. But they do so in order to facilitate the integration of knowledge with practice. In contrast, within the child and youth care field, there is no coherent and agreed upon body of knowledge to acquire or integrate. So instead, the field (out of necessity perhaps) relies heavily – almost exclusively – on the practicum or field experience side of the house. However, a field cannot build a professional foundation on experience, if it does not also insist that certain core areas of knowledge define it and must be mastered and demonstrated before entry into the field.

So, can we require such knowledge at job entry for child and youth care practitioners? Well, according to Arieli (1996), '... child care workers create new knowledge rather than relying on previously acquired information'. Thus, selection criteria consist of ensuring that '... the prospective employee is not a deviant, that he or she is reasonably intelligent, warm, communicative and basically schooled' (Arieli, 1996, p. 290) or (as another administrator put it) can 'fog a mirror' (Christiansen, 1996, p. 306). For Arieli then, you determine whether a child and youth care practitioner '... can do the job' after he or she is hired and '... begins the real frontline work' (Arieli, 1996, p. 290).

But is this the inclusion and exclusion process we want? Do such standards suggest quality or inspire pride? Would we hire a psychologist, social worker, counsellor, minister, or psychiatrist on the basis of the following reasoning: 'Well, they say they can and want to do the job and I don't see any basic problems, so let's give 'em a go!'. If we do not accept such dismal entry standards for these other professions (and we do not), why is child and youth care any different? Are the consequences of inadequate job-entry knowledge any less dire for children and youth who have been or may be removed from their homes?

But if child and youth care practitioners should have specific knowledge at job entry, *what should that knowledge be*? Although an empirical question still, two separate samples of the best and brightest child and youth care line staff and supervisors in the field suggest that practitioners should know about child development, methods and theories of counselling, ethical standards of conduct, and diagnosis and medication, among many other areas (cf. Shealy, 1996a, 1996b, 1997, 1999). Why have practitioners who are among the best educated, most experienced, and highly skilled in the field emphasized such knowledge areas?

It is not all that mysterious, really. After all, how can you possibly work with children and youth that have been, or may be, removed from their homes if you do not have some rudimentary knowledge of attachment theory? How can you possibly make sense, at any deep level, of what happens when attachment processes are disrupted or inadequately established in the first place if you do not know about this core concept from developmental psychology?

And, if you know little or nothing about family systems theory, do you really have a way to grasp what is going on in the families that come before you? Can you recognize when a child has been scapegoated or triangulated and why, and can you intervene in an understanding rather than blaming manner?

If you do not know about boundaries (your own or your clients), if you don't know what a dual-role relationship is and why it may cause problems (especially in child and youth care), do you really have a way to evaluate and check your own conduct or that of your colleagues?

And if you do not have a basic grasp of what diagnoses mean and what medications do – or the economic, political, and self-abnegation forces that may promote both – can you think intelligently about the labels and medication your child receives? Can you critically evaluate the 'disease model' or the oft-made statement that Johnny behaves as he does because he has a 'chemical imbalance in the brain' or 'bad genes'? If you have neither the knowledge nor conceptual framework to question such views, is it really possible to advocate for more human and life-affirming ways of seeing *and being* with children, youth, and families? Without basic knowledge in these and other areas, child and youth care practitioners are at the whim of forces they do not understand and cannot negotiate. They fly blind and don't even know it. No matter the reason or rationale, ignorance of knowledge that is critical for competent performance within a field is not professional, and cannot be ethically justified.

A Model of Professional Child and Youth Care

Toward the objective of catalyzing additional professional development within the child and youth care field, I have offered a model that seeks to integrate being, doing, and knowing perspectives within the larger field (Shealy, 1995, 1996a, 1996b). It is called the *Therapeutic Home Parent (THP) model* and is grounded in decades of data and theory from the counselling/therapy effectiveness literature as well as sub-fields within developmental psychology. The basic rationale for the THP model has been stated as follows: 'Because many of the clients within child and youth care facilities are the product, at least in part, of disturbed or disturbing parental and familial behaviour, it stands to reason that child and youth care workers should not exhibit similar harmful conduct or characteristics. Likewise, if there are characteristics common to all successful therapies, regardless of orientation, it makes sense that child and youth care workers should exhibit similar healing conduct or characteristics' (Shealy, 1995, p. 567).

Personal Characteristics (PCs) of Child and Youth Care Workers

At the most basic level, the THP model is grounded in two comprehensive and time-tested literatures, which represent, in effect, two sides of the same coin. The first literature is concerned with those therapeutic factors or processes that tend to be associated with 'positive or negative outcomes across all therapies or therapists. For example, establishment of a positive therapeutic alliance between patient and therapist is associated with successful treatment outcome regardless of a clinician's unique theoretical framework' (Shealy, 1995, p. 567). As stated by Lambert, Shapiro and Bergin (1986), 'Those factors that are common to most therapies (such as expectation for improvement, persuasion, warmth, and attention, understanding, encouragement, etc.) should not be viewed as theoretically inert nor as trivial; indeed they are central to psychological treatments and play an active role in patient improvement' (p. 163).

In the original model, Table 6.1 provides a 'representative sample of therapist factors commonly identified as therapeutic or counter-therapeutic with their respective authors' (Shealy, 1995, p. 568).[3] The second half of the THP model is principally derived from the larger field of developmental psychopathology (e.g., Cicchetti & Cohen, 1995; Cummings et al., 2000), a field of inquiry that seeks to understand how, when, and why developmental processes and events across the lifespan are associated with 'normal' and 'pathological' outcomes. One segment of this broader literature is concerned with parental and family factors and behaviours that appear to be associated with 'poor' emotional, behavioural, and mental outcomes for offspring. These 'parental correlates of offspring psychopathology' encompass a wide range of findings and programmes of inquiry over the past several decades, exemplified, perhaps, by research in 'expressed emotion, in which familial expression of criticism, hostility, and emotional over-involvement has been shown to predict relapse in previously hospitalized schizophrenics (see Kavananagh, 1992; Kuipers, 1992; Vaughn, 1989)' (Shealy, 1995, p. 568). Representative findings for the original model are presented in Table 6.2.

Taken together, these two literatures provided an empirical and theoretical basis for the THP model, in that the kinds of experiences and environments that successful and unsuccessful therapists tended to produce (as in Table 6.1, the 'therapist' half) seemed to represent the mirror image of the kinds of parental and familial behaviours and contexts that were associated with poor outcomes for children and youth (as in Table 6.2, the 'parent' half). Obviously, the relationship between psychopathology and treatment is typically complex and non-linear; and in this regard, no claim

Table 6.1 Common factors of therapist efficacy

Common factors	Citations
Congruency	Cooley & Lajoy (1980); Gibbs (1975); Marshall (1977); Rogers (1957)
Acceptance / unconditional positive regard	Cooley & Lajoy (1980); Lorr (1965); Rogers (1957)
Empathy	Free et al. (1985); Marshall (1977); Miller et al. (1980); Rogers (1957); Strupp (1986)
Understanding / communicate understanding	Cooley & Lajoy (1980); Cross et al. (1982); Lieberman et al. (1973); Lorr (1965); Rogers (1957); Strupp (1986)
Encourage autonomy / responsibility	Cooley & Lajoy (1980); Cross et al. (1982); Lorr (1965); Ricks (1974)
Ability to relate / develop alliance	Bennum & Schindler (1988); Cross et al. (1982); Luborsky et al. (1985, 1986); Staples et al. (1976)
Well-adjusted	Luborsky et al. (1985)
Interest in helping	Lorr (1965); Luborsky et al. (1985); Ricks (1974)
Provide treatment as intended	Luborsky et al. (1985, 1986)
Exploration of client	Rounsaville et al. (1987)
Expectation for improvement	Gibbs (1975); Ricks (1974)
Emotionally stimulating / challenging / not afraid of confrontation	Lieberman et al. (1973)
Firm, direct; can set limits	Lieberman et al. (1973); Lorr (1965); Ricks (1974)
Work hard for client; persistent	Ricks (1974)
Nurturing	Lorr (1965)
Excessive need to change others	Lorr (1965); Sachs (1983)
Negative attitude	Rounsaville et al. (1987)
Hostile / critical	Lorr (1965); Sachs (1983)
Exploitative / Retaliative	Lorr (1965); Sachs (1983)
Cold	Lorr (1965)

is made here that exposure to a specific therapeutic antidote, though perhaps necessary (as say, the experience of therapeutic warmth and acceptance in therapy by a client who experienced chronic hostility and criticism during development) will also be sufficient for therapeutic healing and growth (cf. Cummings et al., 2000). Nonetheless, when actual child and youth care line staff, supervisors, and administrators from twelve different child and youth care facilities representing 'the spectrum of child and youth care' (Shealy, 1995, p. 569) were asked to describe the 'best' child and youth care practitioners (see Table 6.A, Appendix) and 'worst' child and youth care practitioners (see Table 6.B, Appendix), they identi-

Table 6.2 Parental correlates of offspring psychopathology

Parental correlates	Citations
Hostility	Brown et al. (1972); Rutter & Quinton (1984)
Criticism	Brown et al. (1972); Doane (1978); Hooley et al. (1986); Miklowitz et al. (1988); Nihira et al. (1975); Vaughn & Leff (1976)
Mixed messages	Wynn & Singer (1963)
Blurred boundaries	Bernstein & Garfinkel (1988); Doane (1978); Gross (1984); Hoare (1987); Jansen (1982); Minuchin et al. (1978)
Rigidity	Bernstein & Garfinkel (1988); Doane (1978); Minuchin et al. (1978)
Lack of conflict resolution	Bernstein & Garfinkel (1988); Cooper et al. (1977); Doane (1978); Hoare (1987); Minuchin et al. (1978)
Inconsistency	Chawla & Gupt (1979); Gross (1984)
Coercion	Patterson (1982)
Demandingness	Nihira et al. (1975)
Affective inhibition	Bernstein & Garfinkel (1988)
Enmeshment	Bernstein & Garfinkel (1988); Bjornsson (1974); Brown et al. (1972); Chawla & Gupt (1979); Gross (1984); Jansen (1982); Kashani et al. (1987); Minuchin et al. (1978); Nihira et al. (1975); Parker (1984)
Disengagement	Bjornsson (1974); Doanne (1978); Gross (1984); Jansen (1982); Parker (1984)

fied characteristics that were remarkably similar to those descriptors on either side of the THP model.

In fact, the author attempted to link these two literatures with the 'best' and 'worst' findings from the child and youth care practitioners (that is, Table 6.1 with Table 6.A, and Table 6.2 with Table 6.B), as is evident in Tables 6.3 and 6.4 respectively. To assess the reliability of the author's linkages, 'two independent raters (clinical psychology interns) completed the same linkages and achieved an average 84% of agreement with the author; this comports with Kazdin's (1982) observation that historically, agreement levels have been considered acceptable if they 'met or surpassed .80 or 80 percent' (p. 73)' (in Shealy, 1995, p. 570).

Table 6.3 Linkages between common factors of therapist efficacy and the characteristics of the best child and youth care workers

Common factors	Best personal characteristics
Congruency	Self-aware; good self-image; unpretentious
Acceptance / Unconditional positive regard	Non-defensive
Empathy	Nurturant / Firm
Understanding / Communicate understanding	Interpersonally adept
Encourage autonomy / responsiblility	Responsible; empowering
Ability to relate / develop alliance	Interpersonally adept; unpretentious
Well adjusted / Interest in helping	Good self-image; stable; self-aware
Provide treatment as intended	Predictable/consistent; cooperative
Exploration of client	(no equivalent comparison)
Expectation for improvement	Good self-image; empowering
Emotionally stimulating / challenging / not afraid of confrontation	Interpersonally adept
Firm, direct; can set limits	Nurturant / firm
Works hard for client / persistent	Responsible
Nurturing	Nurturant / firm

Table 6.4 Linkages between parental correlates of offspring psychopathology and the characteristics of worst child and youth care workers

Parental correlates	Worst personal characteristics
Hostility	Angry / Explosive
Criticism	Critical
Mixed messages	Passive-aggressive
Blurred boundaries	Inappropriate boundaries
Rigidity	Rigid
Lack of conflict resolution	Avoidant; defensive
Inconsistency	Inconsistent / unpredictable
Coercion	Authoritarian / Coercive
Demandingness	Selfish; inappropriate boundaries
Affective inhibition	Avoidant; defensive
Enmeshment	Inappropriate boundaries
Disengagement	Inappropriate boundaries

Work Behaviours (WBs) and Knowledges, Skills and Abilities (KSAs)

In addition to Personal Characteristics (PCs), these same child and youth care line staff, supervisors, and administrators were also asked to identify the Work Behaviours (WBs) that were integral to child and youth care practice (that is, what these practitioners actually did on the job) and the Knowledges, Skills and Abilities (KSAs) that were necessary to execute these WBs.

Nine separate Work Behaviours were identified: 1) Assess pre-placement residents; 2) Evaluate residents; 3) Develop/evaluate placement goals and/or treatment plans; 4) Provide counselling; 5) Teach life skills; 6) Supervise residents; 7) Maintain facility routines; 8) Maintain personal and professional proficiency; and 9) Perform administrative duties.

Although space limitations here preclude a complete definition of all WBs (see Shealy, 1996a), it may be useful to include one of the WBs in its entirety: *Provide counselling* reads as follows: 'Provide counselling such as individual and group using educational materials, sociograms, counsellor handbooks, new games books, ropes courses, brochures, interviews, group therapy meetings, evaluations, therapeutic modalities (e.g., reality therapy, role planning) and tests and measurements in order to identify residents' strengths and weaknesses, modify behaviour, facilitate growth and development, and increase residents' interpersonal skills, life skills, and self-awareness' (Shealy, 1996a, p. 222).

Specific and concomitant 'task statements' for the work behaviour of *provide counselling* are as follows:

1. Observe residents' verbal and non-verbal language.
2. Provide feedback and clarification (e.g., asks leading questions, facilitate emotional release, rephrase comments).
3. Identify resident problem(s).
4. Identify goals and objectives of counselling (e.g., educational, vocational, emotional release).
5. Confront beliefs and behaviours (e.g., denial, irrationality, irresponsibility, inconsistency in words and actions, aggression, low self-esteem).
6. Give support and acceptance verbally and non-verbally (e.g., smiles, praise, body position, head nods, voice tone).
7. Specify the ground rules/parameters of sessions (e.g., who attends, where, time, topics).
8. Promote group and individual counselling processes (e.g., provide direction and closure, solicit involvement, promote effective communication).

9. Utilize/implement counselling/therapeutic methods (e.g., role playing, transactional analysis, rational-emotive therapy, behaviour modification, client-centred therapy, high ropes courses).

As noted above, it is not enough to specify what care practitioners must do 'on the job' (i.e., the 'Work Behaviours'); it is also crucial to understand what knowledge areas, skills, and abilities are necessary in order to do what they do. In the original study, child and youth care line staff, supervisors, and administrators identified sixteen separate Knowledges, Skills and Abilities or KSAs that were necessary for competent child and youth care practice: 1) Knowledge of child development; 2) Knowledge of teaching and counselling; 3) Knowledge of professional and ethical standards; 4) Knowledge of agency; 5) Knowledge of residents; 6) Knowledge of health; 7) Knowledge of first aid and CPR [cardiopulmonary resuscitation]; 8) Knowledge of medication; 9) Skill in operating vehicles and equipment; 10) Ability to interact with others; 11) Ability to meet physical and emotional demands of programme; 12) Ability to think logically; 13) Ability to read, comprehend, and interpret written materials; 14) Ability to communicate in writing; 15) Ability to communicate orally; 16) Ability to add, subtract, multiply, divide, and compute fractions, decimals and basic trigonometry.

As with Work Behaviours, it may be useful to include one KSA in its entirety: *Knowledge of teaching and counselling*. It reads as follows: 'Knowledge of Teaching and Counselling to include theories and techniques of counselling (e.g., active listening, empathic listening, interpretation of body language, eliciting responses, role playing, modelling, behaviour modification, transactional analysis, limit setting, unconditional positive regard, life skills and therapies such as Adlerian, client-centred, eclectic, reality, and rational-emotive) as needed to observe, interpret, and confront behaviour and affect, execute treatment plans, modify behaviours, diffuse crisis situations, create an environment conducive to personal growth and development, resolve and prevent emotional conflict of residents and demonstrate flexibility, empathy, support/acceptance, patience, open-mindedness, self-control, and honesty' (Shealy, 1996a, p. 226).

The Therapeutic Home Parent Model

In the original study (Shealy, 1995, 1996a), a separate and representative group of child and youth care practitioners and supervisors (again from 12 different facilities across the spectrum of child and youth care) analyzed these data – Personal Characteristics, Work Behaviours, and Knowledges, Skills and Abilities – through a *Job Analysis Questionnaire* (*JAQ*) in order to determine 'which work behaviours, KSAs, and PCs were least and most important, and how they were interrelated' (Shealy, 1996a, p. 236). That is, at the most basic level, participants provided a quantitative rating for each PC, WB, and KSA in terms of 1) its relative (i.e., rank ordered) importance to child and youth care practice, and 2) which PCs, WBs, and KSAs were necessary upon job entry (i.e., when a practitioner was hired), and which could be developed 'on the job'. With such methods, it is not only possible to provide a composite or comprehensive sense of how these 'subject matter experts' (SMEs) described child and youth care practice, it is also possible to identify what aspects of child and youth care are most and least important for competent practice. Because such data allow for both descriptive and prescriptive levels of analysis, and given the connection between such perspectives and the above empirical and theoretical literatures (common factors of therapist efficacy and parental/familial correlates of offspring psychopathology), it is possible to represent all of this together in the form of the model called the 'Therapeutic Home Parent' (see Table 6.5).

The Therapeutic Home Parent Model consists of two levels – those PCs, WBs, and KSAs that child and youth care practitioners *must* (Level I) or *should* (Level II) possess or exhibit at job entry – and the following four factors – being, not being, knowing, and doing – which emerged directly from the original PC, WB, and KSA data. Because these data are rank-ordered, aggregated, and averaged – and linked to what is actually required to do child and youth care – it is possible to represent a continuum of sorts, which can account for which aspects of child and youth care are most and least important, across levels and factors. For example, note from Table 6.5 that only one KSA – Knowledge of teaching and counselling – is listed under Level I. This designation was not arbitrary, but resulted from the fact that participants rated (e.g., '... to what extent each KSA was needed when performing each work behaviour [0=KSA is not used, to 3=KSA is necessary]', Shealy, 1996, p. 235) this KSA as 'essential for entry-level child and youth care workers ... According to SMEs, such knowledge is necessary in order for child and youth care workers to 1) observe how people behave, 2) understand why people behave as they do, 3) know how to change and modify that behaviour, 4) know how and when to intervene in crises, 5) know what the requisites are for healthy emotional development, and 6) know how to create and maintain such an environment (e.g., by demonstrating 'flexibility, empathy, support/acceptance,

Table 6.5 The Therapeutic Home Parent Model

THERAPEUTIC HOME PARENTS

	I. MUST	II. SHOULD	
A. BE	1. Predictable & Consistent 2. Responsible 3. Common Sense 4. Good Judgement 5. Mature 6. Good Role Model 7. Self-Control 8. Integrity	1. Nurturant & Firm 2. Non-defensive 3. Stable 4. Cooperative 5. Responsive to Authority 6a. Interpersonally Adept 6b. Self-Aware 7. Flexible 8. Good Self-Image 9. Appropriate Values 10. Unpretentious 11. Empowering	A. BE
B. NOT BE	1. Abusive 2. Angry or Explosive 3. Exhibit Pathology 4. Abuse Drugs or Alcohol 5. Dishonest 6. Irresponsible 7. Unethical 8. Authoritarian or Coercive 9. Passive-Aggressive	1a. Inappropriate Boundaries 1b. Poor Role Model 1c. Uncooperative 2. Critical 3. Defensive 4. Rigid 5a. Doesn't Learn from Experience 5b. Inconsistent/Unpredictable 5c. Selfish 6. Poor Self-Esteem 7. Avoidant	B. NOT BE
C. KNOW	1. Teaching and Counselling	1. Residents 2. Professional & Ethical Standards 3. Child Development 4. Health 5. Agency 6. First Aid & CPR 7. Medication 8. Basic Math	C. KNOW
D. DO	1. Supervise Residents 2. Provide Counselling 3. Think Logically 4. Interact with Others 5. Communicate Orally 6. Meet Programme's Physical & Emotional Demands 7. Read, Comprehend & Interpret Written Materials 8. Communicate in Writing 9. Operate Vehicles & Equipment	1. Maintain Facility Routines 2. Teach Life Skills 3. Evaluate Residents 4. Develop & Evaluate Placement Goals & Treatment Plans 5. Maintain Personal & Professional Proficiency 6. Perform Administrative Duties 7. Assess Pre-placement Residents	D. DO

patience, open-mindedness, self-control, and honesty'). By this point, the relevance of the common factors of therapist efficacy and parental correlates literatures to goals like these should be apparent' (Shealy, 1996a, pp. 249-250).

Of course, as Level II, Factor C indicates, 'knowledge areas other than teaching and counselling were seen as very important as well, including – but not limited to – knowledge of professional and ethical standards (e.g., confidentiality, staff/resident relations), child development (e.g., theories, stages), and basic health issues (e.g., hygiene and nutrition, human sexuality)' (Shealy, 1996a, pp. 250-251).

Implications of the THP Model

There are at least three primary implications of the Therapeutic Home Parent model – for 1) professional practice, 2) selection and screening, and 3) education and training, all of which have been discussed at length by the author, and by other commentators on the model (e.g., see *Child and Youth Care Forum*, vol. 25, nos. 4 and 5, 1996; Shealy, 1997, 1999).

Briefly summarized, the 'first and most fundamental' implication of the model is that it provides '... a comprehensive framework for what child and youth care professionals – as therapeutic [home] parents – should and must be, not be, know, and do. Because the model is both descriptive and prescriptive, and is embedded within an applied, theoretical, and empirical context, it could help provide a more coherent sense of professional identity to the child and youth care field as well as its practitioners. Second, two content-valid, legally-defensible selection and screening procedures have now been developed [and are currently in use in the United States], both of which accompany the therapeutic [home] parent model. With additional validation, these procedures could lead to standardized selection and certification of child and youth care practitioners with concomitant gains in the quality, legitimacy, and professionalism of child and youth care. Third, a comprehensive audit of education and training needs has also been identified via this model and its accompanying job analysis. The knowledge and skills child and youth care workers must acquire and apply are specified in great detail, thus paving the way for a coherent, intensive, and inclusive curriculum' (Shealy, 1996a, pp. 267-268).

In Conclusion

Whether or not the therapeutic home parent model or some variation thereof – or any model for that matter – is up to the task of 'knowing a way toward professional child and youth care' is ultimately an empirical question with a split-level answer. At a pragmatic level, such a model should point the way toward a coherent professional identity, clear inclusion and exclusion criteria, and basic education, training, and certification processes and requirements. At a conceptual level, the model should be grounded in relevant data and theory, consistent with the best practices and professional aspirations of the field, and congruent with who we are and are not, what we do, and what we must know.

In the end, without such a comprehensive and integrated framework and approach, it will be difficult for the field to secure lasting professional recognition, mainly because the child and youth care field does not have the power to confer professional status upon itself. Legitimate professional status is only granted via recognition from the external context in which that field is embedded. To earn such status, we must set our own being, not being, doing and knowing standards, make them accessible to current and future practitioners, and then monitor, refine, and strengthen them over time. Ultimately, our external constituencies will take notice of our comprehensive efforts to professionalize. More importantly, so will the children, youth, and families who depend upon us to provide compassionate, competent, informed – and thereby professional – care.

Notes

1. Tables 6.1-6.4 and Appendices 6.A and 6.B were printed previously in Shealy (1995). © 1995 by the American Psychological Association. Reprinted by permission of the publisher. Table 6.5 was printed previously in Shealy (1996a). © 1996 by Human Sciences Press, Inc. Reprinted by permission of the publisher.
2. This statement was discussed by the author in a plenary debate with Dr. S. Lasson during the FICE/EUSARF Conference on (Residential) Child and Youth Care at Maastricht (The Netherlands), May 2000.
3. Note that 'common factors of therapist efficacy' can be associated with 'postive' therapeutic outcomes and processes (as in 'congruency' or 'empathy') as well as 'negative' therapeutic outcomes and processes (as in an 'excessive need to change others' or 'being hostile/critical').

References

Arieli, M. (1996). Do Alabama and the New-Moab belong to the same child care universe? A response to Shealy. *Child and Youth Care Forum, 25*, 289-291.

Baizerman, M. (1996). Can we get there from here? A comment on Shealy. *Child and Youth Care Forum, 25*, 285-287.

Baizerman, M. (1997). The source of our expertise: A response to Krueger. *Child and Youth Care Forum, 26*, 417-419.

Bennum, I., & Schindler, L. (1988). Therapist and patient factors in the behavioural treatment of phobic patients. *British Journal of Clinical Psychology, 27*, 145-150.

Bernstein, G.A., & Garfinkel, B.D. (1988). Pedigrees, functioning, and psychopathology in families of school-phobic children. *American Journal of Psychiatry, 145*, 70-74.

Bjornsson, S. (1974). Epidemiological investigations of mental disorders of children in Reykjavik, Iceland. *Scandinavian Journal of Psychology, 15*, 244-254.

Brown, G.W., Birley, J.L., & Wing, J.K. (1972). Influence of family life on the course of schizophrenic disorder: A replication. In C.E. Vaughn (1989). Annotation: Expressed emotion in family relationships. *Journal of Child Psychology and Psychiatry, 30*, 13-22.

Chawla, P.L., & Gupt, K. (1979). A comparative study of parents of emotionally disturbed and normal children. *British Journal of Psychiatry, 134*, 406-411.

Christiansen, M. (1996). We need a new profession – Not just an upgraded direct care worker! A response to Shealy. *Child and Youth Care Forum, 25*, 305-309.

Cicchetti, D., & Cohen, D. (1995). Perspectives on developmental psychopathology: In S. Ciccetti, & D. Cohen (Eds.), *Developmental Psychopathology, Volume 1: Theory and methods* (pp. 3-20). New York: John Wiley & Sons.

Cooley, E.J., & Lajoy, R. (1980). Therapeutic relationship and improvement as perceived by clients and therapists. *Journal of Clinical Psychology, 36*, 562-570.

Cooper, S.F., Leach, C., Storer, D., & Tonge, W.L. (1977). The children of psychiatric patients: Clinical findings. *British Journal of Psychiatry, 131*, 514-522.

Cross, D.G., Sheehan, P.W., & Khan, J.A. (1982). Short-and long-term follow-up of clients receiving insight-oriented therapy and behavior therapy. *Journal of Consulting and Clinical Psychology, 50*, 103-112.

Cummings, E.M., Davies, P.T., & Campbell S.B. (2000). *Developmental psychopathology and family process: Theory, research, and clinical implications.* New York: Guilford Press.

Doane, J.A. (1978). Family interaction and communication deviance in disturbed and normal families: A review of research. *Family Process, 17*, 357-376.

Free, N.K., Green, B.L., Grace, M.C., Chernus, L.A., & Whitman, R.M. (1985). Empathy and outcome in brief focal dynamic therapy. *American Journal of Psychiatry, 142*, 917-921.

Gibbs, M.S. (1975). Two studies involving expectancy of the therapeutic agent. *Psychological Reports, 36*, 523-532.

Gross, D. (1984). Relationships at risk: Issues and interventions with a disturbed mother-infant dyad. *Perspectives in Psychiatric Care, 22*, 159-164.

Hoare, P. (1987). Annotation: Children with epilepsy and their families. *Journal of Child Psychology and Psychiatry, 28*, 651-655.

Hooley, J.M., Orley, J., & Teasdale, J.D. (1986). Levels of expressed emotion and relapse in depressed patients. In H.W. Koenigsberg, & R. Handley (1986). Expressed emotion:

From predictive index to clinical construct. *American Journal of Psychiatry, 143,* 1361-1373.

Jansen, H.A.M. (1982). The nuclear family as a mediator between class and mental disturbance in children. *Journal of Comparative Family Studies, 13,* 155-170.

Kashani, J.H., Hoeper, E.W., Beck, N.C., Corcoran, C.M., Fallahi, C., McAllister, J., Rosenberg, T.J.K., & Reid, J. (1987). Personality, psychiatric disorders, and parental attitude among a community sample of adolescents. *Journal of the American Academy of Child and Adolescent Psychiatry, 26,* 879-885.

Kavanagh, D.J. (1992). Recent developments in expressed emotion and schizophrenia. *British Journal of Psychiatry, 160,* 601-620.

Kazdin, A.E. (1982). *Single-case research designs: Methods for clinical and applied settings.* New York: Oxford University Press.

Krueger, M. (1997). A contribution to the dialogue about the 'soul' of professional development. *Child and Youth Care Forum, 26,* 411-415.

Kuipers, L. (1992). Expressed emotion in 1991. *Social Psychiatry and Psychiatric Epidemiology, 27,* 1-3.

Lambert, M.J., Shapiro, D.A., & Bergin, A.E. (1986). The effectiveness of psychotherapy. In S.L. Garfield, & A.E. Bergin (Eds.), *Handbook of psychotherapy and behavior change* (3rd ed.). New York: John Wiley & Sons.

Lieberman, M., Yalom, I., & Miles, M. (1973). Encounter groups: First facts. In H. Grunebaum (1975). A soft-hearted review of hard-nosed research on groups. *International Journal of Group Psychotherapy, 25,* 185-197.

Lorr, M. (1965). Client perceptions of therapists: A study of the therapeutic relation. *Journal of Consulting Psychology, 29,* 146-149.

Luborsky, L., Crits-Christoph, P., McLellan, A.T., Woody, G., Piper, W., Liberman, B., Imber, S., & Pilkonis, P. (1986). Do therapists vary much in their success? Findings from four outcome studies. *American Journal of Orthopsychiatry, 56,* 501-512.

Luborsky, L., McLelland, A.T., Woody, G.E., O'Brien, C.P., & Auerbach, A. (1985). Therapist success and its determinants. *Archives of General Psychiatry, 42,* 602-611.

Marshall, K.A. (1977). Empathy, genuineness, and regard: Determinants of successful therapy with schizophrenics? A critical review. *Psychotherapy: Theory, Research and Practice, 14,* 57-64.

Miklowitz, D.J., Goldstein, M.J., Nuechterlein, K.H., Snyder, M.A., & Mintz, J. (1988). Family factors and the course of bipolar affective disorder. *Archives of General Psychiatry, 45,* 225-231.

Miller, W.R., Taylor, C.A., & West, J.C. (1980). Focused versus broad-spectrum behavior therapy for problem drinkers. *Journal of Consulting and Clinical Psychology, 48,* 590-601.

Minuchin, S., Rosman, B.L., & Baker, E.R.L. (1978). Psychosomatic Families. In Hoare, P. (1987). Annotation: Children with epilepsy and their families. *Journal of Child Psychology and Psychiatry, 28,* 651-655.

Nihira, K., Yusin, A., & Sinay, R. (1975). Perception of parental behavior by adolescents in crisis. *Psychological Reports, 37,* 787-793.

Parker, G. (1984). The measurement of pathogenic parental style and its relevance to psychiatric disorder. *Social Psychiatry, 19,* 75-81.

Patterson, G.R. (1982). *Coercive family processes.* Eugene, OR: Castalia Publishing.

Ricks, D.F. (1974). Supershrink: Methods of a therapist judged successful on the basis of adult outcomes of adolescent patients. In D.F. Ricks, M. Roff, & A. Thomas (Eds.), *Life history research in psychopathology.* Minneapolis: University of Minnesota Press.

Rogers, C.R. (1957). The necessary and sufficient conditions of therapeutic personality change. *Journal of Consulting Psychology, 21*, 95-103.

Rounsaville, B.J., Chevron, E.S., Prusoff, G.A., Elkin, I., Imber, S., Sotsky, S., & Watkins, J. (1987). The relation between specific and general dimensions of the psychotherapy process in interpersonal psychotherapy of depression. *Journal of Consulting and Clinical Psychology, 55*, 379-384.

Rutter, M., & Quinton, D. (1984). Parental psychiatric disorder: Effects on children. *Psychological Medicine, 14*, 853-880.

Sachs, J.S. (1983). Negative factors in brief psychotherapy: An empirical assessment. *Journal of Consulting and Clinical Psychology, 51*, 557-564.

Shealy, C.N. (1995). From Boys Town to Oliver Twist. Separating fact from fiction in welfare reform and out-of-home placement of children and youth. *American Psychologist, 50*, 565-580.

Shealy, C.N. (1996a). The 'therapeutic parent': A model for the child and youth care profession. *Child and Youth Care Forum, 25*, 211-271.

Shealy, C.N. (1996b). To be and not to be, to know and to do? That is the question (and the therapeutic parent model has an answer). *Child and Youth Care Forum, 25*, 311-348.

Shealy, C.N. (1997). Brush strokes and empiricism are not mutually exclusive philosophies: A response to Krueger. *Child and Youth Care Forum, 26*, 421-423.

Shealy, C.N. (1999). Ask a simple question, get a complex answer. Why 'the relationship' in child and youth care is neither 'sentimental' nor 'bogus'. *Journal of Child and Youth Care, 13*, 99-124.

Staples, F.R., Sloane, B.R., Whipple, K., Cristol, A.H., & Yorkston, N. (1976). Process and outcome in psychotherapy and behavior therapy. *Journal of Consulting and Clinical Psychology, 44*, 340-350.

Strupp, H. (1986). The nonspecific hypothesis of therapeutic effectiveness: A current assessment. *American Journal of Orthopsychiatry, 56*, 513-520.

VanderVen, K. (1996). Toward a professional dead end or a dynamic process of professional development? The paradoxes of Shealy's 'The Therapeutic Parent: A model for the child and youth care profession'. *Child and Youth Care Forum, 25*, 297-304.

VanderVen, K. (1999). You are what you do and become what you've done: The role of activity in development of self. *Journal of Child and Youth Care, 13*, 133-147.

Vaughn, C.E. (1989). Annotation: Expressed emotion in family relationships. *Journal of Child Psychology and Psychiatry, 30*, 12-22.

Vaughn, C.E., & Leff, J.P. (1976). The measurement of expressed emotion in the families of psychiatric patients. In C.E. Vaughn (1989). Annotation: Expressed emotion in family relationships. *Journal of Child Psychology and Psychiatry, 30*, 13-22.

Wynn, L.C., & Singer, M.T. (1963). Thought disorder and family relations of schizophrenics: I. A research strategy. *Archives of General Psychiatry, 9*, 191-198.

Appendix: Table 6.A Personal characteristics identified in Workshop 2 to describe the best child and youth care workers

1. *Flexible*: ability to respond to varying settings in a range of ways; ability to reverse directions in similar situations; can make appropriate exceptions.
2. *Mature*: makes sound decisions (i.e., judgements); demonstrates self-control; absence of adolescent authority conflicts; does not perceive challenges in every hierarchy; can focus on other's needs without sacrificing own needs.
3. *Integrity*: the ability to behave honestly, professionally and ethically in a manner consistent with values.
4. *Good judgement*: ability to take the 'right', proper, appropriate course of action to ensure the safety and welfare of clients.
5. *Common sense*: ability to use appropriate judgement in the absence of written guidelines or established procedures; can distinguish between critical and non-critical events (e.g., recognizes pre-suicidal behaviour, does not stand under a tree in lightning).
6. *Appropriate values*: values are congruent with those of the treatment programme.
7. *Responsible*: ensures clients are supervised; completes assigned tasks; takes initiative in trouble-shooting; does not allow clients to dispense medicine.
8. *Good self-image*: feels good about 'self'; realizes strengths and weaknesses and works toward self-improvement.
9. *Self-control*: reacts appropriately when 'under fire'; reaction appropriate to situation.
10. *Responsive to authority*: willing to take direction; awareness of limits to authority; listens non-defensively; communicates pro-social attitudes to clients; models appropriate behaviour.
11. *Interpersonally Adept*: communicates clearly; able to mediate conflict; able to 'get along with' others.
12. *Stable*: emotionally consistent; high tolerance for frustration.
13. *Non-Pretentious*: ability to be open and honest; not 'hiding behind role'.
14. *Predictable/Consistent*: punishment and reinforcement are consistent; behaviour is reliable and dependable; provides counterbalance to previous inconsistent environment.
15. *Non-Defensive*: ability to consider alternative perspectives; ability to handle criticism; admits when wrong.
16. *Nurturant/Firm*: ability to be warm; empathizes with the client while providing support and structure; sets appropriate limits on behaviour.
17. *Self-Aware*: possesses clear but flexible boundaries; can distinguish their problems from clients; ability to identify the source of aggravation or frustration; recognizing what 'pushes their buttons'; understands that clients respond on the basis of past learning not necessarily to the child care worker.
18. *Empowering*: encourages independence, autonomy, a sense of self-esteem, and control over the environment.
19. *Cooperative*: ability to work with the philosophy of the programme; adheres to programme/treatment guidelines but questions and modifies when appropriate.
20. *Good Role Model*: provides the 'right kind' of example; advocates a 'do as I do' philosophy to clients (e.g., positive coping strategies, cooperating with authority, honesty).

Appendix: Table 6.B Personal characteristics identified in Workshop 2 to describe the worst child and youth care workers

1. *Exhibits pathology*: exhibits psychosis, personality disorders, and especially character disorders.
2. *Selfish*: consistently places own needs above others.
3. *Defensive*: unable/unwilling to hear or respond to feedback; always projects blame.
4. *Dishonest*: does not relay facts or events in a truthful manner; falsifies records; omits important information.
5. *Abusive*: abuses clients physically, verbally, emotionally, or sexually.
6. *Abuses drugs/alcohol*: excessive drinking; illicit drug use.
7. *Uncooperative*: unable/unwilling to work with others; tendency toward dominance; unable to accept the limits of their role in the treatment plan.
8. *Poor self-esteem*: feels poorly about 'self'; does not realize strengths and weaknesses; does not work on self-improvement.
9. *Rigid*: unable to change perspectives in the face of obvious contradictory data; able to see something from only one perspective.
10. *Irresponsible*: does not complete assigned tasks; takes no initiative in trouble-shooting; leaves clients unsupervised; allows clients to dispense medicine.
11. *Critical*: demonstrates a negative attitude; pessimistic; never accentuates the positive; cannot see the strengths of a client.
12. *Passive-Aggressive*: exhibits covert hostility; resists and sabotages treatment programme; unable or unwilling to communicate perspectives directly.
13. *Inappropriate boundaries*: approval needs met from clients; get worse when kids get better; cannot distinguish between own and child's needs; overly or under involved; unable to separate professional role from personal values; cannot separate being a friend/date from role as staff member.
14. *Unethical*: violates confidentiality; obtains personal benefits from clients; does not protect the client's rights.
15. *Authoritarian/Coercive*: misuses power; confrontational/threatening toward staff and clients.
16. *Inconsistent/Unpredictable*: arbitrary, capricious or unpredictable application and enforcement of policies or treatment of clients.
17. *Avoidant*: inability to confront/deal with conflict; not confrontative when necessary.
18. *Does not learn from experience*: continues making the same mistakes; fails to generalize knowledge across situations or clients.
19. *Poor role model*: actions and words provide a poor standard of conduct; does not 'practice what is preached' or preaches and practices inappropriate attitudes and behaviour.
20. *Angry/Explosive*: outbursts characterized by loss of self-control and temper tantrums which constitute bad modelling or risk of violence (verbal or physical).

Chapter 7

The Role of Residential Child and Youth Care Workers in Care Planning: An Exploratory Study

Erik J. Knorth and Monika Smit

Introduction

A treatment plan that looks ideal on paper, but does not take into account the parents, the group workers who have to carry out the plan, or the circumstances in which the work has to be done, is not a plan, but a useless thing (Kok, 1988, p. 104).

In 1988, Vissers stated that for two thirds of the adolescents in the Netherlands who were admitted to a residential setting by judicial measure, a treatment plan was available. However, in only half of those plans the treatment goals and the ways in which these goals were to be reached were described. His statement was based on a large-scale study. Other studies revealed similar findings (Knorth, 1987).

By now, written treatment plans are available for almost all children and youth in residential care in the Netherlands. In 1995, a study by the Inspectorate for Child and Youth Care and Protection shows that in 95% of the participating child care homes (N=95) it is common practice to make a treatment plan for every resident in care (Inspectie Jeugdhulpverlening en Jeugdbescherming, 1995).

No doubt this is partly due to the fact that since 1991, in the Netherlands, institutions for child and youth care are required by law to make treatment plans, as is the case in several other countries within the European Union like, for instance, Germany and the United Kingdom (Van Unen, 1995). The Dutch *Child and Youth Care Law* (art. 5, AMB) states that a treatment plan has to be geared to the client's problems and has to contain at least a description (based on a diagnosis) of the intended treatment process, and of short and longer term goals. Also, it has to contain an evaluation schedule. Furthermore, the plan has to indicate the professionals who will be involved in the treatment and the ways in which deliberation with the clients will take place.

Working with treatment plans is unarguably one of the most striking features of the professionalization tendency in Dutch child and youth care. This chapter focuses on the meaning of working with these plans for those who deal with the young people in care on a daily basis: the *group workers*. First the literature on working with treatment plans will be explored. Then some findings will be presented from a small-scale study concerning group workers' experiences with and attitudes on this topic.

Working with Treatment Plans

Treatment plans are considered to be of crucial importance for the quality of the work (Van Geffen, 2000; Van IJzendoorn & De Ruyter, 1997). This is illustrated by the fact that in 1997 a government supported, nation-wide project was started, titled *Kwaliteitszorg in de jeugdzorg* (Quality Care in Child and Youth Care) (Van IJzendoorn & De Ruyter, 1997). This programme focuses on improving the quality of care, and 'treatment planning' forms a main point.

Also worth mentioning is the following. Van der Ploeg and Scholte (1997) asked a sample of child and youth care agencies in the Netherlands to name the most important *quality indicators* of the work they were doing. A factor analysis on their data brought two factors to the surface: one referring to organizational requirements and one related to the actual care provided. The second factor contained the following six items: a clear care and treatment programme; transparent and concrete treatment plans; procedures to enhance the co-operation between practitioners; engagement of parents in the care and treatment activities; evaluation of treatment progress; and a planned, well-prepared termination of the helping process. Most of these items, directly or indirectly, have to do with treatment planning.

Advantages and Disadvantages

Several advantages are connected with the use of treatment plans. Among these are the following (cf. De Ruyter, 1997; Knorth & Smit, 1999; Looney, 1984; Van Geffen, 2000; Verheij, 1999):

- *Reflection* Working with treatment plans means that workers have to give an account of the problems with which the young client or his parents struggle, and of which kind of help is considered adequate. In other words: it limits too much intuitivity in the approach.
- *Support* A treatment plan is something concrete for the workers to hold on to during their work.
- *Transparency* The fact that considerations and choices are written down, enhances the transparency and accountability for clients as well as other parties involved (for instance referring agencies, and the Child and Youth Care Inspectorate). Furthermore, it facilitates internal and external information transfer.
- *Gearing* A treatment plan increases the chance that workers pursue roughly the same course, and it ensures continuity in approach in the event that workers are replaced by others.
- *Purposiveness* Treatment plans contain information about the perspective of the treatment, and the goals set. They imply that treatment has to yield results, and that it must end at some point in time.
- *Evaluation and research* A treatment plan offers a good starting point for evaluation of the treatment process at an individual level, whereas analysis of several plans is a means of programme evaluation at an institutional level.

Although research concerning the impact of working with treatment plans is still scarce, some revealing results can be reported. A study among child psychotherapists showed that therapists who state their goals and their approach in advance and who regularly evaluate and report their progress produce the best results (Loeven & Harinck, 1985). The aforementioned study by Vissers (1988) showed that the existence of a treatment plan goes hand in hand with a shorter length of stay. Another study within residential care showed that a planned rounding off of a residential treatment yields to relatively more goals reached (Gerull, 1996; Smit, 1999). In addition, working with clear treatment goals seems to lead to higher worker motivation (Posavac & Carey, 1980).

However, all that glitters is not gold: a panel of Dutch experts observed that there are still quite a lot of snags related to working with treatment plans (De Ruyter, 1997). Apart from their observation that *working with treatment plans is not yet common practice*, De Ruyter mentions four additional shortcomings:

- *Lack of uniformity* There is no uniformity in content and use of treatment plans.
- *Lack of topicality and concreteness* Treatment plans quite often lack topicality and they are sometimes rather vague.
- *The role of clients* It is not clear how clients (children or youth and their parents) can be involved in the formulation of a treatment plan.
- *The role of group workers* It is also not clear to what extent group workers should be involved in the development of a treatment plan, or in what detail the means they typically use in their work, should be described in a plan.

Illustration: Lack of Uniformity

The first point mentioned was demonstrated in a study carried out in three residential settings for child and youth care. The content of their treatment plans was analyzed with regard to the number of statements concerning the 'agogic triad': *problems* of the children or youth and their families, *goals* for the treatment and *means* to be used. In all, 79 randomly selected plans were analyzed. In one setting (A) two different samples of plans were studied, with an interval of half a year. Table 7.1 shows the results.[1]

Table 7.1 Mean number of statements on problems, goals and means in treatment plans (N=79) of three Dutch residential child and youth care centres

	Mean number re to problems	Mean number re to goals	Mean number re to means	Mean number re to $p+g+m$
Centre A [n=24] t1*	14	4	7	25
Centre A [n=16] t2	23	18	39	80
Centre B [n=20]	19	27	32	78
Centre C [n=19]	4	4	9	17

* The numbers between brackets indicate the number of treatment plans investigated.

The three settings differ substantially in the frequency of problems, goals and means mentioned in their plans (compare the column on the right). Setting A at time 1 and setting C produced the briefest plans in this respect; setting A at time 2 and setting B the most extensive ones. Furthermore, the settings differ as far as the 'problem-goal-mean ratio' is concerned. Worth mentioning is that setting A, in between time 1 and time 2, developed a protocol concerning the formulation of care plans. This seems to have resulted in much more extensive plans.

By the way, an extensive plan is not automatically a 'better' plan. Much depends on:

- The *reliability* of the problems mentioned (do they cover reality, or the way those involved experience reality);
- Whether the goals and means mentioned are *concrete* and *manageable*. In this respect it is advisable to prioritize the goals and means, for example in hierarchical chains of goals and objectives (cf. Knorth & Smit, 1995);
- Whether problems, goals and means are *consistently interrelated* (see also Schneider & Loots, 1990).

A Study into the Role of Group Workers

In the Dutch Child and Youth Care Law (1989), the role of the children or youth, their parents or foster parents and the referring agencies in the development and evaluation of treatment plans is mentioned explicitly. But the division of roles between staff members and other workers in residential settings is for them to decide. The law does not mention the position of group workers at all.

Conversely, the literature concerning treatment planning refers to three models with respect to the role care workers could play in the development of a treatment plan: the expert model, the involvement model, and the participation model (Klomp & Van Oeffelt, 1978; Klomp & Van den Bergh, 1999).

In the *expert model* 'experts' (psychologists, academic pedagogues and psychiatrists) are the primary draughtsmen of a treatment plan. Planning is based on diagnostic assessment and on the group worker's observations and reports. A unit co-ordinator plays a consultative role and the group workers are both the informants and the ones who carry out the plan.

In the *involvement model* group workers are the primary draughtsmen of treatment plans. The assumption behind it is that they, as daily counsellors, are the ones who know what the problems are and what approach should be chosen. In this model, the experts are the consultants who can be called for if necessary.

In the *participation model* planning of the treatment is a shared responsibility of both the group workers and the experts. Workers' daily experiences with the youths concerned are evaluated and, together with the results from diagnostic assessment, they form the basis for the development of a treatment plan. The contributions of different disciplines are treated equally. Usually an academic pedagogue, a psychologist, or a unit co-ordinator has the final responsibility for a plan.

In general, it is assumed that the participation model is the best model in the sense that the equal contributions of different disciplines are expected to result in the best-founded vision on diagnosis and treatment. Furthermore, implementation of the plan supposedly goes smoothly because all concerned have had a chance to participate in the planning. Several studies have also shown that participation in different aspects of the work goes hand in hand with more job satisfaction (Van der Ploeg & Scholte, 1998; Romi, 1999). But what do group workers think? This question led to a study that has recently been published (Jongejan, Smit & Knorth, 2000).

The study was conducted in the residential department of a large multi-functional institution for child and youth care (to be precise: in setting A in Table 7.1). The department consists of eleven units with a total capacity of 95 boys and girls with severe psychosocial problems. The residents are aged 9 to 17. In all, 22 group workers (two from each unit) were interviewed about their experiences with, and attitudes on treatment planning. As far as the results are concerned two issues will be discussed in this chapter: a) the role of different disciplines and especially group workers in the process of treatment planning, and b) the usefulness of treatment plans for these workers.

Preferred Division of Roles

A first question was what role the interviewees preferred to fulfil in the treatment planning process. Table 7.2 summarizes their attitudes with respect to two core issues:

- Who should decide on the content of a plan?
- Who should put it down on paper?

With regard to the first question two categories were mentioned most often: a representative of the academic staff (category 1) and the entire team (category 7). As far as this issue is concerned, there seem to be as many protagonists of the expert model as of the participation model. The involvement model is not represented (those in favour of this model would be expected to choose category 3, but no one did). Note that one group worker prefers to put the responsibility in the hands of the youth concerned.

The second issue: who should put the plan down on paper, is much more univocal. All interviewees but one consider this to be an academic staff member's task. Six respondents are of the opinion that a group worker should also take his share in this task (column on the right, categories 5 and 6). In three of these cases, the worker referred to the mentor of the youth concerned.

Table 7.2 Group workers' opinions on respectively who has to decide on the content of a treatment plan and who should write the plan (N=22)

Preferred Actors *	Evaluation Aspect: Deciding on the content of the plan n	Putting the plan down on paper n
1 Academic Staff (psychologist, ac. pedagogue)	8	13
2 Group Coordinator	4	-
3 Group Workers	-	1
4 Ac. Staff + Gr. Coordinator	1	-
5 Ac. Staff + Gr. Workers	1	5
6 Ac. Staff + Gr. Workers + Fam. Worker	-	1
7 Ac. Staff + Gr. Coord. + Gr. Workers + Fam. Work.	7	-
8 Youth	1	-
9 Unknown	-	2

* Ac. Staff = Academic Staff; Gr. Coord. = Group Coordinator; Gr. Workers = Group Workers; Fam. Work. = Family Worker.

Table 7.3 summarizes the opinions of the interviewees with respect to seven aspects of planning. They were asked to what extent they wanted to be involved in these planning aspects. The columns indicating a preferred high or modest degree of participation (the plusses) turn out to be favourite, the only exception being putting the plan down on paper. Again, most workers do not aspire to this task. However, they prefer to be actively involved in every other aspect of the planning. What especially stands out, is their wish to be actively involved in the assessment of the means to be used and the evaluation of a plan.

Not mentioned in this table is that in the institution under study, *actual* participation does not live up to the *preferred* one; the largest discrepancy concerns the assessment of means. This is remarkable, as the policy of this institution is to work according to the participation model.

Table 7.3 Workers' opinions on their preferred degree of participation in seven aspects of treatment planning (N=22)

	Preferred degree of participation *			
Aspect of treatment planning	++	+	-	- -
Assessment of problems	*10*	9	3	-
Assessment of goals	8	*11*	3	-
Assessment of means	*14*	6	2	-
Development of treatment plan	4	*13*	3	2
Putting the treatment plan down on paper	1	5	6	*10*
Evaluation of treatment plan	*12*	10	-	-
Adjustment of treatment plan	*12*	9	1	-
Mean number of times the columns have been marked	8.7	9	2.6	1.7

* ++ high degree of participation preferred; + modest degree of participation preferred; - limited degree of participation preferred; - - no participation preferred. The most frequently mentioned value (the modus) is in italics and bold.

Perceived Usefulness

The interviewees were also asked about the usefulness of treatment plans in daily practice: to what extent and in which ways do plans support them in their work and, conversely, do plans hinder them at all? Table 7.4 shows the interviewees' opinions. Note that the experience of support and of hindrance can go hand in hand; they do not exclude one another.

Table 7.4 Workers' attitudes concerning perceived support and hindrance in their daily work by treatment plans (N=22)

Attitude group workers	Perceived support n	Perceived hindrance n
Agree	6	8
Partly agree	10	-
Disagree	6	11
Unknown	-	3

Sixteen of the 22 interviewees experience support from a plan. Ten of these sixteen indicate that this experience is not the entire story: they partly agree. Eight group workers experience hindrance from the plans.

The group workers explain their *experiences of support* with the following remarks:

- A plan gives information, for example background information, in a compact way;
- A plan serves as a guideline for acting;
- A plan offers a frame work for own observations; and
- A plan discourages too much 'subjectivity'.

One of the interviewees stated: 'Because of a plan, one knows what one is working on and one does not feel like a bungler'.

The workers connect their *experiences of hindrance* with:

- The manageability of a plan (too abstract; complicated language; too long; too poorly organized);
- The content of a plan (too one-sidedly formulated by one discipline; focussed on problems; too imperious, or too noncommittal); and
- Institutional preconditions (not enough time or personnel, and lack of training).

The second problem or objection mentioned shows a difference in opinion, which is also mentioned in the literature (De Ruyter, 1997): some group workers prefer a plan in outlines (and they object to dirigism); others have a need for very concrete guidelines (and they object to too much liberty). Several interviewees suggested the development and use of a general treatment plan that should be combined with a more concrete, shorter-term 'working plan', meant for the daily work in the group.

Conclusion

Working with treatment plans supposedly improves the quality of child and youth care. No doubt partly due to statutory obligations in the Dutch Child and Youth Care Law, working with treatment plans has become common practice in the Netherlands. However, although group workers are the key persons in residential child and youth care, when it comes to carrying out treatment plans, the law does not give guidelines concerning the role of group workers in the process of this treatment planning. In literature, group worker participation is advocated, for example by working according to the participation model. In this model, planning of the treatment is a shared responsibility of both group workers and 'experts' (psychologists, academic pedagogues, et cetera).

The group workers in the study reported here also prefer to participate in different aspects of treatment planning. However, they experience a discrepancy between actual and preferred involvement. They desire more participation in almost all tasks, except for putting the plan down on paper. They also made it very clear that working with treatment plans is not a simple matter; some group workers experience actual hindrance from the plans. And one care worker told us: *Working with eight or nine youths at the same time means treating them all according to a plan, or rather according to eight or nine different plans!* Regular team supervision or in-service-training seem to be the appropriate means to help group workers with these aspects of their task (Klomp, 1999). In such sessions, attention should also be paid to the formulation of concrete goals and means related to the problems observed. In order to improve the workability of plans and to clarify different goals and means, and their interrelationship, it is advisable to order and subsume goals in so-called hierarchical chains of objectives (Knorth & Smit, 1995).

From supporting students during their apprenticeships, we know that in at least some Dutch institutions for residential child and youth care, group workers are actively involved in the planning of the treatment. So the amount of group worker participation varies over different settings. The exploratory study showed that the frequency of problems, goals and means mentioned in treatment plans also varies, as does the problem-goal-mean ratio. An interesting and so far unanswered question is whether the amount of group worker participation influences the content of plans. A larger scale study of the content of plans in several residential settings for child and youth care, working according to different models of treatment planning as far as group worker participation is concerned, is necessary to shed light in this matter.

In this contribution, the focus was on participation of child and youth care workers in treatment planning. The recommendation that can be derived from the research is: do work according to the participation model when planning treatment. However, obviously, there are other people involved in a treatment process as well, such as the youths concerned, and their parents. Participation of group workers is important, but in itself not sufficient. We plead for a clear and substantial role in this process not only for *workers*, but for the *youth* and their *parents* as well. Many researchers and practitioners plead for this, but unfortunately it is not yet 'normal practice' (Conen, 1996; Lindsay, 2000; Schefold et al., 1998; Sinclair, 1998; Sinclair & Grimshaw, 1997; Smit & Knorth, 1997).

Note

1. Data have been derived from four unpublished research theses, written by master students at Leiden University (Department of Education, Centre for Special Education and Child Care), supervised by the authors, i.e. Horsman (1995) [Centre A at time 1]; Okkerse-Hameetman (1995) [Centre A at time 2]; Aarts (1995) [Centre B]; and Tadema (1995) [Centre C].

References

Aarts, S.T. (1995). *Een onderzoek naar behandelingsplannen van BJ Zuid-Holland/Zuid Regio Dordrecht* (master thesis). Leiden: Leiden University, Centre for Special Education and Child Care.
Conen, M.L. (1996). *Elternarbeit in der Heimerziehung: Eine empirische Studie der Eltern- und Familienarbeit in Einrichtungen der Erziehungshilfe.* Frankfurt am Main: IGfH Verlag (3rd. Ed.).
De Ruyter, D.J. (1997). *Hulpverlening op een hoger plan. Planning en plannen in de jeugdzorg.* Utrecht: NIZW Publishers.
Gerull, P. (1996). Fremdunterbringung: Zukunftssicherung oder Fehlinvestition? Zur Effektivität stationärer Heimerziehung. *Unsere Jugend, 48* (3), 92-109.
Horsman, M. (1995). *Hulpplanning en kwaliteit van residentiële zorg* (master thesis). Leiden: Leiden University, Centre for Special Education and Child Care.
Inspectie Jeugdhulpverlening en Jeugdbescherming (1995). *Kwaliteit van het hulpverleningsproces in de jeugdhulpverlening. Tweede deel: De opname van jeugdigen.* Rijswijk: Inspectie JHVJB.
Jongejan, C., Smit, M., & Knorth, E.J. (2000). *Hulpverleningsplanning in de praktijk: Het perspectief van de groepsleiding.* Amsterdam: SWP Publishers.
Klomp, M. (1999). Planmatige teambegeleiding. In E.J. Knorth, & M. Smit (Eds.), *Planmatig handelen in de jeugdhulpverlening* (pp. 305-323). Leuven/Apeldoorn: Garant.
Klomp, M., & Van den Bergh, P.M. (1999). Werkbare hulpverleningsplanning in de (semi)residentiële jeugdhulpverlening. In E.J. Knorth, & M. Smit (Eds.), *Planmatig handelen in de jeugdhulpverlening* (pp. 251-269). Leuven/Apeldoorn: Garant.
Klomp, M., & Van Oeffelt, P.W.H.M. (1978). Residentiële behandelingsplanning als proces. *Pedagogisch Tijdschrift, 4* (3), 387-404.
Knorth, E.J. (1987). *Opname op maat. Een verkennend onderzoek naar de intakeprocedure als begin van residentiële jeugdhulpverlening.* Leuven/Amersfoort: Acco.
Knorth, E.J., & Smit, M. (1995). A systematic approach to residential care. In M.J. Colton, et al. (Eds.), *The art and science of child care. Research, policy and practice in the European Union* (pp. 171-188). Aldershot: Ashgate.
Knorth, E.J., & Smit, M. (1999). Planmatig handelen in de jeugdhulpverlening: theorie en praktijk. In E.J. Knorth, & M. Smit (Eds.), *Planmatig handelen in de jeugdhulpverlening* (pp. 25-54). Leuven/Apeldoorn: Garant.
Kok, J.F.W. (1988). *Specifiek opvoeden: Orthopedagogische theorie en praktijk.* Leuven/Amersfoort: Acco (6th ed.).

Lindsay, M. (2000, May). *Building a professional identity; the challenge for residential care.* Key note address at the International 43rd FICE/7th EUSARF Congress on (Residential) Child and Youth Care 'The Century of the Child', Maastricht, The Netherlands, 9–12 May.

Loeven, L.M., & Harinck, F.J.H. (1985). Praktijk in beeld: Werkwijze en meningen van beeldcommunicatie-therapeuten. In J. Hellendoorn (Ed.), *Therapie, kind en spel* (pp. 257-273). Deventer: Van Loghum Slaterus.

Looney, J.G. (1984). Treatment planning in child psychiatry. *Journal of the American Academy of Child Psychiatry, 23*, 529-536.

Okkerse-Hameetman, M. (1995). *Plannen plannen. Onderzoek naar behandelingsplannen binnen de Stichting Rijnhove* (master thesis). Leiden: Leiden University, Centre for Special Education and Child Care.

Posavac, E.J., & Carey, R.G. (1980). *Program evaluation: Methods and case studies.* Englewood Cliffs (NJ): Prentice-Hall.

Romi, S. (1999). Youth care workers' burnout. *International Journal of Child and Family Welfare, 4* (2), 101-111.

Schefold, W., Glinka, H.J., Neuberger, Ch., & Tilemann, F. (1998). *Hilfeplanverfahren und Elternbeteiligung.* Frankfurt am Main: Deutschen Verein für öffentliche und private Fürsorge.

Schneider, M.J., & Loots, G.M.P. (1990). Werken met handelingsplannen in het speciaal onderwijs. *Tijdschrift voor Orthopedagogiek, 29*, 132-150.

Sinclair, R. (1998). Involving children in planning their care. *Child and Family Social Work, 3*, 137-142.

Sinclair, R., & Grimshaw, R. (1997). Partnership with parents in planning the care of their children. *Children and Society, 11*, 231-241.

Slot, N.W., & Spanjaard, H.J.M. (1999). *Competentievergroting in de residentiële jeugdzorg: Hulpverlening voor kinderen en jongeren in tehuizen.* Baarn: Intro.

Smit, M. (1999). Decision-making on discharge. In H.E. Colla, et al. (Eds.), *Handbuch Heimerziehung und Pflegekinderwesen in Europa* (pp. 741-747). Neuwied/Kriftel: Luchterhand.

Smit, M., & Knorth, E.J. (1997). Involving parents in residential care; fact or fiction? In W. Hellinckx, M.J. Colton, & M. Williams (Eds.), *International perspectives on family support* (pp. 48-66). Aldershot: Ashgate.

Tadema, A. (1995). *Behandelingsplanning. Onderzoek naar behandelingsplanning en behandelingsplannen in de residentiële jeugdhulpverlening* (master thesis). Leiden: Leiden University, Centre for Special Education and Child Care.

Van der Ploeg, J.D., & Scholte, E.M. (1997). *Impliciete kwaliteitscriteria in de jeugdzorg.* Utrecht: NIZW Publishers.

Van der Ploeg, J.D., & Scholte, E.M. (1998). Job satisfaction in residential care. *International Journal of Child and Family Welfare, 3* (3), 228-241.

Van Geffen, H. (2000). *Sikoob: De ontwikkeling van een informatiseringsprogramma voor de orthopedagogische hulpverlening* (PhD thesis). Utrecht: Utrecht University.

Van IJzendoorn, W.J.E., & De Ruyter, D.J. (1997). *Kwaliteitszorg in de jeugdzorg. De plannen tot het jaar 2000.* Utrecht: SOJN.

Van Unen, A. (1995). *New legislation on care for children and young people in England, Germany and the Netherlands.* Amsterdam: Defence for Children International (DCI).

Verheij, F. (1999). Behandelingsplanning met oog voor de ontwikkelings- en levensdomeinen van kinderen en adolescenten. In E.J. Knorth, & M. Smit (Eds.), *Planmatig handelen in de jeugdhulpverlening* (pp. 235-250). Leuven/Apeldoorn: Garant.

Vissers, J. (1988). *De residentiële carrière van jongeren in de kinderbescherming.* The Hague: Ministry of Justice/CWOK.
Wet op de Jeugdhulpverlening (1989). The Hague: Ministry of Justice.

Chapter 8

Professionalization and Institutional Abuse in the United Kingdom

Matthew J. Colton

Introduction

Although the historical antecedents of residential care in Western Europe can be traced back as far as the Middle Ages, the roots of current approaches are more readily found in the 19th century when very large residential institutions were erected in many countries. In the United Kingdom (UK) these institutions were administered by local poor law authorities, churches and charities and were characterised by regimented regimes founded on discipline, training and religion. Their purpose was twofold: to care for the destitute and abandoned, whilst protecting society from the perceived threat to social order posed by 'dangerous' children (Ruxton, 1996). As Hendrick (1994) observes, children take a dual role, both then and now: as 'victims' but also as 'threats'.

After a long period of stagnation, following the Second World War, there was renewed interest in residential care across Europe. Experiments were undertaken with democratic forms of communal living with 'children's republics' and 'children's communities'. Yet by the close of the 1960s, residential institutions were attacked for having repressive regimes and failing to provide individualised care. The following three decades have seen the progressive decline of residential care in all European Countries, with a corresponding growth in foster family care (Ruxton, 1996).

Despite attempts to make residential care a positive choice (see, for example, National Institute for Social Work, 1988), this trend is further advanced in the UK than in other EU countries (Colton & Hellinckx, 1993; Ruxton, 1996). Some 65,000 children and young people are currently looked after by local authority social services in England, Wales and Scotland (NCH, 1996/97), the majority of which are placed with foster carers. In 1992, there were an estimated 15,000 places in residential children homes, 10,000 of which were in the public sector; the remainder were in the voluntary and private sectors. The local authority and voluntary sectors are contracting. Only the private sector has expanded. Currently, there are less than 10,000 children in residential care in England.

In addition to the declining use of residential care, there has been a move away from large-scale institutions towards small-scale homes. In the UK, there is an average of ten child-care places per home (Utting, 1997). These homes are often situated near to children's home localities. This reflects the development of an 'ecological' perspective, which emphasises that effective practice involves taking account of children's origins, family networks and cultural environments.

Around two-thirds of young people in residential care in the UK are there because they have emotional and behavioural problems that preclude other placements. They are typically aged 13 or 14 and have experienced a succession of broken foster care placements. Whilst there are more boys than girls in the homes, nearly all the homes are mixed. About a third of the young people in local authority and voluntary homes, and a quarter of those in private homes, had been sexually abused prior to placement. The significance of this will become clear later when the abuse of young people in residential care is considered (Warner, 1997).

A major European trend in residential child and youth care is the professionalization of caregivers. This trend is driven both by the need to improve the quality of care and the necessity of ensuring that residential workers are able to cope with the increasing challenge presented by very demanding children and youth (Colton & Hellinckx, 1993). However, it appears that the young people placed in residential care in the UK are still looked after by largely unqualified and untrained adults. An estimated 15,000 staff work in children's homes in England. A significant proportion of such staff are employed by private care agencies and work on a peripatetic or temporary basis in different homes. In London, it was found that as many as 13% of the heads of homes and 21% of care staff were employed by care agencies. Roughly 80% of care staff and 40% of heads of homes in the local authority sector have no relevant qualification. Thus, Warner argues that '... there is ... no strong professional ethos around children's homes, as there would be with medicine or nursing, to act as a partial safeguard against abuse and exploitation of vulnerable young people' (Warner, 1997, p. 14).

It would be unwise to proceed further without first clarifying what is meant by key concepts such as 'profession' and 'professionalization' – and how such concepts relate to social work, which is the main occupation associated with child and youth care in the UK. This will be followed by a discussion of the widespread revelations concerning abuse in residential institutions in the UK. An assessment will then be made of the extent to which further professionalization of residential caregivers can help resolve the problems which beset the child and youth care system the UK.

A Caring Profession?

In pre-industrial Europe, the term profession was used to denote certain vocations which were the only occupations outside of commerce or manual work that enabled those without unearned income or wealth to make a living (Mitchell, 1979). The three classical professions were divinity, law and medicine which, according to the Oxford English Dictionary, are the 'learned professions'; although officers in the army and navy were also included in the ranks of the professions.

But the process of industrialisation saw major changes in the structure of the older professions and the rise of new occupational groups, many of which later laid claim to professional status. By the second half of the 20th century, the term profession had been defined as '... a vocation whose practice is founded upon an understanding of the theoretical structure of some department of learning or science and upon the abilities accompanying such understanding. This understanding and these abilities are applied to the vital practical affairs of man ...' (Cogan, 1953, pp. 148-149).

However, since the 1970s, analysis has largely centred on the notion of professional power. Freidson (1970) argued that professional autonomy – that is, the power of the professions to define and control their own work – is the key feature of the professions. On this view, the professionalization process is essentially political in nature. Power and persuasive rhetoric are more important than actual knowledge, training and work (Freidson, 1970; Johnson, 1972). Abbott (1991) considers that professions are exclusive occupational groups that control particular areas of work on the basis of an abstract, esoteric and intellectual body of knowledge. Groups lacking such knowledge have been largely been unsuccessful in their attempts to professionalize.

In the UK residential child and youth work is largely undertaken by social workers. As far back as 1915, Flexner concluded that social work did not qualify as a profession because it was not based on a body of scientific knowledge. Although social workers have attempted to counter Flexner's conclusion, others have argued that social work lacks the autonomy and theoretical knowledge base of a fully-fledged profession. The fact that social work is practised mainly within formal organizations or bureaucracies has been central to discussions about its lack of autonomy (Gary Hopps & Collins, 1995). Etzioni (1969) referred to social work as a 'semi-profession', arguing that it could not be accorded full professional status because of factors such as the relatively short period of training it requires – which is less than for professions such as law and medicine – and its failure to recognise privileged information.

Moreover, commentators in the UK have, from various perspectives, argued that far from moving towards greater professionalization, social work is going in the opposite direction. Lorentson (1990), for example, views social work as a numerically female dominated occupation, imbued with a service ideology that is essentially 'feminine' in its original inspiration, but which is increasingly challenged by masculine rationality within bureaucratic organizations with men predominating in managerial positions. Cannan (1994) argues that 'enterprise culture' in the form of policies designed to reduce state intervention and welfare dependence, and stimulate economic growth have been accompanied by changes in the education and training of social workers. The introduction of employer involvement and a competencies model have challenged social work's professional autonomy and values. Students are now being prepared for work in an increasingly regulated, residualized, welfare system.

Thus, it appears that in the UK, residential work with children and young people is the poor relation of what can at best be described as a developing profession whose legitimacy is subject to ongoing challenge. The education and training, salaries, supervision and support, for residential care workers have, on the whole, all compared unfavourably with that given to other social workers. This does not appear to be the case everywhere. Major differences exist between the UK and other EU countries with regard to the occupations involved in residential child and youth care. In Belgium, for example, there appears to be a distinctive child and youth care profession – that of the social pedagogue or social educator. By contrast, this occupation does not exist in the UK. The role of the 'social educator' is perplexing to the British observer. The difficulty is exacerbated by the fact that it is extremely difficult to distinguish a common list of tasks performed by social educators everywhere. Current practice also makes it difficult in English to link education with the wider range of nurturing services – social, psychological and familial – associated with the term in other European countries. The same is broadly true in relation to the term 'pedagogy'.

It may be significant that the learning, scholarship and vocabulary associated with a distinctive residential care profession are largely missing in the UK. Extensive research undertaken in the 1980s showed that the child-care system was failing badly when judged against the outcomes for children and young people. All aspects of their development were found to be more problematic than those of children cared for by their own families or adopted at a young age (Department of Health, 1991).

Moreover, public confidence in the care system in the UK has been profoundly shaken by numerous highly publicized controversies surrounding the abuse of children and young people, especially those in residential institutions. The Report of the National Commission of Inquiry into the Prevention of Child Abuse (1996, p. 19) in the UK notes: 'The catalogue of abuse in residential institutions is appalling. It includes physical assault and sexual abuse; emotional abuse; unacceptable deprivation of rights and privileges; inhumane treatment; poor health and education'.

A succession of official reports chronicle how the residential care system in all parts of the UK has failed to protect vulnerable youngsters in residential homes. For example, as early as 1985, the Hughes Report on the Kincora scandal exposed widespread homosexual acts and prostitution in nine boys' homes and hostels in Northern Ireland. The Leeways report concerned the head of a South London home convicted in the mid 1980s of taking pornographic pictures of children in his care. In 1991, the Pindown Report revealed how children in Staffordshire, England, were deprived of their liberty and subjected to cruel regimes of social isolation. In 1992, the Williams Report highlighted suicide and self-harm among children in a residential home in Gwent, South Wales. Since then, the Kirkwood Report uncovered large scale abuse by Frank Beck, the head of a home in Leicestershire England and the White Report exposed abuse in residential children's homes in Islington, London. Serious abuse has also been found in Cardiff children's homes and other institutions in South Wales. There have also been a series of well publicised prosecutions associated with widespread abuse in institutions in Merseyside and Cheshire, England. TV documentaries have reported on abuse in other areas. These included a programme on prostitution services operating from local authority homes in the English Midlands; a second programme reported on the activities of Mark Trotter, a social worker who abused children in homes in the Hackney area of London, and who later died of Aids (Warner, 1997).

Most recently, the inquiry into child abuse in residential institutions in North Wales, chaired by Sir Ronald Waterhouse, revealed a quite shocking pattern of sexual abuse by paedophiles operating alone or in semi-organized 'rings' (House of Commons, 2000). Wolmar (2000, p. 18) argues that '… the abuse scandals described in the Waterhouse report …' [House of Commons, 2000] '... are like the tumour which warns of a widespread cancer ...'. It should also be noted that police forces have launched investigations into historical cases of abuse in children's homes in every part of the country. Currently, all but two of the 49 mainland forces in the UK have either completed or are working on such enquiries (Wolmar, 2000, p. 18).

Causes of System Failure

The dearth of appropriately qualified workers has been highlighted as a central problem underlying the poor quality of residential child and youth care in the UK (Utting, 1997). Essentially, the residential child and youth care system in the UK is one in which children with the most severe personal and social problems are being looked after by adults who have the least experience and training in child-care matters. Young, inexperienced, isolated and untrained adults are often left to tend and work with the most problematic young people.

Periodic attempts have been made to improve the training, supervision, management, selection and inspection of residential social workers. But it is clear that the scale of all these efforts was inadequate (Utting, 1997). Many in the UK consider that a pre-requisite for high quality child and youth care services is professional registration. In all the major professions qualified workers are registered by a statutory body, and it is illegal for unqualified persons to describe themselves by the professional title and to practise. Advocates of registration argue that it provides assurance that professionals have achieved a degree of competence and have acquired a basis of knowledge for their practice at a level set by their peers. Significantly, there is no such requirement in child-care. One influential commentator reports: 'According to the law of the land, one can be a bricklayer, stripper or traffic warden one day, and look after children in virtually any type of child care work the next. One does not need to be professionally qualified. Worse than that, one does not need to have been trained at all. People can get into some childcare jobs without their curricula vitae having been checked out. People can get into quite a lot of jobs without police checks. Applicants may not even be the person they say they are ... [Most] ... employers rely on a couple of references and perhaps a check on the main qualifications ...' (Lane, 1998, pp. 8-9). From this perspective, registration of residential social workers represents a vital safeguard for vulnerable children and young people. However, others may be sceptical about the rationale behind registration, and regard it as little more than a means of establishing and defending professional boundaries. Some residential social workers see their work as providing an altruistic service to children and young people. This approach is underpinned by values that may conflict with the less laudable motives that sometimes lie behind the pursuit of professional status and higher salaries. On this view, love and money do not mix. Equally, however, the notion that 'love is not enough' has long been a kind of *Leitmotiv* for those who work directly and indirectly with troubled and troublesome youth. Presumably, such people would tend toward the belief that further professionalization will do much to improve standards of residential child and youth care in UK.

In order to assess the extent to which professionalization can help to ameliorate the failings of the residential child and youth care system in the UK, it is necessary to further explore the possible reasons underlying the failure of the care system. Remarkably little attention has been paid to this fundamental issue. In Wolmar's (2000, p. 18) view, very little effort has been made to tackle the abuse of young people in care homes on a national basis. He argues that '... no one has collected any statistics on the extent or timing of the scandals. There has been no attempt to standardize the investigation methods, or to analyze the fundamental causes of the scandals. Even the Utting inquiry, launched [by Government] in 1996, focused more on the future provision of services rather than on understanding what went wrong ...'.

Wolmar (2000, p. 18) attributes reluctance to investigate the root causes of the problem to fears on the part of central government, local authorities and charities concerning possible compensation claims from victims. He believes that if the authorities were '... forced to accept that there were clear patterns which resulted in the abuse, the victims who are currently seeking compensation through the courts will find it easier to make successful compensation claims. They will be able to argue that the various agencies should have been aware of the risks of the policies which they adopted ...'.

In further contemplating possible causes of the failure of the UK care system, the work of Wardhaugh and Wilding (1993) is enlightening. They distinguish the following eight propositions about systems and patterns of organization that play an important part in the corruption of care in residential institutions:

1. *Neutralization of normal moral concerns* – those who are abused come to be seen as less than fully human.

2. *Balance of power and powerlessness in organizations* – those responsible for highly vulnerable groups such as children and young people have almost absolute power over them.
3. *Particular pressures and particular kinds of work* – children in residential care lack 'value and worth' in the eyes of society; they are easily stereotyped, and this affects the resources made available for their care.
4. *Management failure* – what is striking about the corruption of care is the totality of management failure across most responsibilities at all levels of management.
5. *Enclosed, inward-looking organizations* – these serve to stifle complaints, criticism, and new ideas, and encourage routines and patterns of practice that are rigid and conservative.
6. *Absence of clear lines and mechanisms of internal and external accountability* – thus frontline staff are, in effect, unsupervised, and the organization comes to judge itself by its own internal standards.
7. *Particular models of work and organization* – this includes mistaken notions of professionalism, hierarchical structures, the concentration of those regarded as the most troublesome clients in one place, large size of some institutions; and bureaucracy.
8. *The nature of certain client groups* – children and young people in care are defined as less than fully sentient beings because of their age, and are thus subjected to forms of behaviour and treatment that would be unacceptable with those not so stigmatized.

There is no doubt that improved education and training, supervision, selection systems, and registration can make an important contribution to improving standards of child and youth care in the UK. Yet, it is equally evident from Wardhaugh and Wilding's (1993) account that professionalization by no means represents a panacea for curing the ills of the care system. Indeed, as indicated above, professionalism can, in fact, be part of the problem. Professionalism is widely seen as the hallmark of high standards. At its best, Wardhaugh and Wilding (1993) accept this as true. However, they highlight how certain aspects of professionalism can contribute towards the corruption of care. For example, in some high profile hospital scandals in the UK, narrow models of professional responsibility lead doctors to ignore grossly unsatisfactory physical conditions; mistaken notions of professional autonomy resulted in management failing to set standards and hold professionals to account for their achievement; and, management's faith in the self-sustaining power of professional ethics, irrespective of how demanding the work involved, led to failure to provide staff with the support they frequently required.

Wardhaugh and Wilding (1993) also question the exercise of professional discretion. The professional ability to make decisions in the 'best interests' of the child is a central power of child welfare professionals. Yet the use of such discretion may override any concept of children's rights or natural justice and may, in any case, be illusory with professional decisions often nothing more than routine responses to groups of common problems which the organization must handle. Tellingly, at least half of the eight factors (nos. 1, 2, 3 and 8) that contribute to the corruption of care distinguished by Wardhaugh and Wilding (1993) directly concern the violation of human rights. As much as anything else, therefore, ensuring a better deal for children and young people in residential care in the UK requires increased emphasis on their rights. Groups such as children and young people in care are among those for whom society appears to have little regard. As Wardhaugh and Wilding (1993, p. 14) note: 'Certain kinds of people seem to be particularly at risk from the corruption of care in human services – mentally handicapped people in long-stay hospitals, elderly people, and children in residential care. Policy is built up of fine words but the reality of what is provided for these groups denies their truth. The work is wrapped round with high-sounding terms such as care, reform, rehabilitation, but the resources and facilities made available convey to staff the low value which society places upon their work and upon their clients. Official aspirations and standards are therefore deprived of legitimacy'.

If half of the factors contributing to the corruption of care identified by Wardhaugh and Wilding (1993) concern the transgression of human rights, the other half (nos. 4, 5, 6 and 7) appear to be tied up with bureaucracy. Phrases such as 'management failure', 'closed organizations', 'absence of accountability', 'large institutions', 'hierarchical structures', et cetera connote the vicissitudes of bureaucratic organizations. Colton (1988) questions whether bureaucratisation is a necessary or effective means of social organization in the context of residential child and youth care. Whilst the child and youth care establishments he studied did meet some of the demands placed on them – for example, the control of disparate groups of children – they were not adequately meeting their officially espoused caring role.

Thus, the work of the American sociologist, Irving Goffman still resonates 40 years on from its original publication. He argued that: 'Many institutions, most of the time, seem to function merely as storage dumps for inmates. [The] contradiction between what the institution does and what its officials must say it does, forms the basic context of the staff's daily activity' (Goffman, 1961, p. 73). According to Goffman (1961), the total institution is a social hybrid – part residential community, part formal organization. Local authority run residential homes for children and youth not only share some of the total institution's affinities with formal organizations, but are also part of a much larger formal organization – the Social Services Department (Colton, 1988). These Departments have been said to manifest the worst features of bureaucracies in being 'hierarchic, rule-bound, and slow to respond to changes' (Hadley & Mcgrath, 1980, p. 5). It might be assumed that a potential strength of bureaucratisation in residential child and youth care is that it permits external and internal accountability and supervision of residential staff, and thereby offers a safeguard to vulnerable young people. It is painfully obvious, however, that this was not the case in relation to many institutions in the UK where children and young people have suffered abuse.

Research by Colton and Vanstone (1996) and Pringle (1992) has highlighted issues of masculinity in relation to sexual abuse by men who work with children. Wolmar (2000, p. 18) contends that the fundamental cause of abuse in residential care homes was the replacement of women caregivers by men. He reports that up to the end of the 1960s, women mainly staffed residential care homes in the UK, large numbers of whom were war widows or unmarried. Residential child and youth care not only provided stable employment for such women, but also a home. Thus, in 1967, some two-thirds of staff in care homes were single women and 93 per cent of staff lived in. But, as these women left, they were largely replaced by men who did not live on the premises and who saw the work as more of a career, albeit a poorly paid one. Still more men entered the care system when residential 'approved schools' for young offenders were merged with the network of local authority children's homes following the passing of the 1969 Children and Young Persons Act. With fewer people living on the premises and more men involved in care, the opportunities for abuse were much greater (Wolmar, 2000, p. 18).

Given that most of those who perpetrated the abuse are men convicted of offences against boys, Wolmar (2000, p. 18) fears that it is too easy to jump to the conclusion that only women should be employed in care home for children and youth. Such a policy would, in his view, compound the tragedy. Many young people in care homes are teenage boys of 14 and 15 whom 'desperately need strong role models. Employing good male social workers to help look after them is essential'. However, Wolmar (2000, p. 18) rightly insists that there must be safeguards, both before and after men are appointed to residential social work posts.

This view is shared by Norman Warner, the author of a major report on the staffing and management of children's homes entitled, *Choosing with Care*, which was published in 1992. More recently, Warner (1997) has questioned why children are still taken into public care to protect them from their parents without any guarantee that they will be safe in the children's homes where they are placed. In Warner's (1997) view, there has been a failure to '... take on board the scale of the paedophile problem and the potential sources of harm they represent to children in residential settings of all kinds, not just children's homes ...'. According to Warner (1997), the National Criminal Intelligence Service has a list of about 45,000 convicted or suspected paedophiles in the UK, and there are some 2000 paedophile rings with roughly five members each. Research suggest that, on average, an abuser will have attempted or committed 238 offences before he is caught. A survey of 232 abusers found that they had committed 55,000 offences between them on 16,400 children. Warner (1997) argues that it is the nature and scale of potential offenders, and the attraction to them of residential childcare settings, that makes it vital to have effective checks in place for children's homes and to change their cultures.

Conclusion

In the United Kingdom, residential child and youth care work is the poor relation of a developing social work profession, the legitimacy of which is subject to ongoing challenge. The lack of priority given to residential work is reflected in recent controversy associated with the widespread abuse of young people placed away from home. This chapter has attempted to assess the extent to which professionalization can address the manifest failure of the public care system in the UK. Analysis revealed that although improved education and training, supervision, selection systems and professional registration would all significantly improve standards, professionalism by no means represents a panacea for the ills of British the child and youth care system. Additional measures are necessary in relation to reinforcing children's rights, tackling the adverse impact of bureaucracy, addressing important issues relating to masculinity and the threat posed by paedophile activity.

Therefore, recent measures introduced by the UK Government to improve the quality of care deserve a cautious welcome. In November 1998, following the publication of Sir Williams Utting's review of Safeguards for children living away from home (Utting, 1997), the UK Government introduced an initiative called 'Quality Protects'. This is a major three year programme designed to transform the management and delivery of social services for children in England. A similar programme, entitled Children First, was introduced in Wales. Local authorities are required to demonstrate steady improvement in the management of services and outcomes for children and young people, including those who are placed away from home. The government has committed itself to a series of national objectives. These include ensuring that children looked after by local authorities gain maximum life chance benefits from educational opportunities, health care and social care. A number of sub-objectives are distinguished which are all measurable through the Looking After Children system (Parker et al., 1991; Ward, 1995) now used by most local authorities to trace and promote developmental progress for children placed away from home. A second key objective is to ensure that young people leaving care are not isolated and that they are able to participate fully in the social and economic life of society (Department of Health, 1998). The Quality Protects initiative is accompanied by the injection of substantial financial resources to help local authorities improve the quality of services (Department of Health, 1998, 1999).

It is hoped that the Government's actions signal that the welfare of children and youth in public care is at long last receiving the priority it deserves. However, in view of the tardy, and uneven, progress made by all previous Governments, it would be wise to be cautious in our optimism. Moreover, the quality of care that a society provides for its vulnerable and dependent members reveals much about what it values and what it disdains. Thus, in truth, the appalling abuse suffered by children and young people in residential homes throughout United Kingdom ultimately reflects deeply embedded social attitudes and associated structures of inequality. Historically, children and young people placed away from home have been drawn from the poorest strata of society (Holman, 1988; Parker, 1988). Today, this group is referred to by right wing commentators as 'the underclass' (see Murray, 1994). In 19th century Britain, welfare provision for the poor took the form of a stigmatizing, deterrent, Poor Law founded on such notions as the 'deserving' and 'undeserving' poor (Gregg, 1973; Holman, 1988). Despite over 150 years of staggering social, economic and political change and upheaval, the Poor Law legacy persists in attitudes towards dependent and powerless groups. In relation to children and young people placed away from home, the public attitude is largely one of indifference or, at best, ambivalence. Although generally sympathetic towards child victims of abuse, there is long-standing anxiety about the threat to social order represented by troubled and troublesome youth. Ambivalence is further fuelled by the social class background of these young people and, bearing in mind the disproportionately large numbers of black children and children with disabilities placed away from home, by factors such as racism and negative attitudes towards disability. Thus, the ills of the public care system in the UK will require far more by way of cure than that which political spin doctors are able to conjure.

References

Abbott, A. (1988), cited in: I. Waddington (1996). Professions. In A. Kuper & J. Kuper (Eds.), *The social science encyclopedia* (pp. 677-678). London: Routledge.

Cannan, C. (1994/95). Enterprise culture, professional socialisation, and social work education in Britain. *Critical Social Policy, 42*, 5-18.

Cogan, M. (1953), cited in: G.D. Mitchell (1979), *A new dictionary of sociology*. London: Routledge and Kegan Paul (see pp. 148-149).

Colton, M.J. (1988). *Dimensions of substitute child care: A comparative study of foster and residential care practice*. Aldershot: Avebury.

Colton, M.J., & Hellinckx, W. (Eds.) (1993). *Child care in the EC: A country specific guide to foster and residential care*. Aldershot: Arena.

Colton, M.J., & Hellinckx, W. (1994). Residential and foster care in the European Community: Current trends in policy and practice. *British Journal of Social Work, 24*, 559-576.

Colton, M.J., & Vanstone, M. (1996). *Betrayal of trust: Sexual abuse by men who work with children*. London: Free Association Books.

Department of Health (1991). *Patterns and outcomes in child placement: Messages from current research and their implications*. London: HMSO.

Department of Health (1998). *The Quality Protects Programme: Transforming children's services*. Local Authority Circular (98), no. 28. London: Author.

Department of Health (1999). *The Quality Protects Programme: Transforming children's services 2000-01*. Local Authority Circular (99), no. 33. London: Author.

Etzioni, A. (1969). *The semi-professions and their organizations*. New York: Free Press.

Flexner, A. (1915). Is social work a profession?, cited in: J. Gary Hopps, & P.M. Collins (1995). Social work profession overview. In: *Encyclopedia of Social Work*, 19th Edition. Washington, DC: National Association of Social Workers.

Freidson, E. (1970). *Profession of medicine: A study of the sociology of applied knowledge*. Chicago: University of Chicago Press.

Gary Hopps, J., & Collins, P.M. (1995). Social work profession overview. In: *Encyclopedia of Social Work*, 19th Edition. Washington, DC: National Association of Social Workers.

Goffman, E. (1961). *Asylums: Essays on the social situation of mental patients and other inmates*. London: Penguin.

Gregg, P. (1973). *A social and economic history of Britain 1760-1972*. London: Harrap.

Hadley, R., & Mcgrath, M. (Eds.) (1980). *Going local: Neighbourhood social services*. London: Bedford Square Press.

Hendrick, H. (1994). *Child Welfare: England, 1872-1889*. London: Routledge.

Holman, B. (1988). *Putting families first: Prevention and child care*. London: Macmillan.

House of Commons (2000). *Report of the Tribunal of Inquiry into the abuse of children in care in the former county council areas of Gwynedd and Clwyd since 1974, Lost in Care*. London: The Stationery Office.

Johnson, T.J. (1972). *Professions and power*. London: Macmillan.

Lane, D. (1998). A gap in the armour. *Children's Residential Care Newsletter*, National Children's Bureau, No. 10 (Winter), 8-9.

Lorentzon, M. (1990). Professional status and managerial tasks: Feminine service ideology in British nursing and social work. In P. Abbott, & C. Wallace (Eds.), *The sociology of the caring professions* (pp. 53-66). London: Falmer Press.

Murray, C. (1994). *Underclass: The crisis deepens*. London: IEA Health and Welfare Unit.

National Commission of Inquiry into the Prevention of Child Abuse (1996). *Childhood matters*. London: The Stationery Office.

National Institute for Social Work (1988). *Residential care: A positive choice*. London: HMSO.

NCH – Action for Children (1998). *Factfile 96/97*. London: NCH – Action for Children.

Parker, R. (1988). An historical background. In I. Sinclair (Ed.), *Residential care: The research reviewed. Literature surveys commissioned by the independent review of residential care* (pp. 57-124). London: HMSO.

Parker, R., Ward, H., Jackson, S., Aldgate, J., & Wedge, P. (Eds.) (1991). *Looking after children: Assessing outcomes in child care*. London: HMSO.

Pringle, K. (1992). Child sexual abuse perpetrated by welfare personnel and the problem of men. *Critical Social Policy, 36*, 4-19.

Ruxton, S. (1996). *Children in Europe*. London: NCH – Action for Children.

Utting, W. (1997). *People like us: The report of the review of the safeguards for children living away from home*. London: HMSO.

Utting, W. (1998). People like us: The review of safeguards for children living away from home. In S. Hayman (Ed.), *Child sexual abuse: Providing for victims, coping with offenders* (pp. 8-16). London: Institute for the Study and Treatment of Delinquency (ISTD).

Ward, H. (1995). *Looking after children: Research into practice*. London: HMSO.

Wardhaugh, J., & Wilding, P. (1993). Towards an explanation of the corruption of care. *Critical Social Policy, 37*, 4-31.

Warner, N. (1992). *Choosing with care*. London: HMSO.

Warner, N. (1997). Preventing child abuse in children's homes. In S. Hayman (Ed.), *Child sexual abuse: Myth and reality* (pp. 13-16). London: Institute for the Study and Treatment of Delinquency (ISTD).

Wolmar, C. (2000). The untold story behind child abuse. *The Guardian*, February 16, p. 18.

Chapter 9

Cultural Factors Related to Burnout in Child and Youth Care Workers in Thirteen Cultures[1]

Victor Savicki

Introduction

Many research studies have investigated the impact of the immediate work environment on burnout (Lee & Ashforth, 1996). But there is another level of environment that has powerful effects that has not been well researched in relation to burnout; namely culture (Golembiewski, Scherb & Boudreau, 1993). This broader level of environment, and variations of individuals within it, have been seen as somewhat difficult to operationalize (Triandis, 1996; Van de Vijver & Leung, 1997). The omnipresent, and somewhat ambiguous nature of the concept of culture has made it more the province of anecdotal reports than of systematic scientific investigation. Researchers acknowledge that cultures differ on important issues, but how these differences may affect burnout has not been well described. In this chapter a study will be presented to explore this, as yet, relatively sparsely examined research area. Prior to the report of the study itself, several important concepts relating to burnout and culture will be reviewed.

Burnout

Burnout has been most often defined as a syndrome in which workers feel emotionally exhausted or fatigued, withdraw emotionally from their clients, and perceive a diminution of their achievements or accomplishments at work. The de facto standard of measurement for burnout is the Maslach Burnout Inventory (MBI) (Maslach, Jackson & Leiter, 1996) which contains three sub-scales purported to measure the three factors identified in the above definition: emotional exhaustion, depersonalization, and personal accomplishment. Each sub-scale plays an important role in understanding the quality of the burnout experience.

Burnout has important consequences for child and youth care workers. Both Cherniss (1995) and Maslach and Leiter (1997) have articulated a clear distinction between high and low burnout.

High burnout results in physical and psychological difficulties at work and elsewhere which lead to lower productivity and eventual harm to the individual and to the organization in which they work.

In contrast, low burnout results in the individual thriving and growing in their work. The challenges of work stress invigorate and energize the worker to produce more and to become innovative (Maslach & Leiter, 1997).

Measurement of Culture

The first step in describing the impact of culture is to develop a common language to define its impact. Hofstede (1980) has elaborated a simple, yet powerful set of dimensions of culture based on values encompassing work. Hofstede's landmark study of cultural work values synthesizes information for 40 different countries from over 60,000 individuals. Through factor analysis and other statistical methods he formulated four dimensions of cultural work values:

- power distance;
- uncertainty avoidance;
- individualism – collectivism;
- masculinity – femininity.

These dimensions, which describe critical norms and understandings of cultures, will be described more fully in the methods section of this chapter. By looking at all four dimensions together, it is possible to gain an insight into the character of a culture.

In theory, culture provides another classification of environmental influence at a more general level. Work environment is clearly the proximal environmental condition for burnout; while cultural is more distal. Figure 9.1 illustrates that two cultures; in this case Denmark and the Slovak Republic, can differ significantly on the cultural value of Individualism.

Figure 9.1 Cultural Differences and Cultural Conformity Variations

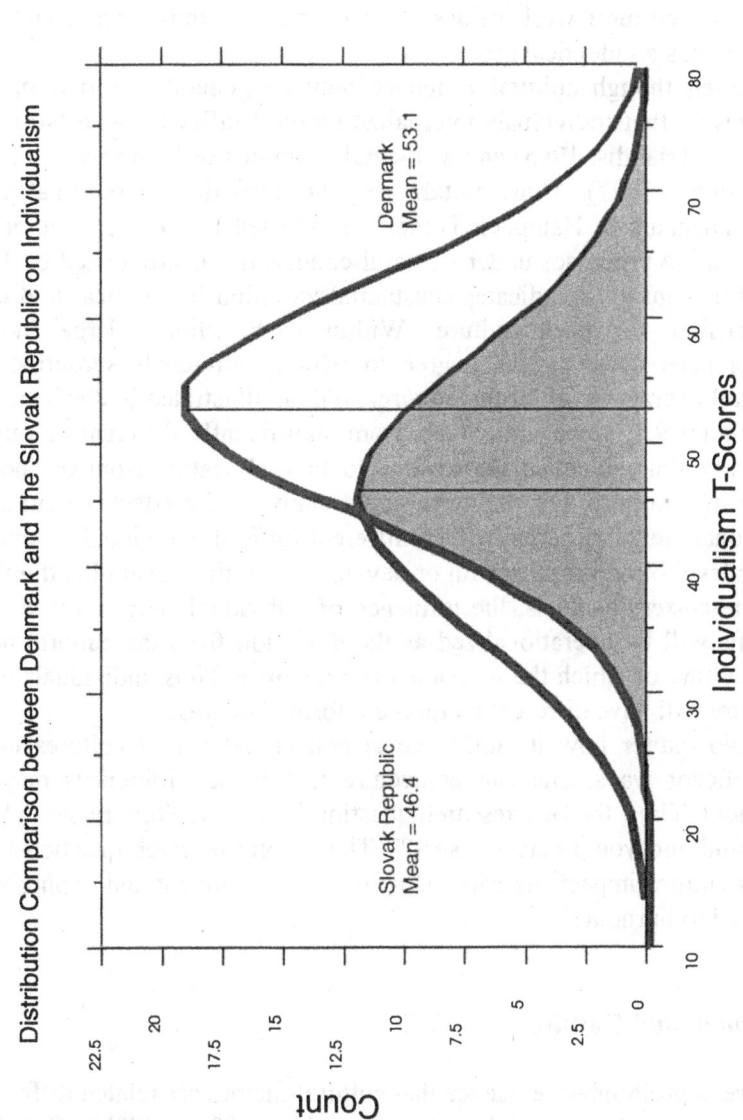

That is, the means for the two cultures qualify as statistically different. Following this example, for the purposes of analysis, the effects of culture as an environmental variable can be construed to impact all members of the culture relatively equally. Therefore, the best representative indicator of overall cultural influence can be seen as the average level of the people comprising the culture. In the current analysis, the overall environmental influence of a cultural environment will be operationalized as the mean score on cultural work values for each culture; thus, each member of a culture has an identical score.

Even though cultural influence may be general, theorists have also suggested that individuals internalize cultural influence as a 'structure of habits' (Triandis, 1995) and as mental programs or 'software of the mind' (Hofstede, 1997). Thus, culture may be carried as a personal variable (Trompenaars & Hampden-Turner, 1998) used in the cognitive appraisal and coping processes under stressful conditions, as articulated by Lazarus (1999). Figure 9.1 indicates substantial variation in the measured cultural dimension for each culture. Within each culture, large individual differences occur in the degree to which individuals subscribe to the overall average score of the culture. And, as illustrated by the shaded area of Figure 9.1, some individuals from significantly different cultures will actually share identical scores due to their deviation from the norms of their own culture. For the purposes of analysis, the effects of culture as a personal mental program will be different for each individual depending on their level of conformity with or deviance from their overall cultural norm. In the current analysis, the influence of individual conformity to cultural norms will be operationalized as the deviation from the cultural norm of the culture of which the individual is a member. Thus, individuals within a culture will have different cultural conformity scores.

No matter how its influence is conceptualized, if cultures differ in significant ways, one can conjecture that those differences may affect burnout. Thus, the first research question is 'Does culture relate to burnout in child and youth care workers?'. The second research question is 'How does culture impact the patterns of work environment and coping that are related to burnout?'.

Burnout and Culture

There is preliminary evidence that cultural factors are related differently to the separate burnout sub-scales (Savicki, 1999a; 1999b). Only a few studies have compared different cultures on the burnout scales. These studies fall into two categories: methodological and cross-cultural.

Methodological studies sought to confirm that the factors of burnout measured by the Maslach Burnout Inventory (Maslach, Jackson & Leiter, 1996) were applicable in other cultures. Confirmation of the three factor structure of the Maslach Burnout Inventory was found in Germany, Finland, Sweden, The Netherlands, Ireland, The United Kingdom, Estonia, and New Zealand (Büssing & Perrar, 1992; Shutte, Toppinen, Kalimo & Schaufeli, 2000; Schaufeli & Janczur, 1994; Green, Walkey & Taylor, 1991). Some caution was advised in interpreting Maslach Burnout Inventory score in differing cultures (Schaufeli & Van Dierendonck, 1995).

Cross-cultural comparisons have been conducted in the countries mentioned above and others (Canada, Pakistan, Japan, and Jordan) on a variety of occupational groups such as forest industry employees (managers, clerks, foremen, blue-collar), teachers, nurses, businessmen, social workers, and human service professionals (Shutte, Toppinen, Kalimo & Schaufeli, 2000; Jamal, 1999; Armstrong-Stassen, Al-Ma'Aitah, Cameron & Horsburgh, 1994; Etzion & Pines, 1986). No cross-cultural comparisons have been published using workers in the child and youth care field specifically. Thus the current study fills a research gap concerning cross-cultural comparisons of burnout in the child and youth care field.

In addition to studying the effects of culture on burnout, another goal of this chapter is to test the generalizability of findings concerning the relationship of burnout to work environment and coping styles. Lee and Ashforth's (1996) meta-analysis of burnout research contained studies predominantly from North America. In that statistical overview of burnout research, strong relationships of burnout to work environment did emerge. Other research has shown the relationship between burnout and coping (Leiter, 1991). For the current study, the question of generalizability and extension is 'Do the patterns of relationship of burnout to work environment and coping found in North America replicate in and across other cultures?'.

Methods

Participants

The thirteen cultures; the thirteen cultures included in this study are Australia (n=37), Austria (n=48), Canada-English (n=48), Canada-French (n=68), Denmark (n=79), England (n=89), Germany-East (n=98), Germany-West (n=47), Israel (n=36), Poland (n=42), Scotland (n=56), The Slovak Republic (n=80), United States (n=97).

Notice that in three cases, culture is defined in a manner so that one nation contains two different cultures; e.g. Canada contains French speaking and English speaking cultures, The United Kingdom contains English and Scottish cultures, and Germany contains the former East and former West sectors. Such a definition of culture is quite consistent with issues concerning culture (Triandis, 1995; 1996). In Germany and the UK, the two cultures are separated geographically, but share the same language. In Canada, the cultures share the same geography, but differ in preferred language.

With the exception of Israel and Australia, the cultures are drawn from North America and Northern Europe. While this representation of cultures was more easily obtained, it is not representative of child and youth care globally. Thus, some care should be taken in extending the findings of this study to regions such as Asia, Africa, and Latin America.

Description of the sample; across the 13 cultures, an attempt was made to match samples to some degree. The 835 participants in this study were all treatment providers, educators, and managers in day or residential treatment facilities dealing with children or youth who might be classified as emotionally disturbed or developmentally delayed. Such a restrictive sample does control for variation that might be introduced by studying participants from variety of different industries or service sectors. However, this is not a precisely matched sample. Rather it is a convenience sample; that is, it is the people who were willing to participate from the agencies or professional groups known to the primary research contact person in each culture.

Research Scales

Four research scales were used in the questionnaire: burnout, cultural work values, work environment, and coping. These scales were selected first because of the desire to determine if results for burnout found in the US were generalizable to other cultures. Secondly, the Cultural Work Values scale was utilized to aid in interpreting any differences between cultures.

Maslach Burnout Inventory (MBI) The factor analyzed sub-scales for this measure include: emotional exhaustion, depersonalization, and personal accomplishment (Maslach, Jackson & Leiter, 1996).

- Emotional Exhaustion is the extent to which a worker feels worn out and drained by the job.
- Depersonalization is the extent to which workers think about and treat children and youth and their families in an unfeeling and impersonal manner.
- Personal Accomplishment describes the extent to which workers feel successful in their work. This last scale becomes lower as workers become more burned out.

The MBI is a widely used instrument in human service professions. The scales have been established as reliable and valid in a number of studies (Maslach, Jackson & Leiter, 1996). The internal consistency reliability for the scales reported in the current study are: emotional exhaustion, .87, depersonalization, .69, and personal accomplishment, .74. In addition, the MBI has shown good reliability in cross-cultural settings. The theoretical relations and factor structure has shown consistency across cultures (Büssing & Perrar, 1992; Green, Walkey & Taylor, 1991; Schaufeli & Janczur, 1994).

Hofstede's Cultural Work Value Scale (CWV) Hofstede's (1980) landmark study of cultural work values synthesizes information for 40 different countries from over 60,000 individuals. The following dimensions are used to describe attributes of cultures, and to gain insight into their character:

- Individualism versus collectivism: Individualistic cultures emphasize personal action and responsibility. Collectivist cultures emphasize interpersonal relatedness and group action.
- Masculinity (career success) versus femininity (quality of life): Masculine cultures emphasize autonomy, assertiveness, and the centrality of work. Feminine cultures emphasize social-consciousness, nurturance and the centrality of social connectedness. Because this dimension is an indicator of a cultural value, Adler (1997) prefers to use the terms career success versus quality of life for this scale because these terms are less likely to be mistaken as indicators of gender. This labelling will be used in the current study.
- Power distance between a boss and a subordinate in a hierarchy is the difference between the extent to which the boss can determine the behaviour of the subordinate and the extent to which the subordinate can determine the behaviour of the boss. In high power distance

cultures bosses believe that they can dictate the behaviour of the subordinate; and subordinates believe that they have little recourse but to follow; whether the behaviour is agreeable or not. On the other hand, in low power distance cultures bosses understand that they must consult and collaborate with subordinates to direct their behaviour; and subordinates understand that they can question and influence the boss's directives.
- Uncertainty avoidance indicates the degree to which cultures establish rules, procedures, and rituals to buffer uncertainties of individual judgement and freedom. High uncertainty avoidance cultures develop rules to cover a broad range of possibilities. Low uncertainty avoidance cultures let individuals react more spontaneously and 'go with the flow'.

Because of the derivation of the CWV scales, internal consistency can only be calculated for Individualism-Collectivism and Career Success-Quality of Life scales. The reliability for these scales in this sample is .74 for both.

Work Environment Scale Selected sub-scales from the Work Environment Scale (WES) (Moos, 1981) were used to measure seven different dimensions of an environmental characteristic called social climate. The 63, true-false items included seven nine-item scales:

- Peer Cohesion (PC): the amount of friendliness and support that is perceived in co-workers.
- Supervisor Support (SS): the support of management and the extent to which management encourages workers to be supportive of each other.
- Autonomy (A): the degree to which workers are encouraged to be self-sufficient and to make their own decisions.
- Task Orientation (TO): the extent to which the work environment emphasizes efficiency and good planning.
- Work Pressure (WP): the extent to which the pressure of work dominates the job milieu.
- Control (Ctl): the extent to which management uses rules and pressures to keep workers under control.
- Innovation (Inn): the extent to which variety, change, and new approaches are emphasized in the work environment.

Internal consistency for the seven WES scales in the current sample is as follows: PC = .64, SS = .71, A = .57, TO = .65, WP = .70, Ctl = .57, Inn =

.76. Two items were dropped from the Control scale to achieve the above level of reliability.

Coping Scale (Latack, 1986) This 28 item scale was developed to measure individual coping strategies in the work place. It is based on research that found more particular coping strategies could be categorized into these two major coping styles:

- Control coping consists of both actions and cognitive reappraisals that are proactive, take-charge in tone. They address the actual source of stress.
- Escape coping consists of both actions and cognitive reappraisals that suggest an escapist, avoidance mode. They are oriented to decrease the negative feelings of stress.

Internal consistency for the coping scales for the current sample are .84 for Control Coping and .79 for Escape Coping.

Procedures

In the typical procedure, the country contact person approached directors of child and youth care agencies to have all of the treatment and management staff from the agencies respond to the research questionnaire. Both burnout and cross-cultural research have a long history of this type of sample (Maslach & Schaufeli, 1993; Van de Vijver & Leung, 1997). A major consideration for burnout research is that participants be actually functioning in a helping profession. It is not possible to conduct simulation studies of burnout. Such a restriction makes it difficult to find qualified participants. The current sample, while not randomly chosen or precisely matched, meets a standard frequently used in such studies.

Results and Discussion

Cross-cultural differences in burnout As Figure 9.2 illustrates, the overall levels of burnout for the 13 cultures differed significantly ($F(36,2433)=5.73$, $p<.001$). Levels of separate emotional exhaustion, depersonalization, and personal accomplishment sub-scales for each of the 13 cultures can be seen as patterns indicating the overall intensity of burnout. Higher emotional exhaustion and depersonalization and lower personal accomplishment are indicative of greater overall burnout, and vice versa. In this graph, by using z-scores, the pan-cultural mean was set to zero so that bars extending to the right of the mid-line indicate scores higher than the mean and bars extending to the left of the mid-line indicate scores lower than the mean.

An analysis of burnout sub-scale scores by cultures indicates substantial differences between cultures. Differences for each sub-scale reach the .001 level of statistical significance. Figure 9.2 shows dramatic differences in the patterns of burnout sub-scales between cultures. For example, the US, England, and Australia show all three sub-scales above the mean; while Slovakia and Germany-East show them all below the mean. Scotland, Israel, Denmark, Canada-English and Canada-French show an overall configuration of sub-scale scores indicating lower burnout; i.e. low emotional exhaustion, low depersonalization, and high personal accomplishment.

In contrast, Germany-West and Austria show the reverse configuration indicating higher overall burnout. When considering this figure, it is important to recognize that there is no absolute level of sub-scale scores that indicates burnout. Further, the figure displays an analysis in which the countries are compared to each other. With more or fewer cultures, or with a different set of cultures the comparison mean for each sub-scale would be different. Therefore, readers should consider these results with some caution.

Pan-cultural analysis of burnout sub-scales In the following sections each burnout sub-scale will be considered separately. As the manual for the Maslach Burnout Inventory suggests, each sub-scale has a unique contribution to make in understanding the general concept of burnout (Maslach, Jackson & Leiter, 1996). Although some previous research has attempted to derive a single burnout score from the three sub-scales (Wright & Bonnett, 1997), the current analysis follows the majority of burnout research and considers them separately (Lee & Ashforth, 1990).

Figure 9.2 Emotional Exhaustion, Depersonalization and Personal Accomplishment Scores for Thirteen Cultures

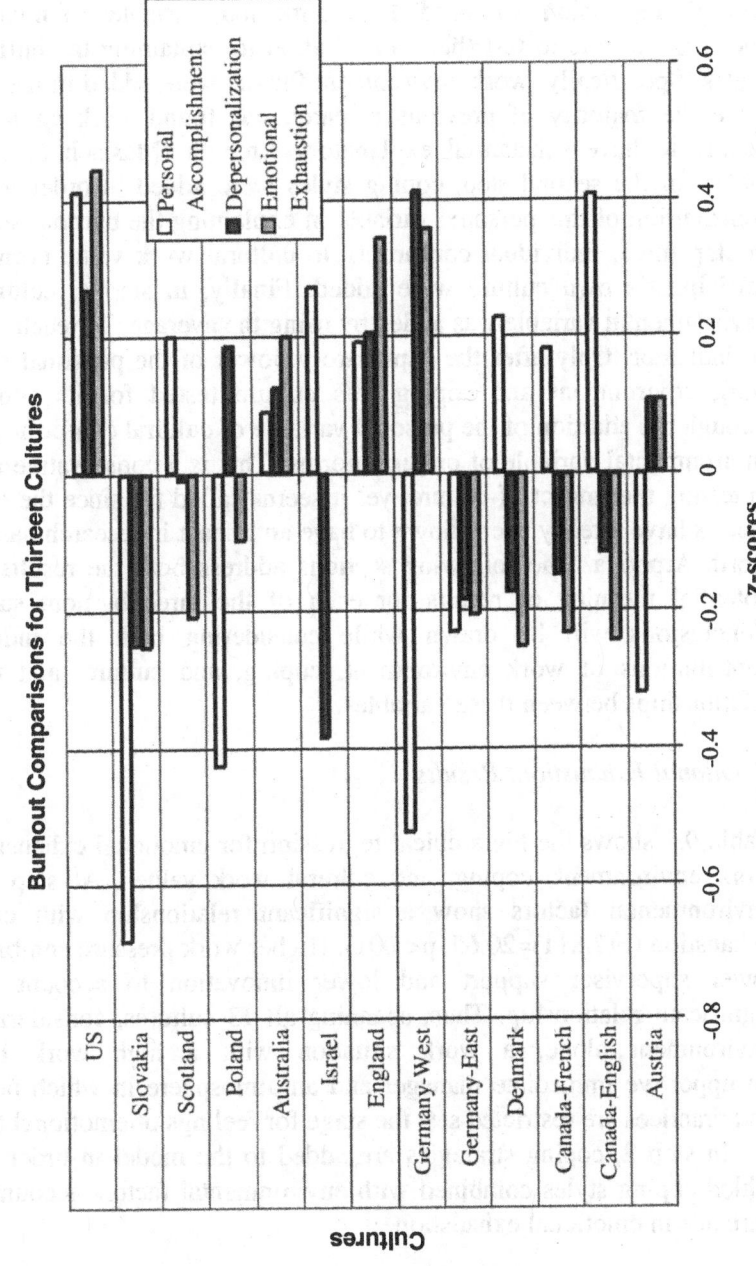

In order to test for the contributions to burnout of work environment, coping styles, and culture, a specific statistical method called hierarchical multiple regression was used. In this method, variables of interest were added in clusters to test their contribution to explaining the burnout sub-scales. Specifically, work environment factors were added in the first step since the majority of previous research has found work environmental factors to have substantial explanatory strength (Maslach & Schaufeli, 1993). In the second step, coping styles were added in order to test the contribution of this personal variable in explaining the burnout sub-scales. In step three, individual conformity to cultural work value norms of the participant's own culture were added. Finally, in step 4, culture as an environmental variable was added by using the averages for each culture as an indicator. Only after the explanatory power of the proximal factors of work environment and coping was culture tested for its contribution through the addition of the personal variable of cultural conformity and the environmental variable of cultural norms. This is a conservative approach to testing the impact of culture, yet it seems called for since the other two factors have already been shown to have an impact in research based in the North America. The following sections address both the results and the potential meaning of results for each of the three burnout sub-scales. Conclusions will be drawn while considering both the independent contributions of work environment, coping, and culture; and the joint relationships between these variables.

Emotional Exhaustion: Results

Table 9.1 shows the hierarchical regression for emotional exhaustion with work environment, coping, and cultural work values. At step 1, work environmental factors show a significant relationship with emotional exhaustion ($F(7,811)=20.65$, $p<.001$). Higher work pressure combines with lower supervisor support and lower innovation to account for this significant relationship. Thus, spanning all 13 cultures, considering work environment alone, a work situation with a high work load, an unsupportive immediate manager and an atmosphere in which new ideas and practices are restricted sets the stage for feelings of emotional fatigue.

In step 2, coping strategies are added to the model in order to show which coping styles combined with environmental factors account for the variance in emotional exhaustion.

Table 9.1 Hierarchical Multiple Regression of Emotional Exhuastion, Depersonalization and Personal Accomplishment with Work Environment, Coping and Cultural Work Values

Variables	Emotional Exhaustion	Depersonalization	Personal Accomplishment
Step 1:	R^2= .151	R^2= .057	R^2= .065
Work Environment	$F(7,811)$= 20.65***	$F(7,811)$= 7.03***	$F(7,811)$= 7.72***
Peer Cohesion	β = -.036	β = -.033	β = .088*
Supervisor Support	β = -.102*	β = -.104*	β = .001
Autonomy	β = .049	β = .054	β = .036
Task Orientation	β = -.060	β = -.117**	β = .051
Work Pressure	β = .312***	β = .109**	β = .023
Control	β = .029	β = .007	β = .071
Innovation	β = -.084*	β = -.52	β = .138**
Step 2:	R^2= .215	R^2= .145	R^2= .208
Coping Style	$F(9,809)$= 24.58***	$F(9,809)$= 15.29***	$F(9,809)$= 23.67***
Control Coping	β = -.019	β = -.057	β = .403***
Escape Coping	β = .259***	β = .311***	β = .017
Step 3:	R^2= .225	R^2= .156	R^2= .215
Cultural Conformity	$F(13,805)$= 17.96***	$F(13,805)$= 11.24***	$F(13,805)$= 16.93***
Power Distance	β = -.009	β = -.058	β = -.007
Uncertainty Avoidance	β = .099**	β = .063*	β = -.011
Individualism	β = -.018	β = -.020	β = .081**
Career Success	β = .020	β = .049	β = -.009
Step 4:	R^2= .250	R^2= .173	R^2= .226
Culture as Environment	$F(17,801)$= 15.73***	$F(17,801)$= 9.85***	$F(17,801)$= 13.76***
Power Distance	β = -.601	β = -.045	β = -.068*
Uncertainty Avoidance	β = .052	β = .074	β = -.035
Individualism	β = -.039	β = .001	β = .061
Career Success	β = .195***	β = .165***	β = -.005

* $p<.05$; ** $p<.01$; *** $p<.001$.

Step 2 is also statistically significant ($F(9,809)=24.58$, $p<.001$) with higher escape coping showing a significant contribution. That is, given the work environment conditions mentioned in the previous paragraph, workers showing increased attempts at reducing the unpleasant feelings associated with stress are more likely to experience emotional fatigue.

In step 3, personal conformity to cultural work values are added to the work environment and coping variables to test whether or not deviation from cultural norms adds to the explanation of emotional exhaustion when the other variables are already accounted for. Again the result is statistically significant ($F(13,805)=17.96$, $p<.001$). Individual deviation above the cultural work value of uncertainty avoidance contributed significantly to the model. Thus, given the work environment and coping results above, individuals who, in their culture, showed a higher than average value for reducing workplace ambiguity and uncertainty by means of rules and rituals show higher emotional exhaustion.

Finally, in step 4 the environmental impact of cultural work values are added to the previous variables to test whether or not general cultural work value norms increases the explanation of emotional exhaustion when the other variables are already accounted for. Again the result is statistically significant ($F(17,801)=15.73$, $p<.001$). When adding the influence of cultural work value norms to the model, cultures that show higher values for career success over quality of life related to higher emotional exhaustion.

Emotional Exhaustion: Discussion

Taken all together, Emotional Exhaustion was related to work environments with high pressure to work, low support from bosses, and low encouragement for changes and new ideas, to dealing with stress by trying to reduce only its unpleasant side effects, to an above average work value of avoiding ambiguity and uncertainty, and to a general cultural norm that emphasizes work and career above other aspects of life.

With regard to the question of generalizability of findings raised in the beginning of this chapter, it is clear that the patterns of work environment and coping do correspond with those specified in Lee and Ashforth's (1996) meta-analysis. Higher pressure to work shows the strongest relationship to emotional exhaustion in both studies. Lower supervisor support and lower innovation both load in the same direction. Also, results for escape coping are consistent with other research (Leiter, 1991; Riolli-Saltzman & Savicki, 2000); higher escape coping relates to emotional exhaustion. It seems that many findings regarding the relationship of work environment and coping can be generalized though the current pan-cultural analysis.

From a personal point of view, worker deviation from the uncertainty avoidance norms of their culture showed higher or lower emotional exhaustion depending on the direction of the deviation. The relationship of uncertainty avoidance and emotional exhaustion seems meaningful from two separate viewpoints. First, Hofstede (1980) indicates that in cultures high on uncertainty avoidance, individuals are likely to have a higher level of anxiety in general and higher job stress in particular (p. 132). Thus, individuals subscribing to high uncertainty avoidance may be more prone to stress, even though they attempt to reduce that stress through rules and other structural or procedural methods aimed at avoiding stress. The higher level of escape coping related to emotional exhaustion may be another demonstration of a higher base anxiety level. Second, Hofstede articulates the difference between good rules and bad rules as attempts to deal with ambiguity (p. 115). Although rules and standard operating procedures can relieve workers from anxiety provoking decisions, they also can take on a life of their own and create additional anxiety when they restrict flexibility and inhibit innovative responses. Cherniss (1995) cites difficulties with bureaucratic restrictions as a major stress factor for his sample. The perception of a lower level of innovation associated with emotional exhaustion may coincide with the restrictive effects of subscription to higher than normal uncertainty avoidance. Hofstede notes that fear of failure, lower risk taking, and intolerance for rule breaking are characteristics of high uncertainty avoidance cultures. These features seem consistent with the perception of lower support for innovation in the work environment.

Finally, culture as a more generalized environmental influence shows a strong relationship with emotional exhaustion through the work value of career success. All of the variables mentioned above may be intensified in an atmosphere in which work is a major source for self-identity and self-realization. Hofstede (1980) indicates that higher career success cultures emphasize greater work centrality, higher achievement motivation, and achievement defined in terms of recognition; additionally, they experience higher job stress (p. 200). In contrast, emphasis on Quality of Life relates to lower Emotional Exhaustion. Such a work value may dampen work related stress factors by construing work as less central to people's lives (p. 20).

Depersonalization: Results

Table 9.1 shows the hierarchical regression for depersonalization with work environment, coping, and cultural work values. At step 1, work environmental factors show a significant relationship with depersonalization ($F(7,811)=7.03$, $p<.001$). Higher work pressure combines with lower supervisor support and lower task orientation to account for this significant relationship. Thus, spanning all 13 cultures, considering work environment alone, a work situation with a high work load, an unsupportive immediate manager and an atmosphere in which work is organized inefficiently sets the stage for feelings of emotional separation and distance from clients.

In step 2, coping strategies are added to the model in order to show which coping styles combined with environmental factors account for the variance in depersonalization. Step 2 is also statistically significant ($F(9,809)=15.29$, $p<.001$) with higher escape coping showing a significant contribution. That is, given the work environment conditions mentioned in the previous paragraph, workers showing increased attempts at reducing the unpleasant feelings associated with stress are more likely to close off emotional contact.

In step 3, personal conformity to cultural work values is added to work environment and coping variables to test whether or not deviation from cultural norms adds to the explanation of depersonalization when the other variables are already accounted for. Again the result is statistically significant ($F(13,805)=11.24$, $p<.001$). The cultural work values of higher uncertainty avoidance, again contribute significantly to the model. Individual deviation above the cultural work value of uncertainty avoidance contributed significantly to the model. Thus, given the work environment and coping results above, individuals who, in their culture, showed a higher than normal value for reducing workplace ambiguity and uncertainty by means of rules and rituals show higher depersonalization.

Finally, in step 4 the environmental impact of cultural work values are added to the previous variables to test whether or not general cultural work value norms add to the explanation of depersonalization when the other variables are already accounted for. Again the result is statistically significant ($F(17,801)=9.85$, $p<.001$). When adding the influence of cultural work value norm to the model, cultures showing higher values for career success over quality of life related to higher depersonalization.

Depersonalization: Discussion

Taken all together, depersonalization was related to work environments with high pressure to work, low support from managers, and inefficient, disorganized work structure, to dealing with stress by trying to reduce only its unpleasant side effects, to higher than average subscription to the cultural value of avoiding or reducing work ambiguity through rules, and to a generalized cultural value of work and career above a more balanced approach to life.

With regard to the question of generalizability of findings raised in the beginning of this chapter, it is clear that the patterns of work environment and coping do correspond with those specified in Lee and Ashforth's (1996) meta-analysis. Again, higher pressure to work shows a strong relationship to depersonalization in both studies. Lower supervisor support and lower task orientation both load in the same direction. Lower task orientation is represented by role ambiguity and role conflict in the Lee and Ashforth study. Also, results for escape coping are consistent with other research (Leiter, 1991; Riolli-Saltzman & Savicki, 2000); higher escape coping relates to depersonalization. For depersonalization, also culture appears to have a significant impact.

From a personal point of view, workers who valued higher than average uncertainty avoidance showed a greater tendency to withdraw emotionally than those with lower than average uncertainty avoidance. This deviation from the norm probably works together with the work environmental condition of lower task orientation. That is, workers who work in somewhat chaotic or unpredictable settings and, at the same time, value structure to control their anxiety seem more prone to escape the resulting conflict between environment and value by building emotional barriers between themselves and their clients.

With regard to the question of the impact of culture as an environmental factor, the value of higher career success enhanced the explanation of depersonalization. The impact of an emphasis on one's career over a more balanced quality of life seems fairly straight-forward. As Hofstede (1980) indicates high career success cultures emphasize the achievement ideal in which people 'live to work' rather than 'work to live' (p. 205) Without balance in one's life, a worker can narrow his or her focus of attention in a way that excludes personal contact with others; especially clients. Particularly under conditions of high workload and chaotic work organization, a worker focused primarily on career success may find it difficult to attain such success. Reducing emotional availability may be perceived as a way of streamlining work responses. Paradoxically, it may result in precisely the opposite outcome.

Personal Accomplishment: Results

Table 9.1 shows the hierarchical regression for Personal Accomplishment with work environment, coping, and cultural work values. At step 1, work environmental factors show a significant relationship with personal accomplishment ($F(7,811)=7.72$, $p<.001$). Higher innovation and peer cohesion combine to account for this significant relationship. Thus, spanning all 13 cultures, considering work environment alone, a work situation with support and encouragement for new ideas and practices and one in which there is a supportive team or set of co-workers is related to feelings of goal attainment at work.

In step 2, coping strategies are added to the model in order to show which coping styles combined with environmental factors account for the variance in personal accomplishment. Step 2 is also statistically significant ($F(9,809)=23.67$, $p<.001$) with higher control coping showing a significant contribution. That is, given the work environment conditions mentioned in the previous paragraph, workers showing increased attempts at direct efforts to reduce the source of stress showed a higher sense of achievement and goal attainment.

In step 3, personal conformity to cultural work values is added to the previous variables to test whether or not deviation from cultural norms adds to the explanation of personal accomplishment when the other variables are already accounted for. Again the result is statistically significant ($F(13,805)=16.93$, $p<.001$). The cultural work value of higher individualism contributes significantly to the model. Thus, given the environmental and coping results above, individuals within a culture who more highly value the importance of self and individual action also show higher personal accomplishment.

Finally, in step 4 the environmental impact of cultural work values are added to the previous variables to test whether or not general cultural work value norms adds to the explanation of personal accomplishment when the other variables are already accounted for. Again the result is statistically significant ($F(17,801)=13.76$, $p<.001$). When adding the influence of cultural work value norm to the model, cultures that show lower values for power distance related to higher personal accomplishment.

Personal Accomplishment: Discussion

Taken all together, personal accomplishment was related to work environments with high cohesion and teamwork with one's co-workers and an atmosphere that encourages new ideas, to dealing with stress by taking direct action to reduce the source of stress, to a higher than average work value of emphasizing individual, independent behaviour over concerns for collective action, and to a general cultural value that favours equity and approachability between workers and managers.

Several areas of research indicate generalizability of findings. Social support from one's co-workers shows a relationship to personal accomplishment (Lee & Ashforth, 1996). Job design theory (Hackman & Oldham, 1980) suggests that innovation results from a well-organized work environment. Also, results for control coping are consistent with other research (Leiter, 1991; Riolli-Saltzman & Savicki, 2000); higher control coping relates to personal accomplishment. For personal accomplishment, culture alsoappears to have a significant impact.

Deviation from the cultural work value of higher individualism enhanced the explanation of personal accomplishment beyond coping and factors in the immediate work environment. It is easy to see how innovation might be supported by an individualist orientation. Hofstede (1980) suggests that high individualism emphasizes 'freedom and challenge' in one's work; likewise, 'individual initiative is socially encouraged' (p. 166). Additionally, taking independent action to diminish stress factors as a method of coping might be supported by individualism. However, at first glance, it is difficult to understand how having good relations with one's co-workers relates to individualistic values. Given past research (Savicki, 1993) it might be speculated that most child and youth care workers function in teams. Therefore, teamwork and good co-worker relationships impact not only one's sense of belonging, but also one's ability to perform well. Much of child and youth care practice occurs in interdependent actions with others. Therefore, good teamwork is likely to produce good results while poor teamwork may create frustrations in actual job performance. Successes arising from team action are more likely to be perceived as individual achievements within an individualistic culture.

With regard to more general cultural effects, lower power distance can be seen to enhance individual achievements that have been supported by innovation, control coping, and higher than average individualism. Cultures that view individuals as inherently equal regardless of placement in the organizational hierarchy allow individuals at any level more permission to act on their own without fear of running foul of those with higher status. As Hofstede (1980) states 'people at various power levels feel less threatened and more prepared to trust people' (p. 94). Recognition for achievement is based on what one is able to achieve rather than their status. Thus individual action is more likely to lead to perceptions of achievement and accomplishment. Cherniss (1995) recounts that individuals in his sample who recovered from burnout were able to do so, in part, because they engaged in some unique activity for which they could feel a sense of accomplishment.

Conclusions and Implications

In general, the research questions posed earlier in this chapter can be answered in the affirmative.

First, culture does seem to relate to burnout. Both general, environmental measures and individual cultural conformity measures showed significant contributions to all of the burnout sub-scales. Second, patterns of work environment and coping related to burnout found in North America did seem to generalize across the 13 cultures.

Several important themes relating to burnout in child and youth care workers emerged from the pan-cultural analysis of burnout across the thirteen cultures. Each theme will be discussed briefly.

Teamwork training and support   Social support aspects of work hold substantial meaning for child and youth care workers since their practice depends on social interaction (Savicki, 1993). Successful practice often occurs within a team context. Unfortunately, workers are not systematically trained in teamwork or group processes within a work team. Such training would be very helpful in establishing and maintaining solid co-worker support both at the emotional and technical performance level. Just being a sensitive and compassionate worker with children and youth does not necessarily translate into being a good team member.

Supportive supervision   Effective interpersonal nourishment from supervisors is also a source of social support. Those individuals in the organizational hierarchy who have responsibility for the working lives of child and youth care workers must balance their focus on the task at hand with the needs of the individual worker. Often, concern for performance and compliance overshadow a more personal awareness of the worker.

Supervisors should be trained to be responsive to both task and socio-emotional aspects of their workers. Classic studies in business and organizational psychology literature (Blake & Mouton, 1964; Fleischman, 1957) have identified the need for such balance.

Planned workplace and manageable pace Work overload is a classic contributor to burnout. Clearly work needs to get done. However, the arrangement of work may have a large impact on how taxing it seems to individual workers. If work tasks can be paced to challenge and not overwhelm workers, they may experience more engagement with their work and find work invigorating in spite of a fast pace (Maslach & Leiter, 1997; Riolli-Saltzman & Savicki, 2000). Likewise, clear, unambiguous work structures allow workers to predict their work activities more clearly; thus reducing the fear of unanticipated demands which may descend in some random fashion. Consistent with this theme, Fleischer (1985) found that child and youth care worker turnover was linked to workload, lack of clear performance feedback, and lack of supervisor support.

Flexible, enriching work Too many rules and structures on the other handcan be stifling of individual initiative and creativity. Part of what engages people with their work is the ability to put something of themselves into it (Maslach & Leiter, 1997). Work structures that allow workers some control over their immediate work environment help the workers perceive their activities as more meaningful and significant. Likewise, support for new ideas communicates the belief that workers may, indeed, be creative people whose contributions can advance the purposes of the organization as a whole.

Coping strategy training Finally, individuals learn coping strategies in a haphazard manner as they grow to adulthood. Thus, some have a broader range of more effective coping resources than others. This haphazardness of preparation for coping should be addressed. Given the stresses that we know exist in child and youth care work, we can expect that workers will need a variety of effective coping strategies. Fuqua and Couture (1986) found internal locus of control positively related to personal accomplishment. McMullen and Krantz (1988) found that higher learned helplessness and lower self-esteem were related to higher levels of emotional exhaustion and depersonalization. Typical burnout workshops have tended to focus on activities such as physical exercise, meditation and guided fantasy, which fall into the escape coping category (Potter, 1987).

While such methods may yield short-term relief, control coping strategies such as systematic problem solving may prove to be more productive in the long run. Systematic training in control coping strategies at both the personal and the organizational level will help workers become more effective at changing both their responses to stress and the environmental context in which the stress occurs (Cherniss, 1995).

In conclusion, it is clear that culture, as a variable, should be accounted for when considering the relationships of work environment and coping to burnout. In the current study, culture added important information to the understanding of the various dimensions of burnout.

Note

1. This chapter is based, in part, on the chapter 'Pan-Cultural Analysis of Burnout' in Savicki, V. (2002). *Burnout Across Thirteen Cultures*. Westpost, CT: Praeger Publishers.

References

Adler, N.L. (1997) *International dimensions of organizational behavior*. Cincinnati, OH: South-Western College Publishing.
Armstrong-Stassen, M., Al-Ma'Aitah, R., Cameron, S.. & Horsburgh, M. (1994). Determinants and consequences of burnout: A cross-cultural comparison of Canadian and Jordanian nurses. *Health Care for Women International, 15*, 413-421.
Blake, R.R., & Mouton, J.S. (1964). *The managerial grid*. Houston: Gulf Publishing.
Büssing, A., & Perrar, K.M. (1992). Die Messung von Burnout. Untersuchung einer deutschen Fassung des Maslach Burnout Inventory (MBI-D) [The measurement of burnout: Examination of a German version of the Maslach Burnout Inventory (MBI-D)]. *Diagnostica, 38*, 328-353.
Cherniss, C. (1995). *Beyond Burnout: Helping Teachers, Nurses, Therapists & Lawyers Recover from Stress & Disillusionment*. New York: Routledge.
Etzion, D., & Pines, A. (1986). Sex and culture in burnout and coping among human service professionals: A social psychological perspective. *Journal of Cross-Cultural Psychology. 17*, 191-209.
Fleischer, B.M. (1985). Identification of strategies to reduce turnover among child care workers. *Child Care Quarterly. 14*, 130-139.
Fleischman, E.A. (1957). A leader behavior description for industry. In R.M. Stogdill & A.E. Coons (Eds.), *Leader Behavior: Its description and Measurement*. Columbus, OH: Bureau of Business Research, Ohio State University.
Fuqua, R. & Couture, K. (1986). Burnout and locus of control in child day care staff. *Child Care Quarterly, 15*, 98-109.
Golembiewski, R.T., Scherb, K.& Boudreau, R.A. (1993). Burnout in cross-national settings: Generic and model-specific perspectives. In W.B. Schaufeli, C. Maslach & T.

Mark (Eds.), *Professional burnout: Recent developments in theory and research*, Washington DC: Taylor & Francis.

Green, E., Walkey, F.H., & Taylor, A.J. (1991) The three-factor structure of the Maslach Burnout Inventory: A multicultural, multinational confirmatory study. *Journal of Social Behavior and Personality, 6*, 453-472.

Hackman, J.R., & Oldham, G.R. (1980). *Work redesign.* Reading, MA: Addison-Wesley.

Hofstede, G. (1980). *Culture's consequences: International differences in work related values.* Beverly Hills, CA: Sage.

Jamal, M. (1999). Job stress and employee well-being: A cross-cultural empirical study. *Stress Medicine, 15*, 153-158.

Latack, J.C. (1986). Coping with job stress: Measures and future directions for scale development. *Journal of Applied Psychology, 71*, 377-385.

Lazarus, R.S. (1999). *Stress and emotion: A new synthesis.* New York: Springier Publishing.

Lee, R.T., & Ashforth, B.E. (1990). On the meaning of Maslach's three dimensions of burnout. *Journal of Applied Psychology, 75*, 743-747.

Lee, R.T., & Ashforth, B.E. (1996). A meta-analytic examination of the correlates of the three dimensions of job burnout. *Journal of Applied Psychology, 81*, 123-133.

Leiter, M.P. (1991). Coping patterns as predictors of burnout: The function of control and escapist coping patterns. *Journal of Organizational Behavior, 12*, 123-144.

McMullen, M.B., & Krantz, M. (1988). Burnout in day care workers: The effects of learned helplessness and self-esteem. *Child and Youth Care Quarterly, 17*, 275-280.

Maslach, C., Jackson, S.E. & Leiter, M.P. (1996). *The Maslach Burnout Inventory (3rd Ed).* Palo Alto, CA: Consulting Psychologists Press.

Maslach, C., & Leiter, M.P. (1997). *The Truth about Burnout: How Organizations Cause Personal Stress and What to do about it.* San Francisco, CA: Josses-Bass.

Maslach, C., & Schaufeli, W.B. (1993). Historical and conceptual development of burnout, In W.B. Schaufeli, C. Maslach & T. Mark (Eds.), *Professional burnout: Recent developments in theory and research,* Washington, D.C.: Taylor & Francis.

Moos, R.H. (1981). *Work Environment Scale Manual.* Palo Alto, CA: Consulting Psychologists Press.

Potter, B.A. (1987). *Preventing job burnout.* Palo Alto, CA: Consulting Psychologists Press.

Riolli-Saltzman, L., & Savicki, V. (2000). The relationship of optimism coping and work environment on burnout and performance. Manuscript submitted for publication.

Savicki, V. (1993). Clarification of child and youth care identity through an analysis of work environment and burnout. *Child and Youth Care Forum, 22*, 441-457.

Savicki, V. (1999a). Stress, burnout und Bewältigungsstrategien in der Jugendhilfe. Ein interkultureller Vergleich [Stress, burnout and coping strategies in youth work: an intercultural comparison]. *Forum Erziehungshilfen, 5*, 232-238.

Savicki, V. (1999b). Udbrændthed inden for børneforsogen i Danmark [Burnout in child care work in Denmark]. *Tidsskrift for Socialpaedagogik, 4*, 37-43.

Schaufeli, W., & Janczur, B. (1994). Burnout among nurses: A Polish-Dutch comparison. *Journal of Cross-cultural Psychology. 25*, 95-113.

Schaufeli, W.B., & Van Dierendonck, D. (1995). A cautionary note about the cross-national and clinical validity of cut-off points for the Maslach Burnout Inventory. *Psychological Reports, 76*, 1083-1090.

Schutte, N., Toppinen, S., Kalimo, R., & Schaufeli, W. (2000). The factorial validity of the Maslach Burnout Inventory-General Survey (MBI-GS) across occupational groups and nations. *Journal of Occupational and Organizational Psychology, 73*, 53-66.

Triandis, H.C. (1995). *Individualism and Collectivism.* Boulder Colorado: Westview Press.
Triandis, H.C. (1996). The psychological measurement of cultural syndromes. *American Psychologist, 51,* 407-415.
Trompenaars, F., & Hampden-Turner, C. (1998). *Riding the waves of culture: Understanding diversity in global business, 2nd Ed.* New York: McGraw-Hill.
Van de Vijver, F., & Leung, K. (1997). Methods and data analysis of comparative research. In J.W. Berry, Y.H. Poortinga, & J. Pandey (Eds.), *Handbook of Cross-cultural Psychology, 2nd Ed.* Boston: Allyn and Bacon.
Wright, T.A., & Bonnett, D.G. (1977). The contribution of burnout to work performance. *Journal of Organizational Behavior, 18,* 491-499.

Chapter 10

Workload and Prevention of Burnout in Special Child and Youth Care Services: A System Analysis

Jef Breda and Elke Verlinden

Introduction

The workload issue is very topical in the private as well as the public sector. Welfare services, schools, hospitals, rest homes, child welfare services and the like are all complaining about excessive workloads and the adverse effect this is having on the quality of the services rendered, and they are demanding measures. However, resolving this matter adequately is not quite as straightforward as it seems, due to the fact that the issue contains several dimensions. Employing additional staff is by no means the only way to deal with the problem of excessive workloads.

One could argue that the quality of the work performed is determined by the organization, the broader context and the commitment of the individual worker. In order to keep the latter's workload under control, it is therefore necessary to steer the system as a whole. A system that cannot be controlled will lead to variable quality and therefore a lack of quality assurance. Moreover, dissatisfaction among personnel may lead to a high staff turnover, protests, resignation and burnout.

In this chapter, we shall approach the welfare sector as a production system. First, we shall outline how a production system in this sector may be defined, which elements are required, and how one can succeed in gaining control inside and outside the system. Subsequently, we shall put our model to practical use in a study of the workload in the special child and youth care services in Flanders.

A Non-Profit Sector considered as a Production System

A systemic but normative model for steering and managing an executive process offers an interesting perspective for keeping workloads under control. In general terms, one can distinguish between three phases where the production process may be controlled.

1. *The input*: i.e. the inflow of requests for assistance (e.g. requests for financial aid or relational guidance). Beside clients and their problems, the social workers and their professional characteristics are also part of the input of the assistance process: number of staff, training, qualifications, et cetera, and the means that are made available to the social services (e.g. the extent and type of administrative support).
2. *The (primary) process*: we refer primarily to the contact between the social worker and the client. More specifically in social work this involves: diagnosing, preparing the decision on whether or not to provide assistance or care, and the assistance itself (counselling, therapy, financial aid, referral ...). But besides the work involving contact with the client, there are other aspects of rendering service that need to be taken into account: passing on and arranging of information, administration on behalf of clients, keeping the team and centre functioning, et cetera. Both processes – the primary, client-oriented and the support function – can be considered as the 'throughput' aspect of the system.
3. *The output*: by this we mean the change that is achieved in the situation of the client. In aggregated terms, it concerns the volume of clients that has actually received assistance from the organization.

In other words, management and control not only concern a variety of client-related parameters (number of cases, composition of client population, et cetera), but also parameters relating to the social workers and the assistance process as such.

A number of further conditions need to be added to this trichotomy, such as the operational objectives of the organization, environmental factors (including any externally imposed standards and procedures) and the organizational structure.

Each of the three phases that were distinguished (input, primary process and output) provides opportunities for attaining control. As we have pointed out, control must involve a number of *predetermined standards*, implying that the nature of processes and results must be laid down beforehand. This holds for the input, the primary process and the output. Hulshof and Hulshof (1980) have designed a general model of management and control in the welfare services. This model is represented schematically in Figure 10.1.

On the basis of this representation, one can describe the three key parameters, i.e. quantity, quality and costs. The *quantity* of services provided concerns the number of clients requesting assistance (i.e. those joining the 'waiting line' or 'queue'). If demand is excessive, i.e. if the queue becomes too long, clients may drop out, additional capacity may be made available, or the nature of the assistance provided may be adapted. The *quality* of the assistance is determined by how clients are dealt with (i.e. the assistance process) and the effects (i.e. changes) that are realized. In keeping with the nature of a professional organization, Hulshof and Hulshof assert that, in the past, the standards for quantity (input) and quality (process and output) were not primarily determined by the organization, let alone the government, but by the professionals themselves, albeit usually not explicitly (Hulshof & Hulshof, 1980). The length of the queue, but also the amount of work that needs to be performed, depends on the volume of demand for service as well as the (implicit, possibly even personal) quality standards by which the professionals operate. In other words, if demand increases, and one wishes to maintain the same professional standards, the only possible systemic response is an increase of capacity.

However, welfare organizations are no longer operating within a system where means can be increased unrestrictedly as in the past. The government, or any other financier, will invariably impose expenditure standards with a view to *cost* control and productivity. These standards are now often detached from standards relating to the quantity and the quality of service rendered. This 'double' rationality is problematic from an organizational perspective: if expenditure is restricted by external cost standards that are detached from quality and quantity standards, then the inevitable consequence of growing demand is greater pressure on staff, as capacity can no longer be increased (or at least, not quickly enough). This suggests that the workload issue is not only connected with excessive demand given the available capacity, but also with quality and quantity standards (and how they correspond with cost standards).

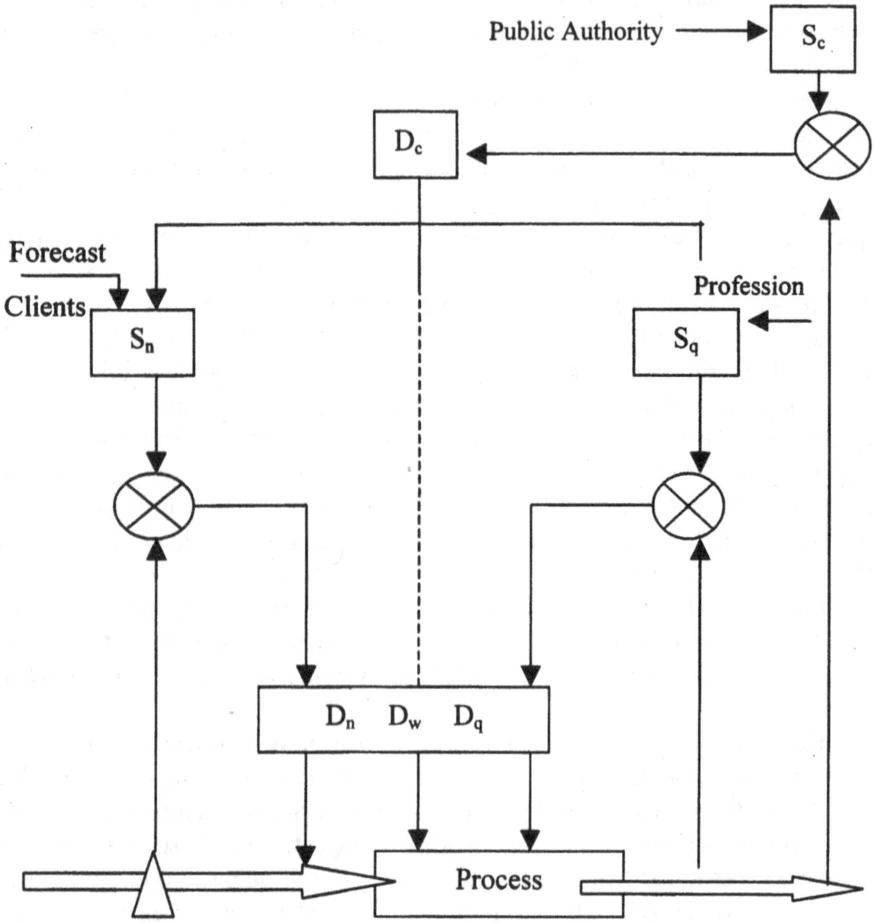

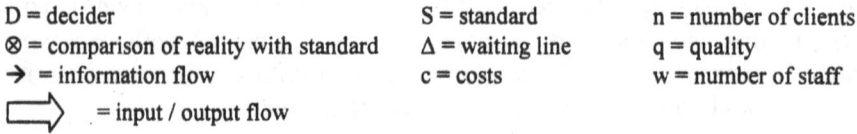

Figure 10.1   Control in the quaternary sector

D = decider   S = standard   n = number of clients
⊗ = comparison of reality with standard   Δ = waiting line   q = quality
→ = information flow   c = costs   w = number of staff
⇨ = input / output flow

Controlling the inflow of clients is of central importance for gaining overall control over the system. Inflow fluctuations and specific demand patterns could, for example, be charted. Hulshof and Hulshof refer in this respect to the demand patterns of specific categories of clients, who also require a specific treatment (in terms of content, intensity and duration). In addition to controlling the inflow, one also needs to control the service processes. The above-mentioned authors assert in this respect that organizations should be aware of the difference in duration and intensity of service to different types of client (Hulshof & Hulshof, 1980).

Besides these specific information needs, one also needs to *tune the different standards to each other*. Among other things, this implies that there must be explicit standards regarding the distribution of means over the different system components (e.g., staff over geographically scattered services), the target group (and those whose request for assistance will be turned down) and the duration and content of the assistance rendered (or, as the case may be, its results or effects). It is the 'superior decision-maker' who must bring prevailing quality and quantity standards in line with intermediate standards, and vice versa. In the proposed control model, the number of clients, the number of social workers and quality are grouped together to indicate that these aspects are all part of one coherent decision process. The model requires: 1) the presence and specification of quantifiable standards, 2) a discourse about quality, and 3) insight into the relation between duration and quality (Hulshof & Hulshof, 1980). For the available time per client, the number of possible contacts and therefore the intensity of the assistance rendered are all essential elements in controlling and optimizing the quality of services provided, both from the perspective of the client and from that of the organization and the social worker.

With this conceptually quite simple control model, it becomes clear that, if one wishes to control and manage the process, one needs to take due account of the relation between the temporal aspects of the assistance (duration, intensity) on the one hand and the combination of demand and supply on the other. However, in many service systems the afore mentioned standards remain disconnected so that the system suffers from many uncontrolled contingencies.

In the system under study, the main environmental disturbances arise from the increase in the number of clients from the unequal spread of cases and resources over the country. Decisions concerning the budget and the staff volume are taken at a much slower rate than the rapid increase in cases and waiting lists. The management has no reliable instruments to measure and adjust to rising demands, so that all kinds of rather spontaneous processes can originate, e.g. a decrease in professional quality and an increase in burden on the staff. In this study we therefore document the actual operation of the system and we design measurement instruments and outline planning norms in order to bring the system under control.

The Production of Social Work in a Specific Sector: Child and Youth Care

Brief Survey of the Sector

Youngsters who find themselves in a situation of 'un-welfare' can call on a range of care services. They can appeal to the general welfare services, the mental health services or community service initiatives. Social workers have been incorporated into the school system. Naturally, there is also a range of provisions for youngsters in so-called 'problematic educational situations' and/or delinquent youngsters. Within these 'special' care sectors, a number of further distinctions are made: there are counselling and educational provisions (ambulatory and residential), and there are the judicial and police authorities. A third group of organizations performs gate-keeping and monitoring functions: they come into operation when youngsters (wish to) enter the special youth assistance service, they follow up the care and the 'special' educational efforts, and they organize the outflow. This study is devoted to the latter group of provisions within the special youth assistance scheme.

Furthermore, within this section of special youth assistance, one can clearly distinguish between voluntary and coercive assistance. The two differ from each other in terms of who are the responsible authorities and which services are involved.

The *Special Youth Assistance Committee (SYAC)* is responsible for providing voluntary assistance, while the *Social Service of the Juvenile Court (SSJC)* prepares and implements legal decisions.

In both instances, the primary task of the social workers involved consists of diagnosis and monitoring of the care efforts. The social workers face the challenge of stimulating co-operation on the part of the client in the (sometimes enforced) assistance process. The output is the number of clients whose cases have been (successfully) concluded.

Both bodies are influenced considerably from the outside, i.e. by channelling as a second-line service of inflowing clients and by the availability of other counselling and care facilities in a given region.

The Production System of Special Child and Youth Care: Empirical Results

Method In general terms, there appeared to be almost no objective information available about each of the system components. With regard to output – the number, nature and quality of concluded cases – we too were unable to collect data. However, we did succeed in gathering data concerning the input and the process itself.

Regarding the *input*, in addition to an estimation of incoming and 'current' cases per regional unit in Flanders, data were collected on staffing levels in each of the units. Both sets of data were expressed as a ratio to the population under the age of 19.

Data regarding the *process* were collected in two ways. First, the average time consumption was measured for each of the principal activities of the social workers involved. Subsequently, a typology was designed for cases where we were able to calculate an average duration on the basis of the average duration for each of the activities involved. In this manner, the current production system was reconstructed in terms of the principal input and process variables.

Process data: nature and duration of the activities Using a time registration form, 73 social workers (from a sample of the universe of social workers, stratified according to size of the workforce of SYAC and SSJC, with a response rate of 90%)[1] kept a log of *all their professional activities* during one week in October 1999.

It appears from these data that a social worker at the SYAC performs an average 8 hours and 38 minutes of work per day, compared to 8 hours and 42 minutes at the SSJC. This is more than one would expect under a 38-hour working week regime. Clearly, then, staff perform overtime on a regular basis.

About 25% of working time is devoted to activities that are not connected directly with the cases that the social worker is dealing with, but have to do with organizational aspects, working in a team, training, et cetera. A further 25% of working time is spent on directly case-related activities (e.g., house calls or telephone calls to clients) and 50% on indirectly case-related activities (e.g. meetings about the case, reporting, or studying the case). The social workers of the SYAC spend more time on meetings, while staff at the SSJC invest more working time in reporting. On ordinary working days, much time is lost on travelling between different locations. During duty periods, staff are required to stay at the office, which reduces the time spent on travelling and increases the time devoted to telephoning (see Table 10.1).

Case-related face-to-face meetings, telephone conversations, travelling and reporting are the principal activities performed by social workers. The duration of conversations varies considerably, which is partly due to the difference in locations and the persons on whose behalf the work is performed. Meetings at the office, for example, are generally shorter than meetings at a residential facility. House calls involving the parents take about as long as house calls involving the youngsters only. But house calls where an external professional social worker is involved take up considerably more time.

Table 10.1 Average duration and proportion of working time spent on selected activities

Activities	SYAC Proportion of working time	SYAC Average duration	SSJC Proportion of working time	SSJC Average duration
Face-to-face with client	23.2%	52 min.	23.1%	56 min.
Telephoning with client	2.2%	13 min.	1.5%	14 min.
Travelling with client	0.7%	51 min.	0.9%	33 min.
Studying case	2.9%	17 min.	4.7%	22 min.
Discussing case	7.1%	24 min.	10.6%	34 min.
Telephoning about case	8.4%	13 min.	6.0%	13 min.
Travelling in connection with case	13.8%	26 min.	20%	29 min.
Compiling file	3.2%	15 min.	3:2%	18 min.
Reporting	7.5%	35 min.	11.0%	56 min.
Meetings about case	4.3%	37 min.	2.1%	67 min.
Conversations, unconnected with case	2.9%	26 min.	1.1%	19 min.
Telephoning, unconnected with case	0.2%	10 min.	1.4%	20 min.
Travelling	1.2%	42 min.	0.8%	40 min.
Administrative activities	5.1%	20 min.	6.0%	27 min.
Meetings	10.8%	77 min.	4.5%	93 min.
Other	6.7%	39 min.	3.1%	32 min.
Total	100%	-	100%	-

Most working time is spent at the office. Working time is also spent at clients' homes, at residential facilities, at foster parents' homes and at schools. As we have previously pointed out, much time is consumed by moving around between locations.

The social workers surveyed work alone most of the time. At the SSJC, almost 48% of working time is devoted to 'solo activities', compared to 36% at the SYAC. This difference is mainly due to the fact that more time is spent at the SSJC on reporting, while staff at the SYAC spend more time in meetings.

Clearly, then, there is a difference between the activity patterns at the SYAC and the SSJC, which is partly due to the fact that the two services deal with different types of cases.

A further analysis of the case-oriented activities allows one to distinguish not only between SYAC and SSJC, but also between new and current cases. The majority of case-oriented time is devoted to current cases: on an ordinary working day, this amounts to about 80% of the working time at the SYAC and about 71% at the SSJC. Almost 13% of working time at the SYAC is spent on new cases, compared to 27% at the SSJC. The rest of the time is taken up by intakes or colleagues' cases. The activity patterns for current and new cases is roughly the same, as is the average time spent on a case. Current cases involve more telephoning. New cases require a greater time investment in reporting.

We may conclude that there are three factors that influence the activity pattern: the body involved (SYAC or SSJC), the nature of the work (duty period or ordinary working day), and the case dealt with (new, current, intake or colleague's case). Besides these three factors, the location where the activity takes place and the persons or bodies that one needs to deal with also influence the average duration of activities.

If one compares regional offices, there are clearly considerable differences. Although staff at all services complain that they are overworked, it is quite noticeable that there are also big differences between services dealing with the same type of case. Staff at some offices spend four times less time on the telephone and in face-to-face meetings than staff elsewhere. There is also a striking divergence in terms of time spent on travelling (this may be partly due to congestion problems in certain areas).

Linking process and input data: cases and activities brought together An attempt was made to draw up a descriptive typology of cases that would allow one to estimate the work and working time involved. A further requirement was that cases had to be easily and instantly identifiable. Therefore, we tried to find objective characteristics that were readily available as routine information. Questions were asked about the sex and age of the youngsters, their family background, place of residence, ethnicity, history of social assistance, and the duration of the case.

In order to gain insight into the input of cases and the time spent on the different types of cases, 48 social workers kept a log of *all their activities* in connection with *five at random selected cases* over a four-month period. As we had already established by means of the time registration what was the average time spent on each activity, we were able to estimate the amount of time invested in each of the five cases.

As with the registration of activities, there appeared to be a significant difference between the SYAC and SSJC. The most complex cases were dealt with by the SSJC. Cases involving a problematic upbringing situation and/or recidivism of an act defined as a criminal offence are most time-consuming. In fact, they require almost three times as much time as the simplest cases dealt with by the SSJC. The latter involve first-time juvenile offenders who have no history of social care besides special youth assistance. At the SYAC, there is clearly a difference between current and new cases. New cases require a more substantial time investment. In these cases, the living condition also plays a role. If the parental home is not located in a so-called disadvantaged municipality, then the case requires a slightly bigger time investment on the part of the social worker. This is probably due to the lower availability of welfare services in these places. Current cases demand less time, especially if there is no involvement of the Mediation Committee.

The pattern of activities for the different cases of the SSJC and SYAC is more or less the same. The main difference is the number of activities involved. New cases encompass twice as many activities.

Workload Distribution in the System

Now that we have gained insight into the time invested in cases, we can compare the workload at the different services. We can, in other words, determine at which youth care agencies social workers must make a more substantial time investment over a given period to process their cases.

The overall mean workload of the system is put as 0 in order to illuminate the pattern of deviance within the system. The variation around this mean is expressed as a percentage below or above the actual mean number of cases in the system as a whole.

Our analysis shows that the workload varies strongly between regional offices. The workload at some SYACs and SSJCs is well above the average, while at others it is well below the mean (see Figures 10.1 and 10.2). Much depends on the nature of the cases involved and the number of staff dealing with the cases.

Input Data: Inflow to Special Youth Assistance Services

Besides the difference in workload, the two bodies also differ in terms of the inflow of cases. In some regions, the proportion of youngsters that is referred to special youth assistance services is four times higher than elsewhere.

Figure 10.1 The workload at the social services of the SYAC, deviation from the mean (75 cases; agencies no. 1 – no. 19)

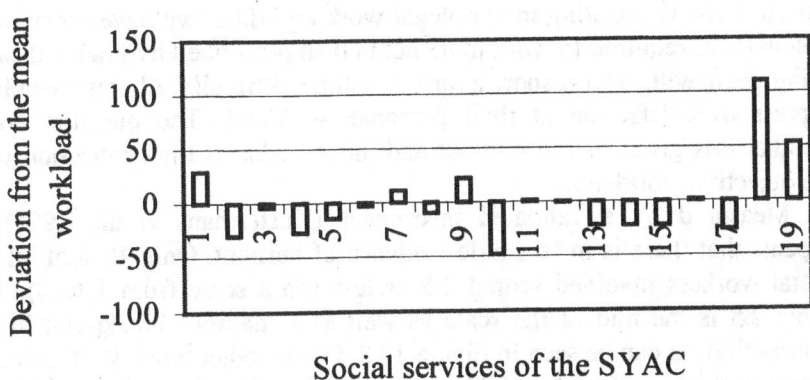

Figure 10.2 The workload at the social services of the SSJC, deviation from the mean (66 cases; agencies no. 20 – no. 33)

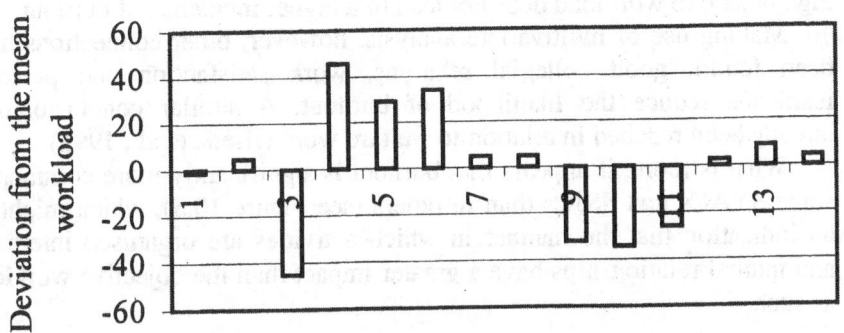

Subjective Work Experiences in the System

Both the central office and the head of the social services of the regional offices (SYAC and SSJC) have asserted that the sector is overburdened. We have demonstrated that this overburdening can be measured and expressed in objective terms, and that there is moreover considerable variation within the sector itself.

As neither body can really dismiss cases or put them on a waiting list, this situation is resulting in extralegal working hours (we have ascertained that staff are required to work more hours than prescribed by law) and cases being dealt with in too short a space of time. Virtually all staff members express dissatisfaction at their personal workload. The question arises whether this gives rise to burnout and indeed what is the connection with the objective workload.

Measured by a validated instrument (Kustermans et al., 1995), it appears that there is in fact little evidence of burnout. Only 10% of all the social workers involved scored 2.5 or less (on a scale from 1 to 4). The value 2.5 is the mid of the scale as well as a 'natural' breakpoint in the distribution, as can be seen in Figure 10.3. On the other hand, staff are quite happy with the extent to which they are able to apply their professional skills, while they are also satisfied with the physical working conditions and their relationships with colleagues. Furthermore, staff are happy with their work situation in general, though dealing with 'problem children and their educational environment' is perceived to be emotionally draining.

The fact that burnout, measured at an individual level, is rare while the objective pressure of work is very high (though variable) seems to indicate that there is little or no correlation in the data between the two variables. A high objective workload does not lead to a higher incidence of burnout.

Making use of multivariate analysis, however, other connections have been found: good collegial relations, work satisfaction and personal resilience reduce the likelihood of burnout. A similar conclusion had already been reached in relation to welfare work (Breda et al., 1995).

What is more, it appears that burnout is significantly more common in some SYACs and SSJCs than in others (see Figure 10.3), which might be an indication that the manner in which activities are organised internally and mutual relationships have a greater impact than the objective workload as such.

Figure 10.3 Average burnout-scores in the regional SYACs and SSJCs (N=33)*

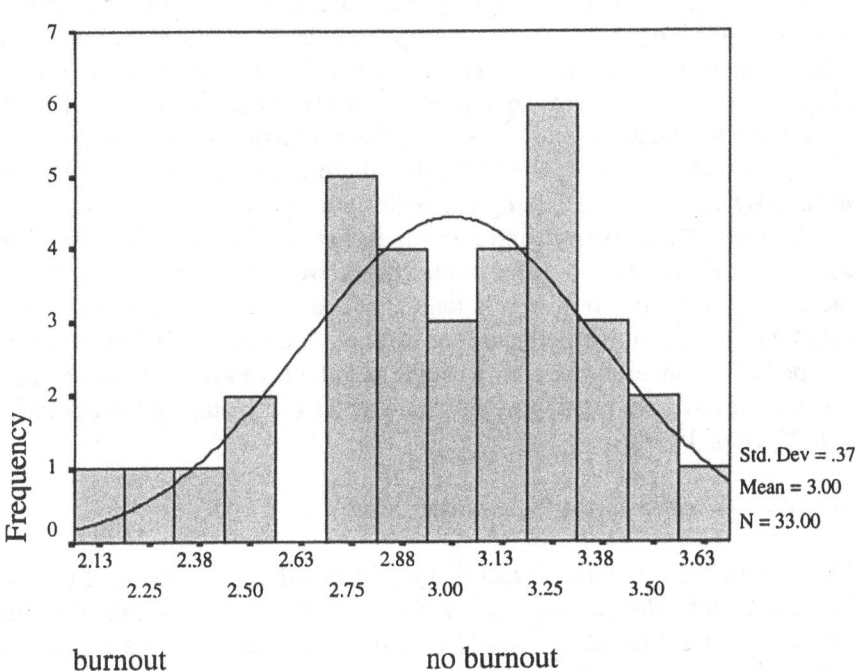

* Scores may vary between 1 and 4. Low scores indicate a high degree of burnout.

Gaining Closer Control over Workload and Production

As we pointed out in the introduction, Hulshof and Hulshof (1980) distinguish between three areas where one can keep a check on the workload and control the production system: input, process and output. In each of these areas, be it separately or in combination, one can take measures to control the rhythm and quantity of work.

Increasing Control through a better Referral Policy

SYACs in particular appear not to have adequate control over the volume and nature of the inflow of cases. Cases which strictly do not fit in with the SYAC's assignment nevertheless present themselves. It may therefore be advisable to give priority to certain types of cases. In particular, one could ask whether the case falls within the SYAC's responsibility. If not, the client could be referred to the appropriate authority immediately. The latter would already contribute to decreasing the workload. At present, priority is given to crisis situations. Consequently, there is a risk that the service will eventually come to deal exclusively with such cases.

In order to gain better control of the inflow, the special youth assistance service must reconsider its position within welfare work in general, and probably also its position in relation to mental health care and care for the disabled. As in The Netherlands, for example, one could restrict the inflow to special youth assistance to a single point of entry, from where cases could be referred to the appropriate authorities (cf. Nota, Van der Schaft & Van Yperen, 1997).

Matching the Inflow with the available Staff

One cannot escape from the fact that the inflow that presents itself needs to be dealt with by the existing bodies. To this end, one could establish certain standards. These standards would determine how many cases a body can cope with given existing staffing levels. The quality of the assistance provided must – in the interest of the client – always be assured. Nobody must be allowed to fall by the wayside. For this reason, determining an average caseload standard may be useful. This average caseload could be calculated and weighted for a combination of typical characteristics. As such, it would provide a guarantee for the quality of the social work performed. Such a standard could be useful at different levels. At central allocation level, it may be used to determine the required workforce and (re)distribute it over the regional offices. These local bodies could in turn use it internally to distribute the work fairly over their staff, to establish priorities, and to inform higher management about the relation between input, performance and quality.

How should such a standard be determined? One could follow a deductive method whereby, starting from a certain case typology, the required activities and time investment are determined by experts, the authorities and fieldworkers. However, this would be a time-consuming method, and it may also prove too abstract. We prefer an inductive method on the basis of the shortcomings identified by the professionals, whereby one could set a standard that is not 'absolute' but merely temporary. If, for example, the nature of the case changes or expectations with regard to output become greater, or the statutory working hours are modified, then the standard could be reconsidered. In concrete terms, we have taken two approaches.

In the present situation, social workers at the SYAC are, on average, responsible for dealing with 75 cases, compared to 66 cases for workers at the SSJC. In both instances, measurements of the subjective and the objective workload have shown the number of cases to be too high. The average number of cases per social worker therefore needs to be reduced. The question remains: by how many cases?

As we have already pointed out, the time registration in our survey revealed that social workers perform more than the required hours of work. If one wants to attain a reasonable distribution of staff over the regions, taking into account the caseload at the regional bodies and the 38-hour working week, then the workforce will need to be increased by 15.3% in the SYAC and by 21.7% in the SSJC. According to this calculation, the number of cases dealt with by the SYAC will decline from 75 to 62, while the social service of the juvenile court will see its caseload diminish from 66 to some 53 cases.

One could also set a standard by considering the nature of the cases and the average time spent on the activities involved. The standard for the SYAC turns out to be 60 cases per social worker, compared to 46 cases for the SSJC.

It is up to the higher authorities to decide which is the most appropriate standard to implement, if need be in the long-run.

Managing the Process

Managing the care process is all about controlling the activities that the social workers perform. It speaks for itself that determining a caseload will enhance one's control over these activities. Yet, there are alternatives, such as increasing the level of professionalism by reducing the number of non case-related activities and saving time by modernizing the administration.

Increasing the level of professionalism Within the services of the SYAC and the SSJC, there is very little personal contact with the youngsters concerned. One tends to talk about the youngsters (with their parents among other people) without actually involving them directly. Also, the number of personal shifts and moves of youngsters around the country looking for places to stay is high. Furthermore, it emerged during our survey that much paper work was duplicated. Again, this is an area for improvement. However, it is important that the quality of the service rendered should always be assured. In other words, it is not a matter of rationing the available means, but of (re)distributing the means more rationally. Controlling the activities will depend on the type of case involved. It is not self-evident, however, how social workers should divide their time between different activities. This is a matter for the different players (clients, social workers, heads) to discuss.

Professional expertise can however be furthered by specializing on certain problems (e.g., mental health, migrants, drugs) in a setting wherein all workers remain within a general caseload but can specialize into such a sub-field.

Administrative modernization Social workers complain about the fact that certain work needs to be performed twice. To an extent, this could be avoided by closer co-operation between the different bodies involved in special youth care system.

By making more use of information technology (including e-mail), information could be disseminated more quickly and more efficiently. It goes without saying, though, that the privacy of the client must always be respected. The time saved in this manner could then be devoted to other, more client-oriented activities, such as face-to-face contact with the youngsters involved.

Heads may also play a significant role in controlling the inflow by deciding which cases fall within the responsibility of the service and which cases ought to be referred to other bodies in the social services.

Improving the general perception of work Our research results show that the occurrence of burnout is due to organizational factors as well as to the relationships between colleagues. Increasing the resilience of staff, enhancing their work satisfaction and improving the atmosphere in the workplace will all contribute towards reducing the incidence of burnout. It will, in other words, be necessary to take account of psychological factors that are in turn affected by how the work is organized and by the type of management. By making the work more professional e.g. putting less time and energy into administration and more into fewer cases, with expertise brought in as necessary, work satisfaction can rise. A strong local leadership at work could have a positive impact on the incidence of burnout by enhancing collegiality. Managers could be trained to this end and so putting more energy into personnel affairs than they used to do. They were in fact very case and paperwork oriented. Eliminating burnout will enhance the quality of the service rendered and it will lead to higher achievements at the output side. It speaks for itself that various system measures at the central level could have a positive effect on these input and processing tools.

Conclusion

First and foremost, our empirical research in the special youth assistance sector has demonstrated quite clearly that analyzing such social services from the perspective of a production system can be very useful. We were, after all, able to ascertain that there is a great deal of variation in terms of the inflow, that there is a considerable (yet not proportional) distribution of the workload over the regional bodies, that cases can differ considerably in terms of the required time investment, and that the production processes – be it professional, administrative, or with regard to mobility – can be seriously disrupted. Moreover, it emerged that there is a discrepancy between the subjective perception of work and the objective working conditions.

The production system perspective would appear to be useful for outlining and adapting policy, both at the central allocation level – cf. the distribution of personnel, assuring that means are distributed fairly – and at local level – cf. positioning within the social services. Within the bodies involved, there is certainly a need for a human resources policy. These distinct, yet mutually affecting policy measures may allow professional social workers to perform their tasks more adequately and in more favourable conditions than when the most essential work is made uncontrollable by an unchecked inflow, an excessive workload and irrelevant activities. It speaks for itself that such change would also be to the benefit of the clients because in such a controlled care system each case can be allowed the time and the effort it deserves. Such a new approach would, however, require regular reassessment of the system (which is in fact an advantage rather than a drawback).

Objectifying and making controllable the underlying production system is an approach that can of course be applied much more broadly than in the sector studied in this particular instance, perhaps even in all easily accessible social services.

Note

1. In the research 19 SYACs and 14 SSJCs participated.

References

Breda, J., & Crets, S. (2000). Managing the quality paradox. Producing welfare services in changing social contexts. *International Social Work, 44*, (1), 43-55.
Breda, J., Crets, S., & Van Raemdonck, I. (1995). *Werken in de hulpverlening. Tijdsbesteding en arbeidsbelasting van maatschappelijk werkers*. Leuven: Acco.
Breda, J., & Verlinden, E. (2000). *Tijdsbesteding en werkbelasting bij de Comités voor Bijzondere Jeugdbijstand en de Sociale Diensten van de jeugdrechtbanken in de Vlaamse Gemeenschap*. Antwerpen: UFSIA.
Hulshof, A.H., & Hulshof, M. (1980). Beheerssystemen in de quartaire sector. *Beleid en Maatschappij, 9*, 250-260.
Kusterman, I., & Vermeire, M. (1995). *Verbeteren van arbeidskwaliteit door organisatieontwikkeling: Strategieën, methoden en praktijkvoorbeelden voor gezondheids- en welzijnswerkers*. Leuven/Apeldoorn: Garant Publishers.
Nota, P.H., Van der Schaft, R.A., & Van Yperen, T.A. (1997). *Toegang tot de jeugdzorg: Functies en systeemeisen*. The Hague/Rijswijk: Minister of Health, Welfare and Sport.

PART III

PARTICIPATION

Chapter 11

The Involvement of Families in Planning and Delivering Care

Mona Sandbæk

Introduction

It is becoming increasingly popular to talk about parents as partners. Empowerment and focusing on competence are other commonly used expressions. There is still reason to question if this is what really happens. Do professionals or informal helpers regard or treat parents as partners when their children have problems? This chapter will discuss the parents' role in the planning and delivery of care when their children are being looked after. Why and how should parents be involved in this process? The role of research in guiding the front line workers, as well as the role of epistemology in terms of professionals' views upon knowledge, will be debated.

Reasons for Involving Parents in the Planning and Delivering of Care

It is reasonable to expect that when the welfare state, represented by the child welfare services,[1] takes a child into care, the child will be provided with stable and nurturing environments. There is also reason to expect some unfortunate exceptions, but basically children in care should get a nurturing and stable home where they can stay, at least until a planned return to their parents is carried out. Empirical research has shown that this is indeed not always the case. A large number of children placed in foster care are exposed to unplanned and for them unwanted breaks (Smith, Gollop & Taylor, 1998). Children placed in institutions also move around quite a bit before a large proportion of them return home. Without going into details about numbers, some figures will be used to indicate the situation. Foster home breakdowns seem to involve 10 per cent for children placed before they were ten, 15-50 per cent for children of older age

(Kagan & Reid, 1986; Thoburn & Rowe, 1988). When it comes to placements in institutions Millham, Bullock, Hosie and Haak (1986) followed 450 children who came into care in five local authorities in England and Wales. After two years 170 children were still in care and 67 of them had experienced breakdowns. Including hasty transfers, the number of breakdowns was 107. The 170 children had experienced 505 different placements. After five years 78 per cent of the children had returned to family or relatives.

Figures will be different among countries, and can surely be debated and interpreted differently also within each country. There is, however, a general agreement that lack of stability is a fact of life for too many children in care. So, one reason why parents should be involved in planning and delivering care, is that they represent stability and continuity in the majority of the children's lives. Feeling they are in charge or at least involved in the whole process, may make it easier for the parents to keep up the contact with the child. The following quote illustrates this point: 'It may be true that some children in care reluctantly go back to relatives because they have nobody else. Nevertheless, whether professionals like it or not, almost all children in care will eventually be restored to their family and our perspectives and interventions need to accommodate that fact'. (Bullock, Little & Millham, 1993, p. 67).

Are Parents Treated as Partners?

As mentioned there is a trend towards talking about parents as partners, and recognising their legal rights. But in practice there is room for judgement, and there are many dilemmas related to when and how parents should be involved in the planning and delivery of care. When parents are asked in various kinds of research, quite a number report that they do not feel treated as partners, on the contrary, they feel excluded and rendered suspect (Cleaver & Freeman, 1995; Thoburn, Lewis & Shemmings, 1995). There seems to be a discrepancy between the professional rhetoric of treating parents as partners and the parents' own experiences. A factor contributing to this problem may be the way professionals' views on parents are frequently reflected in research. There is reason to say that professional explanations – with a few exceptions – place a major responsibility for children's problems upon their parents, and for parents, read mothers (Kristinsdottir, 1991; Parton, Thorpe & Wattam, 1997). When it comes to anti-social behaviour and delinquency, for example, the connections are expressed rather explicitly as can be seen from these quotes.

'Delinquency is statistically associated with a long list of psychosocial risk factors. These span broken homes, single-parent families, teenage parents, family discord, abuse or neglect, coercive parenting, lack of supervision, family criminality, poverty, large family size, delinquent peer groups, poor schooling, and living in a socially disorganised area.' (Rutter et al., 1998).

'A Norwegian study focusing on teachers' views upon the parents' role when the children were receiving special education, found that to a large degree parents were seen as part of their children's problems, either as a cause to their problems or as an obstacle to solving them.' (Fylling & Sandvin, 1999).

'Only a few decades ago it was still common within psychiatry to talk about mothers who provoked schizophrenia in their children.' (Gerdner, 1999).

When parents are portrayed like this in research, why should practitioners treat them as partners? These were just a few examples, and there are some alternative professional approaches where the attention is also drawn to other factors than the parents, but these examples still represent common trends. There is no reason to understate the fact that quite a number of children are taken into care because of their parents' problems. But the rather one-sided focus on parental shortcomings may prevent social workers from looking upon parents as partners – and thus contribute to a practice where they are excluded rather than included. There is a challenge for research to provide a more balanced picture of the parents; with their strengths and efforts to help their children as well as their shortcomings.

The Parents' Efforts to Help their Children

An alternative to blaming the parents, is to focus on their activities and efforts to find solutions and to help their children. Newer literature emphasizes the importance of help-seeking and agency. Uehara and Takeuchi (1998) underline that in recent decades, research on illness and help-seeking has moved away from static, psychological models of medical decision-making toward those that conceptualize help-seeking as a dynamic and inextricably social phenomenon. People change the course and outcome of illness and help-seeking through, for example, the purposeful resolution to solve problems, to reconstruct the meaning of life experiences, and to observe and learn from the past in order to shape the future (Thoits, 1995). The concept of 'agency' tries to grasp the intentions, reflections and efforts of people when they are facing problems (Emirbayer & Mische, 1998). Parents are expected to take care of their children, and there is reason to believe that the concept is relevant also for parents when their children have problems. To what degree or in what ways does agency manifest itself in parents' actions when their children are clients?

In the study, 'Children as clients',[2] parents from 60 families were interviewed twice about various aspects of their and their child's contact with child welfare and protection, school counselling and child psychiatric clinic. The interview also covered the efforts that the parents made to help their children. A few examples will be used in order to highlight parents' efforts to try to sort out the problems (Sandbæk, 1999a, 2000).

- *Informal as well as formal initiatives*
  The parents were the ones who most frequently contacted the child welfare and protective services. They made half of the requests to the school counselling and child psychiatry and one third of the requests to the child welfare services – which is pretty much in accordance with official statistics (NOS, 1997). Other studies have also underlined the parents', particularly the mothers', efforts to find solutions to their child's problems. Farmer and Owen (1998) found that the mothers were actively involved in seeking help from child protection agencies. They were the single largest group to initiate actions that led to a child protection referral. This occurred in 27 per cent of the cases in their study. Similar results were found in a study where child sexual abuse referrals were examined (Sharland et al, 1996).
- *Acknowledging problems*
  The researchers had no other source of information about the families than what the families told them – but they got to know a lot about the families' problems during the course of the interviews – the children's problems as well as the parents'. The services might have defined the problems in a different way than the parents, but the parents certainly did not deny the existence of problems. The parents did not, however, see any contradiction between having problems themselves – and wanting to help their child at the same time.
- *Parents as co-ordinators*
  When asked to participate in the research project 'Children as clients', one mother replied: *Do you think I have time to talk to a researcher as well? We saw the child welfare officer yesterday, tomorrow we'll meet the school counsellor and next week we have an appointment at the child psychiatric clinic. And I actually have a job and another child.* Her reply illustrated the common experience of having to relate to

several services. Many parents – particularly mothers – run from one office and one service to another. Quite often they were the only ones who attended all the meetings. They filled in the gaps when one case manager quit, waiting for a new one to turn up, they accompanied the children to new services informing them about what the latter services meant, et cetera. There were of course examples of efficient service co-ordination, an experience the parents really appreciated, but such incidents were still more the exceptions than the rule. Thus, the lack of formal co-operation quite often placed the parents into a demanding role as co-ordinators and they were certainly those who represented continuity. There is reason to worry about the children whose parents were not able to handle this task.

- *Efforts to integrate the children*
From the parents point of view it was a problem that professionals could so easily say 'Sorry – we have nothing more to offer!' or 'You broke the rules!' and the adolescents were returned home. Again and again some parents had to make new efforts to help the child establish roots in society – and to take them back when they were expelled from institutions or foster homes or for other reasons had to leave. For some of the adolescents there seemed to be a pattern where the parents kept trying to get the child back into society only to be turned away by various professional institutions. Such examples seem to indicate that professionals have their share in marginalizing and stigmatizing children.

It is important to emphasize that not all parents made all of these efforts, but most of them were involved in at least one of these kinds of activities in order to help their children. Combining an acknowledgement of the families' efforts to help their children with an acceptance of break-downs in professional placements, draws attention to the importance of involving the parents in the placements of their children. This leads to the necessity of keeping up the contact with parents, and an important way to secure such a contact, is to involve the parents, and the children, in all steps of the care process. In addition to valuing the effort the parents make to help their children, the following questions should be discussed with the parents:

- What kind of placements do you think would work for your child?
- How can we help you keep in touch with your child?
- How can we help you sort out the problems that caused the placement?

What is Considered to Be Valid Knowledge?

Parents whose children are in need or are being looked after, are often portrayed as perpetrators. When they are described in terms of their efforts to help their children, a different image occurs. A question that often comes up is whether a description like the one given here is idealizing the parents. There is of course a danger of doing that. But arguing for treating parents as partners does not mean there will not be exceptions. There will certainly be some people who can fill a very small part of a partnership model. But exceptions should not rule the practice. Transactional analyses show that parents are often protective factors and sometimes a risk factor in their children's lives. But there is no doubt that they are a factor of importance. Further, treating parents as partners does not equal treating them as customers; that a worker just obeys the parents' 'orders'. Acting like that would deprive parents of the professionals' judgement and knowledge. It is more about negotiating or securing that all parties have their points of views considered – and there should be concrete reasons to turn down the parents' suggestions about what needs to be done in order to improve the situation.

An important point is, what kind of knowledge and whose knowledge are considered to be valid. It has been argued that social work is highly influenced by a scientific model of knowledge, more precisely a positivist view that rests on the assumption that reality can be measured, tested, and objectively verified. Problems are identifiable, measurable entities susceptible to investigation and solutions. In this model the professionals have the solutions (Weick, 1992). By maintaining a positivist method as the supreme vehicle for gaining legitimate knowledge, a broad category of knowledge is inevitably discounted. What Wilhelm Dilthey (quoted in Weick, 1992) called 'lived experience' sinks under the weight of the scientific superstructure.

If, however, the notion of problem is viewed from a constructivist perspective, the identification of problems reflects not only what one is looking at, but also who is doing the looking. This perspective assumes that all perceptions are mediated by culture, language and meaning and that human experience reflects a dynamic interplay between events and the meanings we attach to them. Human beings constantly shape their reality and negotiate its meanings as a social process. Again; what are seen as problems and as solutions depend upon who is doing the thinking or looking (Gergen, 1981; Weick, 1992). The difference may be summed up in a rather simple way by saying that within a positivist tradition there is a hierarchical view about knowledge; scientific and professional knowledge, are situated at the top; possessing the right solution. Within a constructivist tradition, there is a horizontal view about knowledge; there are different kinds of knowledge, and people's own knowledge and professional knowledge will be more equal. The latter position may give workers more incitement to ask for the parents' own opinions and experiences. Epistemology in terms of professional views about knowledge, may therefore play an important role in developing practices for listening to parents' and children's own experiences and points of views.

Involving Children and Parents in Decision-making

In order to give children and parents real influence over what is happening, there may be a need to change the decision-making procedures. Eriksen and Skivenes (1998) have argued for such new arrangements in the following way:

- The best interests of the child is supposed to be the guideline for decisions about placements of children. However, this is a normative concept – and there will rarely be an agreed upon view about what actually constitutes 'the best interests of the child'.
- Professional knowledge does also not provide clear solutions – on most important professional issues there is considerable debate.
- Since the right answers cannot be found either in the law or in professional knowledge, the decision-making procedures are of importance and should ensure that all parties are heard and able to participate in negotiating the final decision.

They suggest establishing decision-making procedures where all parties are included by instituting deliberative organs or meeting places where free exchange of experiences and opinions should take place. They argue that today's formal organs, are favouring professionals and make it difficult for the private parties to participate on equal terms. Steps must be taken to neutralize power and competence inequalities (Eriksen & Skivenes, 1998). No models will eliminate differences of opinions or prevent conflicts, but how decisions are handled and how the processes are guided might be of importance. If parents feel they are in charge, it may be easier for them to keep up contact with their children while they are in care.

Creating Curiosity

Arnkil and Eriksson (1994) claim that the good work done in social work organizations is hidden behind two dysfunctional sets of practices. Firstly, they claim that service delivery follows a deficiency principle. Experts examine and find problems and deficiency in clients and their systems rather than their resources and competencies. This is easily replicated by research that seeks and finds mainly faults and defects in the activity of professional helpers. This produces two layers of deficiency finding: service professionals find deficiency in the clients and researchers blame them for doing so. Both follow the same principle. The result is that the object stays less competent than the observer. Arnkil and Eriksson (1994) argue that social workers as well as researchers could wear buttons: 'Your defects. My competence!'.

Secondly, the deficiency principle can lead to a practice of seeking competence for problem solving outside the immediate context. If the client and her social network is seen as defective, lacking the necessary resources in one way or the other, resources have to be found elsewhere. They have to be 'imported' and a quest for external resources and a 'more competent resolver' begins. This can be seen in referrals for other professionals, or in acts of intensifying control. There is nothing problematic in calling for extra help per se. The service system is sectorized and specialized and offers specialized resources. However, calling in extra help does become a problem if it replaces curiosity in the resources of the clients and their networks.

As consultants and researchers Arnkil and Eriksson (1994) try not to accept the role as the more competent in problem solving. If they do, they would reproduce the cycle 'Your defects, our competence'. Instead they try to support curiosity and experiments. Their recommendations to organizations are to support reflexive structures and curiosity. They assume that increasing space for subjective curiosity in the teams and emerging openness for a variety of views and hypothesis among the professionals, will effect the client-team relationship. If research stimulates professionals to get a grip of their own subjectivity, this may be replicated in the relationship of professionals with their clients. They anticipate that the clients thus have increased chances to raise curiosity in the teams and to nourish their own curiosity about their own alternatives of action. They argue that providing reflexive space and rooms for alternatives, will make alternatives of action multiply. The approaches chosen by researchers play an important role in promoting such a practice.

Concluding Remarks

Understanding and respecting the identity and agency of parents as well as children are of vital importance. Children have not been the topic of this chapter, but are of course of at least equal importance. Results from interviews with children in the study 'Children as clients' have been discussed in other articles (Sandbæk, 1998; 1999a; 1999b). Combining an acknowledgement of the families as partners with an acceptance of professional shortcomings and limitations might create a more equal and thus fruitful relationship between professionals and the families. This is not only a matter of altering or improving the practice of the front-line workers. It is just as much about the role of research and production of theory. There is a gap between these parents' efforts and responsibilities and the research literature focusing mainly on them as part of the problem. There is a need to develop alternative theoretical constructions regarding why problems occur as well as how to approach them. The following quote from an article by Fiona Williams, who also discusses agency and structure, sum up the points made in this chapter: 'Whatever discourse we work with, we need to be able to develop conceptual frameworks which allow us to move away from seeing people as passive beneficiaries of state and professional intervention, or as inhabitants of fixed social categories. Instead we need to be able to develop ways of researching the complexities of identity and agency but without losing sight of the social relations of power and the broader patterns of inequality through which identity and agency are inscribed' (Williams, 1998, p. 13).

Notes

1. In this context child welfare services are used to cover both preventive and protective interventions, or to use the English term, 'children in need' as well as 'children looked after'.
2. The 60 families, representing approximately 44 per cent of the client population in the community where the study was carried out, consented to participate in the interviews (Sandbæk, 1999a, 2000). In this contribution the children from the three services will be treated as one category – because there were no major differences between them on the phenomenon that will be discussed here. The three services will be named Child welfare and protection services. As is common in client samples, there was an overrepresentation of children from broken homes, and with out of home placements. 26 of these 60 parents consented to interviews with their children. Two children refused, leaving a sample of 24 children. The parents were restrictive in allowing access to their children, mainly because they did not want them to be confronted with questions related to their problems or contacts with the child welfare services.

References

Arnkil, E., & Eriksson, E. (1994). Deficiencies, resources and curiosity. In S. Hänninen (Ed.), *Silence, Discourse and Deprivation* (pp. 134-147). Helsingfors: Stakes Research Reports 43.

Bullock, R., Little, M., & Millham, S. (1993). *Going Home. The Return of Children Separated from their Families*. Aldershot: Dartmouth.

Cleaver, H., & Freeman, P. (1995) *Parental Perspectives in Cases of Suspected Child Abuse*. London: HMSO.

Emirbayer, M., & Mische, A. (1998). What is agency? *American Journal of Sociology, 103*, 4, 962-1023.

Eriksen, E.O., & Skivenes, M. (1998). Om å fatte riktige beslutninger i barnevernet. *Tidsskrift for Samfunnsforskning, 39*, 3, 352-379.

Farmer, E., & Owen, M. (1998). Gender and the Child Protection Process. *British Journal of Social Work, 28*, 545-564.

Fylling, I., & Sandvin, J.T. (1999). The Role of Parents in Special Education: The notion of Partnership Revised. *European Journal of Special Needs Education, 14*, 2, 144-157.

Gerdner, A. (1999). Problem kring begrepet 'medberoende'. *Socionomen, 13*, 4, 53-63.

Gergen, K.J. (1990). Therapeutic Professions and the Diffusions of Deficit. *Journal of Mind and Behavior, 11*, 3/4, 353-368.

Kagan, M.R., & Reid, J.W. (1986). Critical factors in the adoption of emotionally disturbed youths. *Child Welfare, XLV*, 1, 63-73.

Kristinsdottir, G. (1991). *Child Welfare and Professionalization*. Umeå: Umeå Universitets Tryckeri.

Millham, S., Bullock, R., Hosie, K., & Haak, M. (1986). *Lost in Care. The Problems of Maintaining Links between Children in Care and their Families*. Aldershot: Gower.

NOS (1997). *Official Statistics of Norway. Social Statistics 1997*. Oslo: Central Bureau of Statistics.

Parton, N., Thorpe, D., & Wattam, C. (1997). *Child Protection. Risk and the Moral Order*. London: Macmillan Press.

Patterson, G.R., DeBaryshe, B.D., & Ramsey, E. (1989). A Development Perspective on Antisocial Behavior. *American Psychologist, 44*, 2, 329-335.

Rutter, M., Giller, H., & Hagell, A. (1998). *Antisocial Behaviour by Young People*. Cambridge: Cambridge University Press.

Sandbæk, M. (1998). Competence and Risk factors in Norwegian Client and Non-client Children. *Childhood, 5* (4), 421-436.

Sandbæk, M. (1999a). Children with Problems: Focusing on Everyday Life. *Children & Society, 13*, 106-118.

Sandbæk, M. (1999b). Adult Images of Childhood and Research on Client Children. *International Journal of Social Research Methodology, 2*, 3, 191-202.

Sandbæk, M. (2000). Foreldres vurdering av hjelpetjenester for barn. *Tidsskrift for Velferdsforskning, 3*, 1, 31-44.

Sharland, E., Jones, D., Aldgate, J., Seal, H., & Croucher, M. (1996). *Professional Intervention in Child Sexual Abuse*. London: HMSO.

Smith, A., Gollop, M., & Taylor, N. (1998). *Children's Voices in Foster or Kinship Care: Knowledge, understanding and participation*. Paper presented at the Twelfth International Congress on Child Abuse and Neglect. Auckland: New Zealand.

Thoburn, J., Lewis, A., & Shemmings, D. (1995). *Paternalism or Partnership? Family Involvement in the Child Protection Process*. London: HMSO.

Thoburn, J., & Rowe, J. (1988). A Snapshot of Permanent Family Placement. *Adoption & Fostering, 12*, 3, 29-34.
Thoits, P.A. (1995). Stress, coping and social support processes. *Journal of Health and Social Behavior, 36* (extra issue), 53-79.
Uehara, E.S., & Takeuchi, D. (1998). *Understanding the Dynamics of Illness and Help-Seeking: Event-structure Analysis and a Cambodian American Narrative of 'Spirit Invasion'*. Seattle (WA): University of Washington/University of California.
Weick, A. (1992). Building a Strengths Perspective for Social Work. In D. Saleebey (Ed.), *The Strengths Perspective in Social Work Practice* (pp. 18-26). New York: Longman.
Williams, F. (1998). Agency and Structure Revisited: Rethinking Poverty and Social Exclusion. In M. Barry & C. Hallet (Eds.), *Social Exclusion and Social Work. Issues of Theory, Policy and Practice* (pp. 13-25). London: Russel House Publishing.

Chapter 12

Participation by Children in Care Planning: Research and Experiences in the United Kingdom

Ruth Sinclair

Introduction

When we think about the involvement of children in planning their care it is useful to start with the UN Convention on the Rights of the Child, adopted in 1989 and now ratified by almost all countries. The Convention establishes the principles and the standards that nation states should seek to achieve in respect of the protection, participation and provision of services to children. Article 12 of the Convention requires that: 'States Parties shall assure to the child who is capable of forming his or her own views the right to express those views freely in all matters affecting the child, the views of the child being given due weight in accordance with the age and maturity of the child' (Article 12, UN Convention on the Rights of the Child 1989).

Regarding participation, many countries have now incorporated these principles into their national legislation. For example, since the implementation of the Children Act in England in 1991 there has been a legal requirement to draw up *care plans* for children in public care (termed 'children looked after') and for these plans to be reviewed regularly. Further, the Children Act states that: 'Before making any decision with respect to a child ... a local authority shall, so far as is reasonable and/or practicable, ascertain the wishes and feelings of the child' (Children Act 1989, S.22 [5][a]).

The purpose of this chapter is to report on how that requirement is being put into practice in England, drawing on research by the author and others (Grimshaw & Sinclair, 1997). Given that similar legislative requirements pertain in many countries these findings will however have wider relevance.

The Children Act 1989

This contribution starts with a brief introduction to the Children Act, the main legal framework relating to the care of children in England and Wales which was passed in 1989, but which was implemented in late 1991.

The Children Act has been described as the most comprehensive and far-reaching piece of child care legislation enacted in England. Moreover the Act has to be viewed as more than the details of the statute. It was built upon clearly articulated principles and is accompanied by very detailed Regulations and Guidance.

The Regulation and Guidance is particularly detailed – some would say prescriptive – in respects of planning and reviewing; setting out both the content and manner in which care plans shall be drawn up and regularly reviewed. For example, care plans have to be confirmed at a first Review held no more than four weeks after a child becomes looked after, the second at three months and thereafter at least every six months (Sinclair & Grimshaw, 1995).

This Regulation and Guidance is firmly based on the findings from a body of research on social work decisions in child care carried out in the 1980s and which helped establish a set of principles underpinning good practice in child care planning (DHSS, 1985). These can be summarized as:

- open and shared decision-making;
- clear, specific and written decisions;
- involving children and young people;
- working in partnership with parents;
- planning to meet the full range of a child's needs;
- planning with other agencies, especially health and education.

The Children Act Guidance reflects the view that if decision-making is to be open and shared, if it is to be accountable and multi-agency, then the best mechanism to ensure this happens is a *participatory meeting*. In practice, children's involvement in care planning is most often translated as their attendance at review meetings. Obviously this is one opportunity for involving children but it does raise the wider question: what is meant by participation in care planning?

What is Meant by Participation?

It has often been said that planning is a process and indeed the Children Act Guidance says there are four aspects to planning: inquiry, consultation, assessment and decision-making.

Similarly it is possible to see participation as a process. Children can only be actively or purposefully involved at, say, the decision-making stage, if they are involved both before and after that. So participation will be more effective if children are involved at several stages in the process. We can think of the process as having four parts:

Being informed about the process People cannot be active participants in a process if they do not know about or if they do not understand that process. The first step to empowering children is to keep them informed about the planning process, and in ways they find helpful.

Consulted about their views Assessments of children and families are based on a range of information. These assessments must be child centred. That means not only that the child is always kept in focus, but that the child's perspective is included and that someone purposively seeks out, in an appropriate manner, the views, including the wishes and feelings, of the child.

Attend meetings that discuss their care When professionals come together to discuss a case and to make decisions, their discussions and their decisions are likely to be better informed, to be more realistic, and more likely to be implemented, if all those concerned are present. While this is easy to say, it is not always easy to do in a way that is effective and meets everyone's needs.

Receive written record of decisions Having a written record of decisions increases a sense of ownership of decisions and awareness of the part that every one has to play in ensuring the decisions are fulfilled. Having a copy of the decisions (in an appropriate format) is also a very important tool in enabling children and families to hold agencies to account and to monitor subsequent actions to implement decisions.

Evidence of Participation in the Planning Process

All of these activities outlined above are expected under the Children Act

1989. However the evidence from our research on the implementation of this part of the Act suggests a patchy response, at least in the first few years. While there have been some significant and positive changes in practice in some areas, this is not apparent in all aspects. Set out below is the evidence from the NCB research and each of these stages of the process (Grimshaw & Sinclair, 1997; Sinclair & Grimshaw, 1995). First some background to the research.

This three year study, funded by the Department of Health, had four main components:

- a national survey of all local authorities in England and Wales concerning the development of local policy, procedure and paperwork in relation to the planning and reviewing system;
- a detailed examination of the circumstances and decision-making processes in respect of 180 children in care in three local authorities;
- attendance at planning and reviewing meetings in respect of 48 of these children;
- interviews with participants at these meetings, including children and young people.

A selection of findings will be presented here.

Information In our study we found very few examples where children were given information about the planning process. This should be a relatively easy and effective step in making participation more effective, yet it is done rarely.

Consultation There is evidence that children were consulted before the review meetings, as shown in Table 12.1 below.

Table 12.1   Consultations with children (N=180)

Age of child	Proportion consulted
Under 5	9
5–10	56
11–15	88
15+	91
All children	65

This demonstrates a high level of consultation was happening, increasing with the age of the child. But what about the quality of the consultation? We also assessed this using a range of indicators. The results suggested that the consultations were limited in their depth and range: for example in the extent to which they presented the independent voice of the child by using the child's own words, rather than someone else's summary of a child's views. They were also limited in the range of issues discussed. For example, consultations on education might discuss the school which the child would attend, but recorded little about the child's general views on schooling, on achievement, on bullying and so on.

Some authorities now use consultation forms to help children express their views and raise issues of importance to them. Our evidence suggests that consultation can be helped by the use of forms, but only under two conditions: that the forms are well designed and that children are facilitated and encouraged in completing them. There is little chance of getting a meaningful response by simply sending a child a form and asking him or her to complete it.

Attendance at meeting In England this is seen as a key part in participatory child care planning and undoubtedly there have been major changes in this aspect of practice in recent years. Our research suggests a high level of attendance, especially by older children and young people – see Table 12.2 below.

Table 12.2   Children's attendance at Review Meetings (N=180)

Age of child	Proportion attending
Under 5	9
5–10	30
11–15	80
15+	97
All children	55

Of course attendance at meetings is not to be confused with active participation and later in this chapter young people's experience of these meetings will be discussed. Despite the overall high proportion attending, this is likely to be less true for younger children or for children who are disabled (Morris, 1998; Thomas, 2000).

Receipt of a record of decision We found very little evidence that children were given a record of decisions, or encouraged to keep and use these in their dialogue with their social workers or the agency.

Children and Young People's Experience of Meetings

In reporting children's experience of participation this contribution draws on our own research on children's attendance at review meetings but also research on children's participation in other forms of care planning, child protection case conferences and Family Group Conferences (Baldry & Kemmis, 1998; Horgan & Sinclair, 1997; Lupton & Nixon, 1999; Lupton & Stevens, 1998; Shemmings, 1996; Sinclair, 1998; Thomas & O'Kane, 1999).

Of course the experiences of young people will vary, but in pooling the research findings from several studies it is clear that a very similar story is being unfolded. Two general points stand out. First, for most young people, whatever their views about the experience, they take seriously their right to be involved in decisions that affect them, hence the high levels of attendance at meetings which was noted earlier. Second, although children recognized the importance of their attendance at meetings, overwhelmingly they find it an uncomfortable, and often meaningless, experience.

In listening to what young people have said about their experience of meetings some clear themes emerge. Each of these is illustrated with quotations from children and young people.

Lack of preparation for the meeting
> They could have told me more what is actually going to happen there.
> I never know what is going to be discussed.
> When the meetings are about to start they give you this paper ... you're not ready for it ... You don't have time to think about what you are going to do in there. They say: "Is it OK? Is it OK?". And I go: "Yeah that's fine."

Meetings are too large
(In our research the mean size of meetings was 6.2 people, with some as large as 13 attenders.)
> They ask you if you mind if another person comes. But you're already scared when the manager and staff are there and the more people you get scared. You get shy and try not to make a mistake in what you are saying.

You don't really want to sit and talk to a whole room about your problems, though, do you?

I didn't get a chance to say anything because everyone was talking.

Not able to talk freely

There were people there I couldn't speak in front of.

I find it difficult to talk about some things as my foster parents are always there. So I think a lot of things are missed out and they don't find out about them.

I do feel that people listen to me but I don't really feel as if I can say what really goes on.

How can I speak ... they are talking about my family ... I can't talk about what I want with them there.

Being put in the spot light

It's like, what has she been doing – not what has the family unit being doing.

They come into a review and come out with all these questions – you're not sure what to say, afterwards you think – I forgot to say so and so.

Feeling ignored

They talk about you as if you are not there, so you just shut up – and listen without saying a word.

I don't even think we should have reviews. They are the biggest load of rubbish. They talk about you as if you weren't there.

They don't listen to you. They just go by what they want to go by, not what we want.

Repetitious, boring

Its like they're going through a checklist on your CV. "So you're doing this ... Have you got anything to say?" And by the end you're like this ... [mimes sleeping].

The meetings are so boring.

They should have different reviews for different people because most of the questions in the review are totally irrelevant for me.

Lack of trust

We had no one we could actually trust not to go back to our foster parents, or our social workers, people we didn't get on with.

Sometimes you want to hold back, just in case, because they sort of twist your words.

It's like what you're expected to say you say it. It's sort of, like, pressurising you.

Of course it is not all bad. Some young people did have more positive things to say, but this is the overwhelming emphasis of what children tell researchers and indeed tell those from the local agencies who conduct consultation exercises with them.

What comes through from these accounts is the importance that young people attach to reviews. Many young people now report that they are given the opportunity to have their say, but still they do not feel they are listened to or have their views taken into account.

How Can it Be Made Better?

First, there is a need to consider the *style and structure of planning meetings* and ask questions about current practice:

- Do meetings try to do too many things? Is it possible for one meeting to be comprehensive, to be participatory, to monitor practice and to make decisions about the future?
- Are meetings too large? Do all those attending need to be there, or to be there at the same meeting?
- What is the right balance between work/decision-making that needs to be undertaken before a meeting and that which needs to be done in a meeting, bearing in mind the difficulties of really getting to the heart of some matters if several parties are present?

Second, there is a need to think in terms of *processes* rather than events. It seems important not only to see planning as a process, and within this the review process, but most importantly to see participation as a process. This means giving less emphasis to meetings as stand alone events and ensuring positive action in all four stages in the process discussed earlier – relevant information, effective consultation, better preparation and clear, speedy feedback.

Third, we need to address the strongest message that comes from talking to children and young people. That is the need for *proper preparation* of children if they are to be active and empowered participants in decision-making occasions. Children need to know the purpose of meetings, who will be attending, what is going to happen and what will be discussed.

Recent years have seen a growth in materials which address both the principles and practice of effective involvement of children and young people in decision-making (for a research briefing see Sinclair and Franklin, 2000). Many of these have relevance to care planning. However two focus specifically on supporting children and young people to make them feel more empowered within the care planning process. The first, *It's your meeting: A guide to help young people get the most from their review meetings* (Wheal & Sinclair, 1995), is aimed at young people themselves and takes them through the three stages of preparing for a review, attending a review and following up on the review. The second, by Thomas and O'Kane (1999), is aimed at helping staff better support younger children and offers a series of games and exercises.

In Conclusion

Actively involving children is a continuous process facilitated by a participatory culture. Children will only be able to participate in formal processes in a climate that encourages involvement and when they feel empowered. In England local authorities invest significant time and resources on care planning. Acceptance of the principle of participatory planning is now almost total. In practice that means encouraging children to attend planning meetings to discuss their current situation and plan for the future. However there is obviously still work to be done to make the process a meaningful and an effective process for young people. Through research that listens to the voice of children and hears their experiences and their suggestions for improvement we can move in an evidence based way towards changes in practice.

References

Baldry, S., & Kemmis, J. (1998). What is it like to be looked after by a local authority? *British Journal of Social Work, 28,* 129-136.

Department of Health and Social Security [DHSS] (1985). *Social work decisions in child care: Recent research findings and their implications.* London: HMSO.

Grimshaw, R., & Sinclair, R. (1997). *Planning to care: Regulation, procedure and practice under the Children Act 1989.* London: National Children's Bureau.

Horgan, G., & Sinclair, R. (1997). *Planning for children in care in Northern Ireland.* London: National Children's Bureau.

Lupton, C., & Nixon, P. (1999). *Empowering practice? A critical appraisal of the Family Group Conference approach.* Bristol: The Policy Press.

Lupton, C., & Stevens, M. (1998). Planning in partnership? An assessment of process and outcome in UK Family Group Conferences. *International Journal of Child and Family Welfare, 3*, 135-148.

Morris, J. (1998). *Still missing: The experiences of disabled children living away from home*. London: The Who Cares? Trust.

Shemmings, D. (1996). *Involving children in child protection conferences*. Norwich: University of East Anglia Press (Social Work Monographs, 152).

Sinclair, R. (1998). Involving children in planning their care. *Child and Family Social Work, 3*, 137-142.

Sinclair, R., & Franklin, A. (2000). *Quality Projects Research Briefing No. 3: Young people's participation*. Department of Health/Research in Practice/Making Research Count. www.rip.org.uk/openaccess.html.

Sinclair, R., & Grimshaw, R. (1995). *Planning and reviewing under the Children Act: Shaping a framework for practice*. London: National Children's Bureau.

Thomas, N. (2000). *Children, family and the state. Decision making and child participation*. London: Macmillan Press.

Thomas, N., & O'Kane, C. (1999). Children's participation in reviews and planning meetings when they are looked after in middle childhood. *Child and Family Social Work, 4*, 221-230.

Wheal, A., & Sinclair, R. (1995). *It's your meeting. A guide to help young people get the most from their review meetings*. London: National Children's Bureau.

Chapter 13

Early Residential Foster Care: Parental Experiences Concerning Their Co-operation with Professional Workers

Marie-Pierre Mackiewicz

Introduction

This chapter aims to develop an analysis of the experience of parents of very young children who are placed in residential care. The issue to be addressed is: What type of co-operation exists between parents of young children and professional carers throughout this difficult and stressful situation? In order to answer this question, first a reflection will be provided on a number of key concepts like 'respite residential foster care', 'parenthood', and 'collaboration'. Secondly, an analysis will be presented – mainly based on interviews with parents of young children – concerning the experiences with the placement of their child, stressing the elements that concern co-operation between them and professionals.

Key Concepts

In France, residential foster care centres for very young children, in taking over the role of orphanages, are qualified to '... foster day and night, children who can be looked after neither by their parents nor by a foster family' (Decree of January 15th, 1974). The care of children from birth to three years has evolved according to scientific knowledge and according to the ideas of the social work and legal professions.[1] Nowadays, because children are seldom orphans or abandoned, co-operation with the parents has become a crucial issue.

Research has integrated this evolution by proposing an interpretation of the types of care and by developing concepts intended to describe and define them. Thus, the concept of *respite foster care*, proposed in 1986 by

Paul Durning and his team (cf. Durning, 1986, 1991) enables us to distinguish professional intervention from the notion of substitution which was used previously. Respite foster care is therefore defined as a type of '... action which aims to provide the tasks of child-rearing and education usually afforded by the families, developed partially or totally outside the family in a residential setting' (Durning, 1986, p. 102). A recent explanatory model (Mackiewicz, 1998) enables one to connect respite foster care to two other concepts whose definitions are at the centre of present day debates in France: parenthood and co-operation.

The Respite Foster Care Relation

The respite foster care relation is the social relation included in all respite foster systems like boarding schools, family foster care or residential foster systems (Durning, 1995). This relation puts parents, professional foster carers and the children residing in care into contact with each other. One calls *parenthood* the relationship between the parents provided for and the child in residence; *respite foster care* ('fostering') can be used to name the relationship between the professional foster carers and the child; and the concept of *co-operation* indicates the relationship which links parents and professionals (see Figure 13.1).

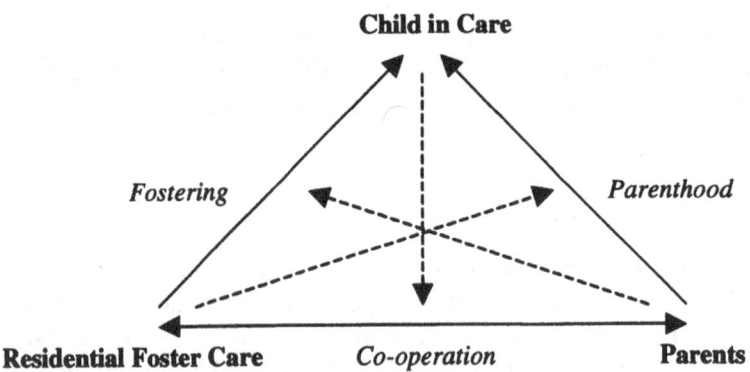

Figure 13.1 Relationships between the three 'parties' concerned

The relationship between respite foster helpers and the family is characterized by an asymmetry in the collaboration between parents and professionals. Indeed, most often parents have to deal with a supervision order: although their parental status and authority is officially still recognized, a child care agency is designated as educational instance in the name of the Child Protection Board.[2]

Any respite foster care relationship is sensitive to the interactions which take place between the three 'parties' involved: the child in care, the parents, and the fostering professionals. For example, the relationships between adults will develop according to the reaction of the child. Moreover, each one is influenced by the perception that the other persons concerned may have of the relationship in which he or she is not directly involved (the dotted lines in Figure 13.1). Thus, the manner in which the parent views the respite foster care professional and the manner in which the professional views parenthood, both influence the professional-child and parent-child interactions. Within this dynamic system, one cannot anticipate the nature of each specific relationship. However one can ask oneself whether there are balanced positions. In the context of early respite foster care breaking points can be seen with a considerable incidence. As a consequence some children are due to be adopted when there is a breaking of the family link.

The Co-operation Relationship

In the course of this chapter the character of the co-operation between parents and professionals will be further explored. The ambiguity of the term 'co-operation' is – at least in French – due to its positive connotations, easily pointed out in its classical opposition to that of the term 'competition' (cf. Deutsch, 1962; Wrightsman, O'Connor & Baker, 1972).

Antagonisms The use of the term 'co-operation' may seem odd in a context where many ingredients are present to potentialize antagonisms between the persons concerned: the emotional *rivalry* inherent to the removal of the child to a different living place; *doubts* concerning the educational and upbringing abilities of the parents; and mutual *stereotypes*. Another negative factor is the *threatening climate* in which 'replaced' parents experience the placement, which engenders, for them, a fear which is difficult to remove (see also Ghesquière, Hellinckx, & Baartman, 1995). The constraints in which they are caught limit their capacity to negotiate and to establish trustful relationships; their adhesion is rendered difficult by differences bearing on values, beliefs and attitudes between them and the professionals.

One should not forget also that the duty of the child protection agency has an important corollary: the assessment of parenthood by respite foster carers. This assessment imposes a transparency of interactions between parents and children and a set of written documents which will be used in order to make decisions. It *hinders the intimacy* necessary for the parenthood relationship and creates *tensions* between foster carers and those who are fostered for, the former watching over the latter.

Legitimations We define co-operation outside a positive connotation, and according to two dimensions (cf. Elias, 1939): the adhesion to legitimations and the taking part in tasks, in our case, of an educational nature. Therefore, the asymmetry of the relationship mentioned above can be examined at two levels: one of legitimations and one of tasks.[3]

Examining the sources of the legitimations to which the two 'educational instances' – parents and professionals – refer, the study leads us to identify four types. The last one, provisionally called 'presence legitimation', is still a matter for reflection.

Table 13.1 Types of legitimation of parents and professionals in the respite foster care relationship

Types of legitimation	Parents fostered for	Professional foster carers
Formal legitimation	Kinship	Appointed
Normative legitimation	Described as deviant	'Judges of normality'
Competence legitimation	Non-specialists	Specialists
Presence legitimation	Sharing of intimacy	Actual care

Formal Formal legitimation stands on established documents proving kinship or appointments, and indicates the importance of official recognition by the parents and court orders. The legitimation by kinship is expressed through genealogical belonging, which the official processes of recognition confirm. In the mental representation it is associated to the idea of natural link and attachment in the long term. The legitimation by appointment on the other hand is associated to an artificial link that might be imposed.

Normative Normative legitimation designates deviant parents according to the evolution of social norms. The foster carers, involved in the assessment process, represent, for their part, an established order of 'normality' (Becker, 1963).

Competency based Parents rely on non-specialist knowledge to bring up their children whereas professionals have been trained to master techniques controlled by the environment in which they are used. The competence legitimation is confirmed by diplomas or linked with experience.

Presence based In the respite foster relationship, the presence of the parents is partial and controlled, whereas that of the professionals is continuous and distributed according to different functions. According to the length of the placement and the rights to visit or to accommodation granted and actually exerted by the parents, either the parents or the professionals can be most often present for longer periods with the children. This presence builds attachment and bonding which the adults have been able to create with the child; it is connected to intimacy issues for the parents and to types of care for the professionals. This is a dimension of paramount importance to the fostering when the child is very young.

Parental Strategies

Based on the agreement of the parents with regard to the legitimation of the intervention and to the competence of the professionals, one can identify principally three different strategies of handling the respite foster care relationship:[4]

- opposition, in which legitimation and competence are refused;
- delegation, in which parents give way to delegation of tasks;
- collaboration, in which parents get involved in the process of participation in a form of co-education (see Durning, 1999, for a review of forms).

It remains to be seen if a 100% collaboration is considered in all cases possible by the foster carers themselves.

According to an empirical study that was done in three residential foster centres for very young children,[5] 11 parents out of a sample of 30 families evolve from opposition or delegation to (some form of) co-operation during the placement. The majority of parents, compelled to admit the intervention but recognizing the competence of the foster carers, prefers to *delegate* to the professionals certain educational tasks. They will admit that the professionals, specialists of child care, can look after their children properly. They feel that there is one risk: that of depreciating the care they provide themselves as parents. The socialization issues are also delegated, probably because they constitute a task which the parents find difficult to cope with, and they will ask for advice. On the other hand, they will often discuss if not refuse the emotional involvement and the moral influence of the foster carers: these are the two spheres where they pay most attention and where they are most critical. In other words, it is on the instrumental level that daily care is delegated while the emotional and moral dimensions should be, according to the parents, reserved to them. This delegation strategy with regard to the foster carers expresses their wish to 'recover' the child and it enables them to avoid conflicts.

Co-operation Granted

Three forms of 'co-operation' thus have been identified in the study:

- an *antagonistic co-operation* (without any possibility for the professionals and the parents to agree concerning the issue of their respective legitimations and without any exchange around the tasks);
- a *neutralized co-operation* (the most frequent, where each one accomplishes his or her tasks without any visible contestation of the legitimations); and
- a *granted co-operation* (where an actual negotiation has a bearing on the legitimations and on the sharing of tasks).

It can be concluded that it *is* possible to achieve a granted co-operation, where fostered-for parents and professional foster carers recognize a mutual legitimation and organize a sharing of educational tasks. In that case we could talk of *co-education*.

What are the conditions which promote this co-education? Even if the placement of their young child remains an intervention which is deemed brutal and disproportionate, the parents are led to admit, if not to wish a helping intervention when they feel that they are not able to afford the necessary protection for their child.

The urgency of solving a problem concerning the child and the interest found in a solidarity among adults sharing a protective function can found a 'common aim' linking parents and foster carers. The necessity of help is often recognized because of parent-child 'distances' or because of the exhaustion of the parents and the very frequent conflicts within the families. The parents discover the mediation role of the professionals of the Child Protection Agency (in France: Protection de l'Enfance). Paradoxically, these professionals are sometimes the only ones to assign the parents a place beside the child, while their own kinship group denies them.

Against the antagonisms of the foster care relationship, the recognition of parental rights (preservation of parental rights) and customers' rights (Laws of 1984 and 1986) are of paramount importance. The recognition of rights encourages parental involvement, even if this may cause periods of conflicts. This is what takes place when the parents are involved in the decision process, formulate demands concerning the education of their child, or criticise the respite foster care. Tensions arise with this involvement, but they are nevertheless appreciated by the foster carers when they can interpret them as the sign of an ability to look after the child and to assume the parental function. Furthermore, the assessment by the fostered-for parent of a help granted could lead to a greater visibility of the foster care. Anyway, one could ask if the professionals are ready to admit that.

Involvement Factors According to Parental Experiences

We have just shown the importance of parental involvement in the co-operation between parents and carers. As a father pointed out, the parents who 'see nothing coming ...' are not sufficiently involved (or adequately involved) to be able 'to recover their child again'. How do the parents mention the factors which hinder or promote their involvement in the placement situation? An analysis of the talks with and documentation concerning parents enables one to identify involvement factors – presented whilst bearing in mind the three relationships which constitute the respite foster relationship, as they have been detailed.

Involvement and Parenthood

For the parents, the placement is a violent event, the source of a great suffering. All the testimonies describe the depressive state which it creates: the absence of the child is felt with much suffering and the short breaks, the visits or the outings, reactivate the pain of separation throughout the placement.[6] The fear of losing the child, reinforced by his or her young age, is more important with the reception at the family's home of an assistant paediatric nurse.

Parenthood is sustained by the active involvement of the child. A strong mutual attachment, of which the professionals can be the witnesses, is one of the main factors of involvement. The parents say that they find in themselves a reverberation of the suffering felt by the child: either an old suffering (they have experienced separations themselves in the course of their childhood) or because they share the actual distress of their placed child.

In the residential centre, the parents attempt to recover a possible intimacy with the child, as a part of the invisible relationship which is necessary for the establishment of a relationship which is neither disturbed by a foreign eye, nor too artificial. This can explain attitudes of staunch reserve: 'When I come, I wish to see only my child', said a mother who tried to avoid any intercourse with the staff or the other parents. Force-feeding, frequent during visits with young children, are probably of the same order and often difficult to bear.

Parenthood is woven into the network of a primary socializing environment (parents, members of the environment, friends). Foster carers often neglect that aspect of the placement. Yet shame causes the severing with the whole of the relationship system: the event of placement is silenced, hidden, minimized. Supportive environments (work, neighbourhood, et cetera) are sometimes absent or distant, sometimes conflicting and sometimes worn out. Nevertheless, the parents may find help with intermediaries, with people close to them who help them to overcome their ordeal.

Involvement and Respite Foster Care

With regard to their young children, several parents fear negative consequences linked to the period of respite foster care: given the young age of the children they would all have preferred to find solutions within the family, even if they had to be monitored. They are somewhat taken aback when they realize that the child feels well in his placement. A father goes so far as to say: 'It mustn't be too good, or else we won't count anymore ...'.

As for the respite foster care, the parents say they feel overcome at having to face professionals who are specialists of childhood and who are present every day. They will nevertheless maintain a presence and at the same time uphold educational demands and establish forms of monitoring or assessment of the respite foster care (for example, they will come outside fixed times, and watch what takes place with the other children without their presence).

Parental expectations toward the professionals concerns a support of parenthood: this can be in terms of mediation for a better social and family integration; of learning for more adequate educational practices; or of a reflection bearing on parental experience.

Involvement and Co-operation

The relationship of parents with the foster carers follows what the parents have experienced previously with other professionals, and it will be in accordance to mental representations and experiences they have had themselves in foster environments. The manner in which the parent felt he or she was treated before the placement and when he or she was taken in, can have repercussions throughout the placement in the relationships one has established with the foster carers, i.e. whether they will be considered as allies or not. Quite often, the relationships with several interlocutors are violent. Parents complain about those who do not warn them or who disappear, and they feel that they are treated in a disrespectful if not offending manner. Some parents admit that they themselves were quite aggressive (threats, shouting, insults) when they were informed the placement would take place.

Parental involvement is expressed as how one claims one's place as a parent in decision processes (see also Sinclair & Grimshaw, 1997): the relationships with the judge and the duration of the placement, for instance, are very important issues. These issues enable the parent to think that the placement is not definitive and that it is possible for them to act so as to 'recover' their child.

After the period of distress, parents often attempt to establish more familiar or co-operative relationships with the professionals (Kohn et al., 1994) to tame a system which they understand only partially, hoping they will be admitted on an emotional register that they wish to master. Next of kin or members of their environment can support them in a better granted form of co-operation: the sister of a grandfather advises him or her to not get over-excited and angry; friends call in at the home during a period of depression; a friend accompanies a mother during her appointments at the Aide Sociale à l'Enfance (Children's Bureau).

Some expectations concern co-operation: the parents are sensitive to a warm, humane welcome; they ask to be informed with regard to their rights and to see that these are respected. Even if they maintain a certain defiance toward professionals, they identify those who could be allies, and they are capable, as we have shown, to modify their strategies.[7]

Conclusion

To conclude, this contribution explored the experiences of parents telling about their suffering, their possible involvement and their expectations, which opens up a reflection bearing on what founds respite foster care practices. It was explained how some parents can talk about their involvement: how it is analyzed and sustained, even when it consists in forms of avoidance or opposition. Co-operation is indeed an interactive relationship in which it would be useful to ask further questions concerning the point of view of the professionals.

A granted co-operation demands a constant vigilance in order to dissolve the antagonisms characteristic of an unequal relationship, bearing rivalries and woven into an assessment of parenthood by professionals. The tensions between the legitimations of parents and professionals in such situations of constraint cannot disappear. To a certain degree they are necessary so that those adults who are determined to protect and to bring up the child can be identified. The tensions found the dynamics of co-operation and rather than attempting to even them out, it would be more worthwhile to analyze them and to consider them as part of the substance of the work.

Notes

1. See, for instance, the juridical obligations defining the rights of the French customers of the 'Aide Sociale à l'Enfance' (the Children's Bureau) (according to Laws of June 6th, 1984, and January 6th, 1986).
2. According to Article 375 of the French Code Civil, concerning educational support. Note that in eight cases out of ten, residential placements of young children are operated following a Court Order (a so-called 'Ordonnance de Placement Provisoire').
3. We will not go into the issue of educational tasks in this chapter.
4. Strategies were constructed in reference to the work of Kellerhals and Montandon (1991).
5. The research study, together with my colleague Dr. Dominique Fablet, was done in 1996 in three residential foster centres for very young children. In total 35 children (from 30 families) were in care. Different research methods were applied: document study, observations, and interviewing. 13 parents or members of the children's environment were actually interviewed. Eight parents were totally out of sight for practitioners as well as for researchers because of disappearance, admission into a psychiatric unit, long prison sentences, or death.
6. Comparable results were described by Jenkins and Norman (1972) and Conen (1997).
7. The analysis chart of social and educational interventions proposed by Boutin and Durning (1994) can be a useful help, especially if one is interested in items bearing specifically on the place that is left to parents.

References

Becker, H. (1963). *Outsiders*. New York: The Free Press.

Boutin, G., & Durning, P. (1994). *Les interventions auprès des parents. Bilan et analyse de pratiques socio-éducatives*. Paris: Unpublished report.
Conen, M.L. (1997). *Elternarbeit in der Heimerziehung*. Frankfurt am Main: IGfH (2nd ed.).
Deutsch, M. (1962). A theory of cooperation and competition. *Human Relations, 2*, 129-152.
Durning, P. (1986). *Éducation et suppléance familiale. Psychosociologie de l'internat spécialisé*. Paris: Centre Technique National d'Etudes et de Recherches sur les Handicaps et les Inadaptations (CTNERHI).
Durning, P. (1991). A psychological approach to foster-parenting in residential care. In W. Hellinckx, E. Broekaert, A. VandenBerge, & M.J. Colton (Eds.), *Innovations in residential care* (pp. 227-235). Leuven: Acco.
Durning, P. (1995). Exploring parenting roles. In M.J. Colton, W. Hellinckx, P. Ghesquière, & M. Williams (Eds.), *The art and science of child care* (pp. 221-236). Aldershot/Brookfield (USA): Ashgate.
Durning, P. (1999). *La partage de l'action éducative entre parents et professionals*. Vaucresson: Centre de Recherche de l'Education et Formation (CREF) (Etude CREF, Instruments et méthodes, CNFE-PJJ, Vaucresson, nr. 1, 12/99).
Elias, N. (1939). *Die Gesellschaft der Individuen*. (Translation of *La Société des Individus*, Paris: Fayard. 1991). Frankfurt am Main: Suhrkamp Verlag.
Ghesquière, P., Hellinckx, W., & Baartman, H.E.M. (1995). Multi-problem families: Investigating the client perspective. In M.J. Colton, W. Hellinckx, P. Ghesquière, & M. Williams (Eds.), *The art and science of child care* (pp. 207-219). Aldershot/Brookfield (USA): Ashgate.
Jenkins, S., & Norman, E. (1972). *Filial deprivation and foster care*. New York/London: Columbia University Press.
Kaiser, C. (1995). Conceptions de la prise en charge socio-éducative de jeunes enfants: Instrument d'exploration auprès d'une population de parents. In R. De Paolis, et al. (Eds.), *Petite enfance en Suisse Romande* (pp. 129-142). Lausanne: Réalités Sociales.
Kellerhals, J., & Montandon, C. (1991). *Les stratégies éducatives des familles*. Neuchâtel: Delachaux and Niestlé.
Kohn, R., Abda, O., Callu, E., & Famery, K. (1994). Les initiatives parentales: La dynamique de leur articulation avec les initiatives instituées pour l'éducation de leurs enfants. In P. Durning, & J-P. Pourtois, (Eds.), *Education et familles* (pp. 163-188). Bruxelles, De Boëck.
Mackiewicz, M-P. (1998). La coopération dans la relation de suppléance: Quelle transaction sociale? *Chronique Sociale* (pp. 90-97). Paris: L'Harmattan.
Sinclair, R., & Grimshaw, R. (1997). Partnership with parents in planning the care of their children. *Children and Society, 11*, 231-241.
Wrightsman, L., O'Connor, J., & Baker, N. (Eds.) (1972). *Co-operation and competition: Readings on mixed motive games*. Belmont: California Books.

Chapter 14

Listen to the Client. (Foster) Children about 'Difficult' Parents: How to Handle Conflicts with Them

Elly Singer, Jeannette Doornenbal and Krista Okma

Introduction

In the 1920s Vygotsky, one of the founders of a socio-historical approach to developmental psychology, was apprenticed to an experienced clinical psychiatrist (Vygotsky, 1936/1993). Vygotsky witnessed several consultations with parents, and these experiences made him realize what the challenge of developmental pathology should be. For instance, take the consultation of a mother with an unmanageable boy of eight. The mother had noticed problems at home, but since he started school the problems had become more marked. According to the mother, 'the child had strong and unmotivated fits of temper, passion, wrath and anger. In such a state he could be dangerous to those around him; he might throw a stone at another child or attack someone with a knife' (p. 242). After questioning the mother, the psychiatrist concluded: 'Your child is epileptoid.' (Today one would say he had a Conduct Disorder or Attention-Deficit Hyperactivity Disorder). Vygotsky continues: 'The boy's mother became attentive and started to listen closely. "What does that mean?" she asked. "It means that the boy is irritable, wrathful, and temperamental; it means that when he is angry, he forgets himself and can be dangerous to those around him; he might throw a stone at another child, and so forth." Disillusioned, the mother exclaimed: "But I have just told you all this myself."'(p. 242). Vygotsky, analyzing this episode, concludes that the problem is that the Epileptoid diagnosis cannot solve the practical problems of this mother. Epileptoid is only a descriptive concept. What failed was a theoretical analysis of the dynamics of the boy's behaviour from a developmental and pedagogical perspective. Without understanding the psychological functioning of the boy, the psychiatrist cannot give practical advice to the mother. Focussing on descriptive labels keeps the psychiatrist or pedagogue from listening to the child and understanding his or her inner logic (Vygotsky, 1936/1993, p. 274).

Thanks to the Diagnostic and Statistical Manual of Mental Disorders (American Psychiatric Association, 1994) or Child Behavior Checklist (Achenbach, 1991), the descriptive diagnostic categories are refined. But nowadays theoretical frameworks are still needed to understand the development of problem behaviour. This challenge forms the background of this study on how (foster) children deal with conflicts with their parents (Singer, Doornenbal & Okma, 2000).

A theoretical framework and an interview instrument were developed to study the dynamics of children's behaviour from their own perspective. The aim was to understand children's *inner logic*, that is, the connections children make between their actions, the goals and values they pursue, and their emotions and emotion regulation.

The main research questions are: What do children do in situations of conflict with their parents? Which goals do they want to obtain? Which underlying interests/values and emotions are at stake? Do foster children differ or resemble children who live with their own parents – we call them 'own children' – in these respects?

The reason to compare foster children with own children is that foster children are presumed to be 'problem children' (Robbroeckx & Bastiaensen, 1992; Scholte, 1995). As a result, they are often approached as being problem children. And the more problematic children are, the more often they are labelled and become objects of concern, instead of subjects with their own views (Johnston, Yoken & Voss, 1995; Smart, Wade & Neale, 2001). But when we talk seriously with (foster) children and begin to understand their inner logic, maybe their strange and sometimes fierce behaviour becomes understandable.

This chapter begins with some theoretical considerations. (For an extensive explanation of the theoretical framework used, readers are referred to Singer, Doornenbal & Okma [2000].) Then brief methodological remarks will be made about the research group and the methods used. The main goal of this contribution is to present some of the research results which shed light on the inner logic of children in a disciplinary situation. In conclusion, the implications for child and youth care will be discussed.

Theoretical Considerations

This research into the inner logic of children is related to three recent developments in developmental psychology and pedagogy.

The first development is the acknowledgement at a theoretical level that not only parents and other educators (including child and youth care workers) are raising children. Children, too, are active participants in these processes. Children contribute to their own development and upbringing. Subscribing to this assumption, children's knowledge about and insights in themselves have to be taken into consideration (De Winter, 2000; Garbarino, Scott & Bass, 1989; La Greca, 1990). In every family, parents and children disappoint or do not understand one another, and even disagree about vital issues (Waksler, 1996). In these conflicts at least two parties are involved. To solve these conflicts, mutual understanding is essential. Thus when clinicians and/or care workers want to mitigate these tensions, they have to focus not only on the parents' perspective, but on the children's perspective as well. This insight motivated us to talk in depth with children about their ways of dealing with conflicts with their parents.

The second development is the insight, rapidly gaining ground, that people's psychological functioning is context-bound. Pretzlik (1997), for example, found that in different situations children cope differently with stress. Children confronted with an injection by a doctor use other coping strategies than they do when confronted with teasing at school. Consequently, if professionals want to know how children deal with conflicts with their parents, they will probably not find any unifying answers. On the contrary, they would have to ask them explicitly about their activities, goals, values and emotions in different specific situations. This insight motivated us to talk to children about their ways of dealing with difficult parents in three problem situations.

The third development is the neo-Vygotskyan theories and constructionist theories of the affective (emotional and moral) development, which shed new light on the development of cognitive-affective schemes (Day & Tappan, 1996; Diaz, Neal & Amaya-Williams, 1990; Van Emde, Biringer, Clyman & Oppenheim, 1991; Haste, 1993; Killen & Hart, 1995; Miltenburg & Singer, 1999, 2000). These theories assume a unity between cognitive and emotional processes which are distinguishable only at an analytical level. In human activities this unity becomes visible. The nature of the cognitive-affective schemes is situational and social, because they are based on and acquired through social relations and through repeated experiences with certain people in certain contexts. The concept of a cognitive-affective scheme is the cornerstone of the theoretical framework in this research for analyzing children's inner logic (Singer, Doornenbal & Okma, 2000). In this study, studying how children deal with difficult parents in different situations means analyzing the cognitive-affective schemes that are evoked. On which underlying 'decisions' about reality do they base their activities, goals, values and emotions? What affects their activities and emotion-regulation: what are their goals, values and emotions?

Method

A semi-structured interview was developed which was administered to 45 foster children and 48 'own children' (children living with at least one of their biological parents) aged 8 to 13 years old. Most children had Dutch native parents; 25% had immigrant birth parents. The research group consisted of 50 girls and 43 boys. The foster children were recruited with the assistance of five regional organizations that counsel foster care families. The counsellors selected children of the right age group who were in the same foster care family for at least six months. They passed letters describing the research to the foster parents and children. The parents and children who wanted to co-operate contacted us by phone or mail. The children living with their biological parent(s) were recruited with a letter for the parents and children through the schools. A selection of own children was made to match the foster children qua age, sex and socio-economic background.

The children were presented with three *fictitious* situations in which a child (named *Maarten* for boys, and *Merel* for girls) is confronted with a problem caused by a parent. The first case is about a disciplinary situation. The child asks the father if (s)he may watch a television programme which other children are allowed to see. The father refuses. The second case is about a crisis of confidence. A mother is telling her neighbour a child's secret. While the women are laughing, the child comes in. The third case is about a false accusation. A father accuses the child of losing his pen, but it is the father's own fault. Subsequently, the child was asked if she or he had a *real-life* example of such a situation. If so, she or he was asked to recount the event, and the same questions as about the fictitious situation were posed: What would the child do? What does the child want to achieve, what makes the child want that, what does the child feel and how?

The interviews took place at the child's home, in the child's room preferably – for privacy reasons. Most interviews lasted between one-and-a-half to three hours. To get and hold the children's attention and to engage them in the task, some props were developed: pictures of the standard situation, a thermometer on which the child can indicate the amount of severity, emotion faces, and pictograms to remember their own event. To give the children control over the interview, they were given a stop sign to indicate that they did not want to answer a question, to stop the interview or to take a break (Garbarino & Scott, 1989; La Greca, 1990).

The stories of the children were transcribed and entered into the computer. The data were analyzed with a qualitative data program, *QSR Nud*ist* (1997). The analyzing process was started with a deductive procedure, based on our theoretical assumptions. Based on the interview material the categories were inductively altered and readjusted. This turned out to be a labour-intensive process, because every new situation added new (sub)categories. The main categories we worked with were:

Severity of the situation	Very severe; fairly severe; not severe.
Acts	Towards parents; towards yourself.
Goals	To get your own way; to persuade the parents by taking their limits into account; to pursue mutuality; to obey; to save yourself.
Interests	Moral (you have to keep a secret, children ought to be treated equally, you have to make up after a quarrel); social (I want to belong to the peer group, I don't want be laughed about); personal (I'm afraid to lose control, I want to be proud of myself).
Emotions	Angry; sad; guilty; ashamed; proud; happy; neutral; confused; scared; fake.
Emotion-regulation	Strategies to communicate your emotions; strategies to hide your emotions; strategies for inner regulation of emotions.

Findings

This chapter presents the results of an analysis of the *disciplinary situation*: What would children do, feel and think, and what do they want to obtain when a parent refuses something which other children are allowed? Firstly, some quantitative data about the reactions of the children to the fictitious situation and in their own stories will be discussed. 91% of the children told a story about a disciplinary situation (41 foster children and 44 own children). To see if there were any significant differences between the foster children and the own children, the chi-square statistic was computed for each separate category within the main categories of acts, goals and emotions. An alpha level of .05 was applied. Only differences that were significant according to this level are pointed out in the tables. Secondly, the psychological processes are discussed in more depth by presenting the inner logic of two children.

Children Talking about a Disciplinary Situation: Quantitative Data

On the question: How severe do you find the parent's refusal?, the majority of the children answer that it is fairly severe or not severe at all. In the real life situation 34-39% find it very severe.

Table 14.1 Severity of the situation (in percentages)

Severity	Foster Fictitious	Foster Real life	Own Fictitious	Own Real life
Very severe	33	34	19	39
Fairly severe	47	29	58	41
Not severe	20	24	21	16
Missing values	-	12	2	5

A remarkable difference between the foster and the own children is that the foster children find the fictitious situation more often very severe, while the own children more often think that their real-life story is quite severe.

Subsequently, the child was asked what he or she did in this situation. Most children name more than one act, mostly combining parent-related and self-related acts.

Table 14.2 Main actions of children (in percentages)

Actions	Foster Fictitious	Foster Real life	Own Fictitious	Own Real life
Parent-related actions:				
Sneaky	47	2	56	2
Exercise pressure	45	15*	40	36*
Asking why, arguing	44	68	48	70
Communicate emotions	20	46*	33	68*
Withdraw	31	32	33	39
Obey, give up	16	49	13	39
Self-related actions:				
Distraction and cognitive restructuring	20	51ª	33	58ª
Express emotions when alone	7	27ª	8	32ª

* $p < .05$ according to X^2.
ª The numbers for these categories in real life stories are higher than the numbers in the fictitious stories, because in real life stories the inner emotional regulation is explored further.

Table 14.2 shows a considerable difference between the acts the children put forward in the fictitious situation and in the own story situation. For example: doing what is forbidden in a sneaky way is almost reduced to zero in the real life stories, whereas it is one of the most favourite actions in the fictitious situation. Asking why and arguing with their parents and communicating emotions are more common acts in the real life stories than in the fictitious situation.

The most remarkable difference between the foster children and the own children concerns the act 'exercising of pressure on parents'. Pushing a parent is a loved strategy of own children, both in the fictitious situation and in their own story. This is not the case for the foster children (the own children use this strategy significantly more often than foster children, $X^2=5.2$, $p < 05$). In the fictitious situation they often imagine this strategy, but in their own stories they seem to fear the consequences. The foster children seem more restrained. They try to persuade their parents by showing their anger or sadness less often than the own children ($X^2=4.1$, $p <.05$).

What do you want to reach by doing so? is the next question the children had to answer. Table 14.3 reveals the goals the children say they strive for.

Table 14.3 Goals (in percentages)

Goals	Foster Fictitious	Foster Real life	Own Fictitious	Own Real life
Get your own way	62	15	68	30
Persuade the parent	36	54	36	50
Obey	11	10	6	2
Mutual solution	2	12	6	11
Save yourself	18	32*	19	11*

*$p <.05$ according to X^2.

In the fictitious situation, the children mainly want to get their own way, but in their own story they more often want to persuade their (foster) parents (by communicating emotions, asking questions and by bringing arguments forward). The children want to see where they can get by taking into account the parents' limits. Just obeying parents is not generally a normal goal for children. Most children are searching for more space. Mutual solution is often not their goal, either. Most children act from their own point of view in disciplinary situations.

With regard to children's goals, the same phenomenon of restraining – as seen previously – can be found in the foster children. The foster children try to save themselves (significantly more than own children), whereas the own children more often try to get what they want.

As said before, another aspect of inner logic is the interests and/or the motives at stake. To find out which interests are touched upon in the disciplinary situation, the children were asked: What makes that goal so important to you? Table 14.4 gives an overview of the interests touched upon.

They answered this question as follows. They say: 'I want that because I like to see that movie. It's funny. So I try to persuade them' (personal interest). Two other vital values are, firstly, the social value of being with other children or not being laughed at or teased – both in the fictitious situation and in their own story – and secondly, the moral value to be treated the same as other children – especially in the fictitious situation.

Table 14.4 Most mentioned moral, social and personal interests/values (in percentages)*

Interests/values	Foster Fictitious	Foster Real life	Own Fictitious	Own Real life
Moral: equal treatment	60	37	52	30
Social: other children	76	76	67	67
Personal: my own way	89	80	98	82
Personal: to avoid worse/punishment	22	24	6	9

*All children mentioned several interests.

The foster children, in comparison to the own children, are more frequently motivated by the fear of making things worse. This fear makes them in real life more reserved in trying to get their own way than own children. But the foster children probably share the same desires as the own children: in the fictitious situation they mention the goal of 'having their own way' at the same rate.

Another interview item is questions about the emotions provoked in this disciplinary situation (see Table 14.5). Most kids say this situation makes them feel angry and sad. These feelings – especially sadness – are mentioned in the fictitious situation more often than in the own story. Although guilt is a rare emotion in this situation, foster children mention it more often. No remarkable differences between the foster and the own children were found.

Table 14.5   Evoked emotions (in percentages)

Emotions	Foster Fictitious	Foster Real life	Own Fictitious	Own Real life
Anger	80	66	79	73
Sadness	82	49	69	48
Shame	11	7	8	9
Guilt	16	7	2	-

Table 14.6   Strategies to regulate emotion in the real life situations, i.e. anger (in percentages)

Strategies	Foster	Own	Total
Only strategies to communicate to parents	31	15	23
Only strategies to hide from parents	45	24	34
Strategies combining communication and inner Regulation	17	61	40

More foster children than own children try to hide their anger from their parents, while more own children use a double strategy: on the one hand, they communicate their anger to their parents, and on the other hand, they use strategies for inner regulation so that they can dose their anger towards their parents. Strategies for hiding and inner regulation of anger which the children often mention are distraction, relativeness, and expressing your anger when you are alone. Some children have well-developed rituals for self-regulation of anger.

The foster children and the own children do not differ in their strategies for regulating their sadness. Half of the children try to hide their sadness from their parents, and even more children (59%) only express their sadness when they are alone.

The General Picture

The general picture is that most children find it (a little bit) bad that a parent forbids them something that other children are allowed to do. In such a situation, most children try to get their own way, mostly by asking why and showing their emotions, especially their anger. They want to persuade their parents without going too far. In the first place, they are strongly motivated by their personal interests to get what they want. Yet most children do not want to make their parents angry or to spoil the relationship. In the second place, the children are motivated by the moral value that it is unfair that they are not treated as other children. Besides, they are afraid that they may lose their social position at school or in their peer group.

It is clear that Dutch children do not accept parental authority right away. Maybe we can best characterize the dominant pattern as living in an *emotion culture*. Children want to get their own way because they *feel* they want something; personal interests seem to be more important than moral and social interests. Children call on their emotions to get what they want. Knowing how to regulate their own emotions, they play on the emotions of their parents. Moreover, their behaviour is the result of their affective relationships with others. They restrain their emotions because of their bond with their parents and they want something because of their bonds with other children.

Most children also try to argue with their parents. However, it can be questioned whether 'asking why' and 'arguing' can be labelled as a process of negotiating. On the one hand, the line between arguing and nagging is thin. According to some children, their parents dislike their ongoing argumentation and why-questioning, and the children therefore use these actions to exercise pressure. On the other hand, arguing with a parent is difficult for children under 13 years, because adults have more verbal power. A girl reported that she could never win a dispute with her mother. So she had to use more 'childish' emotional behaviour.

The overall picture of living in an emotion culture is stronger for the own children than for the foster children. Foster children call on their emotions less often to influence their parents; they withdraw more often to express their emotions on their own or to seek distraction; they are more afraid of making things worse and they try to prevent their foster parents' anger. An explanation for this is that foster children do not feel as secure in their relationship with their foster parents as own children do with their parents. If this is the case, they lack an important and essential tool for living in an emotion culture: the possibility of working on the emotions of their foster parents. Besides, this presupposes that the child is convinced that she or he is of value to the parent; that the parent will be concerned when the child is angry or sad, disappointed or unhappy. Own children, on the other hand, probably presuppose that their bond with their parent(s) is unconditional. However difficult they behave, they are not really afraid of destroying their relationship with their parent(s). Some own children seem to think that they can get what they want, and that kicking, shouting or threatening is acceptable behaviour.

The Inner Logic of Individual Children: Qualitative Data

To examine this general picture of the data in more detail, one must take a look at the logic of children on an individual level. To do this Liza, a foster child, and Jeroen, an own child, are introduced. Both children say that they behave oppositionally in the real life situation; i.e. they communicate fierce feelings of anger, they put pressure on their parent(s) to get what they want. Nevertheless, whereas their visible behaviour is similar, their logic is very different. In Liza's story, inner conflicts and confusion become clear. As shown in Table 14.2, exercising pressure on parents was rare in foster children and if they do so, in almost all cases these rebellious acts are related to inner conflicts. Jeroen's story shows a conflict in which exercising pressure on his parents is a means to get his 'rights'; this type of inner logic is found in a fifth of the own children and in none of the foster children.

> *Liza, an eleven-year-old foster child*
> Liza told us that she, being the youngest, must go to bed earlier. Sometimes when she gets out of bed, she finds the family together with chips and cola. She wants to join them, have a cookie too. But her mother refuses, because she has already brushed her teeth. 'When I'm not getting very angry, I'm asking over and over again: why don't I get a cookie just like the others? In the end, I leave the room without saying goodnight. But when I'm very, very angry then I smash the door and stamp up the stairs. I hope it will wake up one of the babies and make them cry. When my mother or father comes to my room, I try not to talk to them because I'm very angry. I think to myself: why haven't I slapped them in the face, because I didn't dare! I think they're stupid! I'm glad they are not my own parents. I will never talk to them again. I hope they get angry at me so I can show them: you see, you never loved me anyway! That's what I'm thinking then. But my mother can't sleep when I'm angry, so she always comes to me. At the end we talk to each other and then it's over.'

On the basis of this story hypotheses about Liza's logic can be made.

- When Liza feels herself set back compared to the other children, her belief that she is not welcome and loved is confirmed.
- This hurts very much, often too much. Uttering her pain through anger has several advantages. Angry thoughts soften the pain. When Liza thinks 'she's not my own mother' or 'I want to break with them', it hurts less.
- Besides that, when she makes her parents angry, she can show them that they never loved her anyway. Then her world is predictable: the

behaviour of her parents fits in with her belief that she is not loved. Then she is no longer confused.
- In addition: by acting out her anger she can manipulate her mother. Her mother will do everything to smooth things out. Then she can feel that her mother cares for her.
- Yet maybe, because she has forced her mother, this good feeling cannot beat her basic belief of not being welcome. So, after some time, she has to repeat this procedure.

Jeroen, an eleven-year-old boy, living with his own parents
Jeroen told us that he wanted to play laser games for his birthday party. His mother refused. First, he kept nagging. His mother promised him that she would talk about it with his father. The next day, his parents let him know that their answer was definitely no. Then 'I got red and a little bit impudent and went to my room stamping my feet. I wished my mother and father would be angry at me and that they would give in within a few days. It was very important for me – other kids were allowed, so why not me. And I thought laser games were very cool. I showed my parents my anger by sitting in my room for three hours, playing music very loudly. I wanted to get their attention, so that they would feel pity for me and would say yes in the end. But instead my father gave me a fiery sermon. Then I stopped. If I am confronted with such a situation again, I think I must tackle it harder. So keep nagging and go on with it till they relent. Then I will say: you don't have much to say about me, you're not the boss. I am allowed to set my own rules'.

On the basis of Jeroen's story, the following hypotheses about his inner logic can be distilled.

- He thinks: I am my own boss. If I use my power, I have a big chance of winning. My parents' weak spots are: they feel pity for me when I'm unhappy and they want to get rid of my problem behaviour. Only if my parents stick to their guns will I see that they have a point and will I give in.
- His main interest is personal: to get his own way. His moral interest is to be treated equally as other children. His social interest is that he wants to be one of the kids.

Liza's and Jeroen's behaviours are both oppositional. They nag, stamp their feet, try to have it their way. Despite this, their inner logic is fundamentally different. To exaggerate the differences: Liza lacks confidence in the love her parents feel for her. They must prove it to her again and again. On the other hand, Jeroen has so much confidence in his parents' love that he takes over the power position when they do not set rigid limits. He is an epitome of a child living in what we called an emotion culture. This cannot be said of Liza.

Conclusions

On the basis of the research results, five conclusions can be enumerated which have consequences for parents and educators, and child and youth care in general.

The first conclusion is that in order to understand children's behaviour it is necessary to look further than their observable behaviour. This means that a diagnosis based on descriptive behavioural terms only, like the Diagnostic and Statistical Manual of Mental Disorders (American Psychiatric Association, 1994), is insufficient. Theoretical frameworks are needed to understand the dynamic psychic mechanisms behind observable behaviour. A possible way of achieving this is to analyze children's inner logic to understand why they do what they do. It is easy to interpret the nature of Liza's behaviour in the same way as Jeroen's – but then we fail to see the different inner logic at the basis of the same observable behaviour. When a child's inner perspective is unknown, it is not possible to support the child adequately and to give it what it needs. An intervention might even make things worse. Liza needs help in solving her inner conflicts. For instance, she may need to learn more constructive ways to test her foster parent's trustworthiness in case she is overwhelmed by emotions of insecurity and sadness, related to her history of being abused and abandoned. Jeroen does not ask for lenience, but rather for parents who do not confuse upbringing with indulgent love.

Second, oppositional behaviour on the part of the foster children was strongly related to inner confusion and conflicts. In own children, oppositional behaviour was predominantly a means to get their own way. Many foster children in this study made a great effort to suppress their anger and to not be oppositional. They tried to conform because of a fear of punishment or due to the conviction that it would not be successful.

Third, this study has shown that school children have well-developed psychological theories about their parents' and their own behaviour. If good interview techniques and instruments are used, they appear to be able to talk about their theories. When the right questions are asked, they are very capable of making explicit which goals, which moral, social and personal interests, and which emotions lie at the basis of their behaviour.

A fourth conclusion concerns the important differences between what children say about the vignette situation and about their real life experiences. Children demonstrated more guts when talking about the vignette situation and they set other goals, et cetera. Consequently, if professionals wish to find out more about the children's inner lives and/or their own perspective, they cannot base their knowledge on children's talk about fictitious situations only. Nevertheless, much research on children's perspectives is based on what children say about fictitious situations (Dodge, 1993; Kohlberg, 1984; Orobio de Castro, 2000).

Fifth, the two other situations are currently being analyzed. The assumption of *contextuality* seems to be reaffirmed. For example, whereas getting their own way is the main goal in a disciplinary situation, in a situation of damaged faith, saving your self-respect is the aim of most children. Their acts, feelings and thoughts are connected with that aim. This means that problem behaviour should not be seen as a treat or disorder of people, but as actions occurring in specific situations. A general diagnosis of problem behaviour fails to take this contextuality into account. Essentially, pedagogical help to children is about making contact, finding common ground and fitting in with the child's motivation for learning and change. So, *we must listen to them* and try to understand their inner logic for their behaviour in a specific context.

References

Achenbach, T.M. (1991). *Manual for the Child Behavior Checklist/4-18 and 1991 Profile.* Burlington, VT: University of Vermont, Department of Psychiatry.

American Psychiatric Association [APA] (1994). *Diagnostic and statistical manual of mental disorders* (4th ed.). Washington DC: Author.

Day, J.M., & Tappan, M.B. (1996). The narrative approach to moral development: From the epistemic subject to dialogical selves. *Human Development, 39,* 67-82.

De Winter, M. (2000). *Beter maatschappelijk opvoeden. Hoofdlijnen van een eigentijdse participatie-pedagogiek.* Assen: Van Gorcum.

Dodge, K.A. (1993). Social-cognitive mechanisms in the development of conduct disorder and depression. *Annual Review of Psychology, 44,* 559-584.

Díaz, R.M., Neal, C.J., & Amaya-Williams, M. (1990). The social origins of self-regulation. In L.C. Moll (Ed.), *Vygotsky and education* (pp. 127-154). Cambridge: Cambridge University Press.

Garbarino, J., & Scott, F. (1989). *What children can tell us.* San Francisco/London: Jossey Bass.

Haste, H. (1993). Morality, self, and sociohistorical context: The role of lay theory. In G.G. Noam, & T.E. Wren (Eds.), *The moral self* (pp. 175-208). Cambridge, Mass.: The MITT.

Johnson, P.R., Yoken, C., & Voss, R. (1995). Family foster care placement: the child's perspective. *Child Welfare, 74,* 959-974.

Killen, M., & Hart, D. (1995). *Morality in everyday life.* Cambridge: Cambridge University Press.

Kohlberg, L. (1984). *Essays on moral development. Vol 2: The psychology of moral development.* San Francisco: Harper & Row.

La Greca, A.M. (1990). *Through the eyes of the child. Obtaining self-reports from children and adolescents.* Boston: Allyn & Bacon.

Miltenburg, R., & Singer, E. (1999). Culturally mediated learning and the development of self-regulation by survivors of child abuse: A Vygotskyan approach to the support of survivors of child abuse. *Human Development, 42,* 1-17.

Miltenburg, R., & Singer, E. (2000). A concept becomes a passion. *Theory and Psychology, 10,* 547-570.

Orobio de Castro, B. (2000). *Social information processing and emotion in antisocial boys.* (PhD dissertation). Duivendrecht: Paedologisch Instituut Amsterdam.

Pretzlik, U. (1997). *Children coping with a serious illness. A study exploring coping and distress in children with leukaemia or aplastic anaemia.* Amsterdam: University of Amsterdam, SCO-Kohnstamm Institute.

QRS Nud*ist. User guide. (1997). California: Thousand Oaks.

Robbroeckx, L.M.H., & Bastiaensen, P.A.C.M. (1992). De Nederlandse pleegzorg tegen het licht gehouden. Een inventarisatie van 20 jaar onderzoek en beleid omtrent pleegzorg in Nederland. *Gezin, 4,* 108-133.

Scholte, E.M. (1995). Het plaatsen van jeugdigen in pleeggezinnen en residentiële centra. *Tijdschrift voor Orthopedagogiek, 34,* 99-114.

Singer, E., Doornenbal, J., & Okma, K. (2000). *(Pleeg)kinderen over 'moeilijke' ouders. Een onderzoek naar de manier waarop kinderen omgaan met alledaagse conflicten met hun (pleeg)ouders.* Utrecht/Groningen: Universiteit Utrecht/Rijksuniversiteit Groningen.

Smart, C., Wade, A., & Neale, B. (2001). Object van bezorgdheid? Kinderen en echtscheiding. In C. Van Nijnatten, & S. Sevenhuijsen (Eds.), *Dubbelleven: Nieuwe perspectieven voor kinderen na echtscheiding* (pp. 11-30). Amsterdam: Thela Thesis.

Van Emde, R.N., Biringer, Z., Clyman, R.B., & Oppenheim, D. (1991). The moral self of infancy: Affective core and procedural knowledge. *Developmental Review, 11,* 251-270.

Vygotsky, L.S. (1993). The diagnostics of development and the pedological clinic for difficult children. In R.W. Rieber, & A.S. Carton (Eds.), *The collected works of L.S. Vygotsky, vol. 2. The fundamentals of defectology* (pp. 241-291). New York: Plenum Press (original published in 1936).

Waksler, F. (1996). *The little trials of childhood and children's strategies for dealing with them.* London/Washington: Falmer Press.

Chapter 15

Listen to the Client. Battered and Abusing Women Speak of Their Early Victimization in Out of Home Placement

June Price

Introduction

It was their whispers that pushed you, their murmurs over pots sizzling in your head. A thousand women urging you to speak through the blunt tip of your pencil. Kitchen poets, you call them ... These women, they asked for your voice ... And this was your testament to the way that these women lived and died and lived again (Danticat, 1996, pp. 222, 224).

This study focuses on the relational experiences of two vulnerable populations who were in foster care and residential placement. Participants included women reported for child abuse and battered women. A qualitative, phenomenological method was used which enabled the researcher to give a voice to the participants, to tell the story of their experience in their own words, and also to synthesize the core of that experience.

For these women, that essence encompassed early trauma, devising survival techniques, revictimization, and as adults, re-enactment of the earlier traumas. Battered women would re-enact their experience with men, and child abusing mothers with their own children. Both populations were unaware of the connections between their past history and their present relationships.

Researchers have documented that a foster child is seven to eight times more likely to be identified as abused while in care, and a child in residential care is six times more likely (Hobbs, Hobbs & Wynne, 1999, p. 1246). Chernoff (1994) reported that 81% of children in placement have a prior history of abuse. Trauma theories address the phenomena of attachment disorders, the likelihood of victims to be re-victimized, and the little understood potential for victims to re-enact their earlier experiences (Herman, 1992; Terr, 1991; Van der Kolk, McFarlane & Weisaeth, 1996). Yet little is known about the meaning of personal relationships in these populations, and no prior work is available that explores the experience of being in relationships throughout their life spans.

Method

Six mothers, all previously reported for child abuse, and five women who had been chronically battered were interviewed in depth about the history of their relationships with people important to them – including biological or blood parents, fantasy families, relatives and fictional kin, out of home caretakers, friends, peers, boyfriends, pimps and husbands. Interviews were based, in part, on the drawing of relational maps that covered their life spans (Josselson, 1992).

Using the phenomenological methods of Giorgi (1985) and Van Manen (1990), interview transcripts were coded for small, unique meaning units, or 'de-contextualized' (Tesch, 1990, p. 118). Later, these codes were 're-contextualized' (Tesch, 1990, p. 122), a process that involves identifying related concepts, developing themes, and interpreting meaning. Stories or narrations resulted that illustrated the essence of these relationships. Further analysis developed and examined metathemes and patterns that expressed the totality of their experiences. Related phenomenological literature, such as fiction, poetry, and autobiographies were also used to further the hermeneutic process. Interpretations were member checked with the participants.

Findings

The words of one of the participants will tell the story of how our systems abet in the creation of characters out of the Odyssey, moving from Scylla to Charybdis. As a young child, *Lisa* was neglected and exploited by her mother and her mother's boyfriend. She was later placed out of home ten times before her sixteenth birthday.

Lisa's Story

'My mom, she wouldn't have much time to spend with me. She used to be sick all the time, drinking, and my brother ain't notice me. We were crazy poor, had no electricity and little to eat. My mom would let me do whatever I want. My ma got a boyfriend who was homeless. She brought him in, my brother threw him out, but she kept taking him back. And he would keep buying her beer, beer, beer. She used to take me out at night with her, and I'd hate it. She wants to go sit in the park drinking, and he'd be doing his bumming scam. We'd be standing there and he'd walk up to a car, and the next thing you know, people would be looking at you. Cause he'd say: "We need money, that's my little girl over there". Then when I was eight, my mother died. She didn't wake us up, and I went into the living room and I was shaking her. She didn't wake up and she had blood on her nose and in her eyes. I was like, "Oh, why won't she wake up! What's the matter with her?".

When my mother died, I go to my aunt's house. My aunt used to dress me nice, buy me good clothes, do my hair. My aunt was like: no TV, no nothing. Wanted me to do my homework. I used to cry every night. They gave me Christmas, and I had everything under the tree. I never had a tree before. I stayed with them for one year, and she decided to put me in foster care. They had no room.

One day, the Lady came. She says, "You're going to live in a house, going to be with a family". I'm going to have a sister! Later, it felt like my family gave me up. Here I was with this other lady, have to call her 'Mom'. Like your first day is really weird. The first family was Jamaican, I couldn't understand a thing they said. But after two years I start sounding just like them. I thought I was going to stay with them. I didn't know they didn't want me. One day, I go to the agency, and they told me that they're putting me with another family. By then, I was like: "Oh, well, I don't care". I just had an attitude. "Well, I didn't want to stay with them anyway." But I was attached to them. I went to another family, they was Spanish. I tried to call them 'mom' and 'dad', but it didn't come out right. There was no bonding there. I felt like I ain't fit in there. This funny feeling you get. They told the agency that it didn't work out.

Now, I'm 12 years old. I go to the Brown's. Mrs. B., she was like color funny. She's from down South, and they have light colored skin. She used to call me 'big nose' and names like 'darkie'. Say, "How evil you are". She didn't like my braids, said it was too niggerish. She talk about you like a dog. Call me 'fast ass'. Say, "You're going to be like your mom". I had told her how it was with my real mom, the welfare and the boyfriends, and she'd just throw it up in your face. And her husband, he was always grabbing me, trying to feel me up. By then, you catch an attitude. And she hit on me too much. One time, she told me to cut a lettuce. There's a certain way to do it so it doesn't fall apart. I'm looking at it – saying which way?

So I just cut it, and it falls apart. My mom, she comes in and says, "I'll tell you, you little black heifer, what to do with it!". So she pushes me up against the refrigerator with the knife at my throat.

I went back to the agency, and told them how she hit me. They call her in and she says: "Listen, I ain't got no time to be taking off work for this nonsense. That's right, I hit her 'cause she was being fresh". So the agency was like, "Well Lisa, you're too old now, ain't nobody else going to take you". Me and her never got along. So I've been in group homes ever since, in and out, in and out.'

Ping Pongs

As the poet Maya Angelou (1971) once wrote: 'Why they send us away? And what did we do so wrong? So wrong ...' (p. 43). Lisa was placed so often, she always felt like second hand goods. The natural children of foster parents taunted her, and the adults assured her of her status by their verbal battering and banishment. Participants in both studies were continually bounced around from place to place, batted back and forth from caretaker to caretaker. This inconstancy of relationships was described by the participants as the natural course of events. It neither surprised nor shocked them, it was simply the way it was. Ping pong relationships at times reflected problem solutions for the participants' families. Child care arrangement were complex and frequently reconstructed. Adverse conditions such as death, the inability to financially care for a child or a desperate need to escape an abusive partner, led to children being placed out of the home. Sometimes, these placements were triggered by a parent's need to maintain a relationship with a partner, and the child was perceived to be in the way. Since the participants' parents often had multiple partners, the children would appear, disappear, and reappear, batted back and forth between various extended families and agencies.

Anya, who was severely physically abused and had been raped as a child, moved to a relative's home at the age of nine where she was sexually abused by her uncle. Yet she recalled that experience as 'being in heaven', comparatively, she was better cared for in that home. By the time Anya was sixteen, she had moved seven times between the homes of blood and fictive kin. *Yvonne* moved from her grandmother's home, to her mother's, to three foster care placements by the time she was sixteen. *Simone* was also eight years old when her mother disappeared and left her alone in the apartment. She was placed in foster care and spent two years locked in an attic with another foster child before the system intervened. *Daisy* was placed in foster care when her mother ran away from her battering boyfriend, and her grandmother refused to care for her.

Survival Techniques

Dissociation

The American author Toni Morrison (1988) called it 'dismemory', George Orwell (1984) called it 'memory holes', and trauma theorists call it 'dissociation'. There may be a repression of traumatic events, a dreamlike quality of recollections, and a massive denial of one's own history where it is unavailable to the individual.

Emotional responses are split off and also unavailable. While reducing pain, dissociation also leads to a lack of awareness and insight into one's own behaviour, to impaired judgements about others, and to the misreading of social cues, all of which are associated with problems in interpersonal relationships. At the same time, it is 'one of nature's small mercies' (Herman, 1992, p. 43), minimizing the stress of life events.

The foundation for future relationships has been set: participants 'get an attitude' – being in relationships is dangerous, and connections to others are ambivalent, often ephemeral. Pain and betrayal are the expectations.

Dodging Bullets

The only way to avoid the subsequent pain and the label of 'You're no good, you're just trash' was to never love again, to never let anyone get too close or too important. Participants became 'possessed by their ghosts' (Fraiberg, Adelson & Shapiro, 1975, p. 388), haunted by their early experiences of attachment to others. Without the experience of being held dear, and held securely, the participants had no tools available to them to banish the ghosts, to put the stake through the heart of the beast. Being chronically humiliated, *Lisa* 'disinherited' everyone: 'It's just me. I ain't got no family members. I don't want to be bothered'.

Future relationships were modelled on previous experience. In fact, supportive relationships could not be assimilated or accommodated. Safe, secure, and nurturing relationships were too foreign and too frightening. The individual had expectations of pain and betrayal, and knew how to cope – she had survived those experiences after all.

Substance abuse also served the psyche, nurturing the dissociative process through chemicals – a few hours of peace, no pain, and no memories. *Evalynn* described this phenomenon of spacing out as 'I'm just floating from place to place'.

The Sitting Duck Syndrome

Participants repeatedly placed themselves in danger. Due to their use of dissociation, they did not appear to remember past experiences that were dangerous or harmful, and could not recognize cues of danger in the present. Extremely vulnerable, they exhibited what Kluft (1990) termed, the 'sitting duck' syndrome. Out of home placement was the first chapter in their stories of being re-victimized. Other forms of re-victimization included rape, prostitution, battering, poverty and homelessness.

Researchers are now beginning to gain a better understanding of the physiology of trauma, the 'black hole of trauma' (Van der Kolk & McFarlane, 1996, p. 3), including lasting changes in the limbic system, a decrease in inhibitory control, fragmentation of emotional memory from informational memory, and an increase in endorphins creating an actual 'high' when revictimized. Experiences are not forgotten, but rather 'dismember'-ed (Morrison, 1988, p. 188), disallowing connection with one's own life story.

The Ugly Duck Syndrome

Through out of home placement, participants were alienated from their own roots and lacked a sense of community or belonging to a social group. They were like the ugly duckling that never found a world of swans. Lacking this sense of belonging, they had no model for creating a world of family-marriage-children. They had never been included, or sensed the feeling of 'you-are-part-of-us'. They could not identify a sense of belonging to either their family of origin, which was never a stable concept, or to their ethnic or racial background.

Re-enactment of Traumatic Events as the Victimizer

Severe and chronic childhood abuse, dissociation, and re-victimization set the stage for later dysfunctional and destructive relationships with their men and with their children. As mothers, they perpetrated abuse on their own children, frequently recreating identical scenarios of their own traumas without any recognition or awareness of the repetition. There was a deafness, a blindness, and a chilling emotional distance (for a summary – see Table 15.1).

Table 15.1 Analysis of participants' experiences: categories and themes

I. A history of chronic and severe child abuse
emotional and/or physical
sexual
neglect
witnessing abuse
multiple abusers
betrayal
traumatic bonding
'you're no good' – unwanted and unloved
'ping pongs' – inconsistent caretakers

II. Survival techniques
'dismemory' and 'memory holes' – dissociation
'gettin' an attitude' – belligerence
'dodging bullets' – avoiding relationships
substance abuse
attachment disorders

III. Re-victimization: the 'Sitting Duck' syndrome
'ping pongs' – multiple out of home placements
rape
prostitution
battering
poverty and homelessness
the 'ugly duckling' – alienation from community

IV. Re-enactment of traumatic events as the victimizer

Lisa had suffered physical, sexual and emotional abuse in foster care and out of home placements. She had spoken of 'the Lady' who would always come to move her to the next placement. Years later, 'the Lady' reappears in her story as she talks about her own children: 'Sometimes I get so ... I think if I didn't have the kids, I would really be working. There's been times that I walked down to foster care, and I said to the Lady: "What's it like to be in care?". Karen keeps crying. Sometimes I get into a good sleep, and she wakes me up, screaming. It just makes me crazy 'cause she gets me so mad. And like as soon as I walk, all of a sudden she'll be right underneath me, and I'll be falling over her. And Maya, I don't understand her no more. She's the reason this place be a mess. I'd straighten up and then by the end of the day, toys be all over, and I'm like ... So, lots of times, I sit and think about it.'

Implications and Conclusion

Knowledge of a history of abuse is essential, with an understanding that violence may be a way of life, a world view, not simply a symptom of pathology. The notion of social support is a concept that has been imbued since childhood with danger and betrayal. Sequelae of an abuse history, including fear, distrust, and feelings of entrapment will effect any attempt to develop a helping relationship.

Clinicians should consider the possibility that behaviours they are taught to recognize as symptoms of deviant behaviour, may in fact be problem solving solutions for victims of trauma. Truancy, running away, substance abuse, and child abuse can serve as escape routes from an impossible situation. These behaviours provide the exit doors from the living hell of chronic trauma victims.

Vulnerable populations such as child abusing mothers and battered women must be helped to remember their own experiences. Violent behaviour will not change until there is integration of the traumatic experience with the appropriate affects of anger, pain, and sadness (Herman, 1992). The trauma victim needs to learn to feel safe, to feel empowered, and eventually, to be in control of her own life story.

Researchers on resilience to traumatic events in childhood support the idea that the consistent presence of a caring adult plays a critical role in resisting the long term effects of maltreatment (Heller, Larrieu, D'Imperio & Boris, 1999). Emotional support from a caring person, including a foster care parent or relative has been noted to be a factor in breaking the intergenerational cycle of abuse (Egeland, Carlson & Sroufe, 1993; Hunter & Kilstrom, 1979; Werner, 1989).

There is also evidence that resilience is not a fixed trait, but rather a fluid concept (Herrenkohl, Herrenkohl & Egolf, 1994), 'dependent on environmental context' (Heller et al., 1999, p. 334). This evidence allows for the potential to intervene, to develop a meaningful relationship with a caretaker, even in adolescence.

In conclusion it must strongly be recommended to listen to the client. *Anya* concluded her interviews by saying: 'Even though I had people in my life, I had no one. And that's the end of my life story. Remember the damage. The hurt. Remember me! Remember me! The pain. Remember you sent me away to a loveless place. Remember you murdered my soul'.

References

Angelou, M. (1971). *I know why the caged bird sings.* New York: Bantam Books.
Chernoff, R. (1994). Assessing the health status of children entering foster care. *Pediatrics, 93,* 594-601.
Danticat, E. (1996). *Krik? Krat!* New York: Vintage Books.
Egeland, B., Carlson, E., & Sroufe, L. A. (1993). Resilience as process. *Development and Psychopathology, 5,* 517-528.
Fraiberg, S., Adelson, E., & Shapiro, V. (1975). 'Ghosts in the nursery'. A psychoanalytic approach to the problems of impaired infant-mother relationships. *Journal of the American Academy of Child Psychiatry, 14,* 387-421.
Giorgi, A. (Ed.) (1985). *Phenomenology and psychological research.* Pittsburg (PA): Duquesne University Press.
Heller, S.S., Larrieu, J.A., D'Imperio, R., & Boris, N.W. (1999). Research on resilience to child maltreatment: Empirical considerations. *Child Abuse and Neglect, 23,* (4), 321-338.
Herman, J. (1992). *Trauma and recovery.* New York: Basic Books.
Herrenkohl, E.C., Herrenkohl, R.R., & Egolf, B. (1994). Resilient early school-age children from maltreating homes: Outcomes in late adolescence. *American Journal of Orthopsychiatry, 64,* 301-309.
Hobbs, G.F., Hobbs, C.J., & Wynne, J.M. (1999). Abuse of children in foster and residential care. *Child Abuse and Neglect, 23,* (12), 1239-1252.
Hunter, R.S., & Kilstrom, N. (1979). Breaking the cycle in abusive families. *American Journal of Psychiatry, 136,* 1320-1322.
Josselson, R. (1992). *The space between us.* San Francisco: Jossey-Bass.
Kluft, R.P. (1990). Editorial: The darker side of dissociation. *Dissociation, 3* (3), 125.
Morrison, T. (1988). *Beloved.* New York: Penguin.
Orwell, G. (1984). *1984.* New York: Signet (original work published in 1949).
Terr, L. (1991). Childhood traumas: An outline and overview. *American Journal of Psychiatry, 148,* (1), 10-20.
Tesch, R. (1990). *Qualitative research: Analysis types and software tools.* London: Falmer Press.
Van der Kolk, B.A., & McFarlane, A.C. (1996). The black hole of trauma. In B.A. Van der Kolk, A-C. McFarlane, & L. Weisaeth (Eds.), *Traumatic stress* (pp. 3-23). New York: The Guilford Press.
Van der Kolk, B.A., McFarlane, A.C., & Weisaeth, L. (Eds.) (1996). *Traumatic stress.* New York: The Guilford Press.
Van Manen, M. (1990). *Researching lived experience.* London, Ontario: State University of New York Press.
Werner, E.E. (1989). High-risk children in young adulthood: A longitudinal study from birth to 32 years. *American Journal of Orthopsychiatry, 59,* 77-85.

PART IV

EPILOGUE

Chapter 16

The Challenge in Child and Youth Care Research and Practice: Professionalization *and* Participation

Erik J. Knorth, Peter M. Van den Bergh and Fop Verheij

Introduction

In Chapters 2 and 3 two conceptions of the position of the child in the last century were critically discussed: the 20th century as the 'Century of the Child' (Dekker) and the 20th century as the 'Century of the Participating Child' (De Winter). Both images proved to be open for discussion, and neither the romantic portrayal of a child nor the engaged portrayal of a child corresponded (or corresponds) with reality. The conclusions that were drawn in these chapters are that child and youth care is characterized as: increasingly professional but (still) hesitantly participatory.

An important challenge at the beginning of the 21st century is, we think, to critically follow and guide both tendencies. This means first further designing, and if necessary experimenting with these concepts in practice, with specific emphasis on enhancing the active involvement of those in need of care. And second, using scientific research to explore the meaning of 'p&p practices' for the quality of child and youth care. As a conclusion to this book we will now further reflect on this challenge.

Professionalization

Garfat and Newcomen (1992), in the following quotation, give an interesting sketch of the development towards a professional child and youth care (short: cyc): 'In the early days, before the introduction of training opportunities, academic degrees, conferences, and the development of a body of child and youth care literature, most front-line workers had no alternative but to intervene with children without any models to guide their actions. They were expected to do the job *as if* they knew what they were doing. With the increasing complexity of the field, it became evident that this was not an acceptable way to proceed and, in more recent years, the field has responded to the need. There is now a wealth of literature specifically addressed to the work of child and youth care workers ...' (p. 277).

The authors comment that today the understanding of the *content* of the cyc-work has grown. Gradually more is known about the nature and background of children, youth and parents that are in need of support from youth care services. Also, the amount of literature about intervention variables and models is extensive.[1] In Chapters 5, (Lindsay) and 6 (Shealy) in Part II of this book, it is also demonstrated that it requires a good and long-term education and training to become familiar with important parts of this continuously growing body of knowledge. Furthermore, more and more is known about relevant organizational variables. In Chapters 8 (Colton), 9 (Savicki) and 10 (Breda and Verlinden) evidence-based suggestions are given on how to tackle and/or prevent two important problems in child and youth care, unacceptable behaviour and burnout of practitioners.

However Garfat and Newcomen also signal an, in their eyes, important omission: attention for cyc-work as a *process*. 'Like all professionals, child and youth care workers need to develop a way of thinking about the process of their work ... It is not enough to understand the content; one must also have a way of organizing one's interventions with children in a clear manner. Although the available literature successfully addresses the content of child and youth care work, there is little that addresses process ...' (Garfat & Newcomen, 1992, p. 227). By process is meant the way in which cyc-workers organize *their own thinking* about client needs and interventions. The model they offer in this context, called with a playful acronym AS*IF, consists of five phases:

- *A*ssessment (careful mapping of the situation of the troubled children and families);
- *S*election (selecting the intervention that is the most appropriate for the situation);
- * pause and preparation (aimed at reconsidering the selected intervention and preparing the implementation, including care and treatment planning);
- *I*ntervention (carrying out the intervention process);

- *Follow-up* (closely observing, evaluating and if necessary adjusting the chosen approach).

This model shows strong resemblance to process models like those developed by Van Strien (1986), Knorth & Smit (1995; 1999), and Verheij (1998; 2001) in The Netherlands,[2] and a model developed by Taylor and Devine (1995) in the UK. The latter authors suggest that a four phase model (assessment – planning – implementation – evaluation) is basic. However all authors emphasize the cyclic character of the models they propose.

In research literature indications can be found that structuring the thinking process of a practitioner according to one of the earlier mentioned patterns, contributes to more transparency both in the considerations that are made during the treatment process and the treatment process itself (Knorth & Smit, 1999). In fact, a growing number of countries already put such a process into operation with the emphasis that is placed on working with care and treatment plans (Chapter 7) (also see Van den Bergh & Klomp, 1998). In the Netherlands an extensive protocol has been developed by Verheij (1998) and others.

... *and* Participation

What is remarkable in these models is that the position of the client is not strongly articulated. That is not surprising when considering that these concern primary models to support the practitioner's process of reasoning and acting ; the models capitalize on the professional expertise of child and youth care staff. However, Part III of this book has shown why it is necessary to attune the professional process to the needs and views of children, youth and parents, and why it is profitable for all parties involved that clients play an active role. Sandbæk (Chapter 11) asks that attention be given to the parents of children and young people in care, and states that they often already fulfil a crucial, but largely unrecognized role. Mackiewicz, who also sheds light on the position of parents (Chapter 13), demonstrates that a good co-operation can be built with most parents, but this requires an active effort from cyc-workers. The same message is offered by Sinclair (Chapter 12), but this is now directed towards children and youth: good preparation of and active listening to young clients in the context of a review-meeting will influence, in a positive sense, the involvement of youth, and will therefore advance the care process. In fact this implies that giving more attention to the process, as above described, concerns not only the professional but also the client. *In each phase* of the care process the dialogical character of this process should take shape. This is reproduced in a schematic way in Figure 16.1, in which the phases model of Taylor and Devine (1995) is taken as starting point.[3]

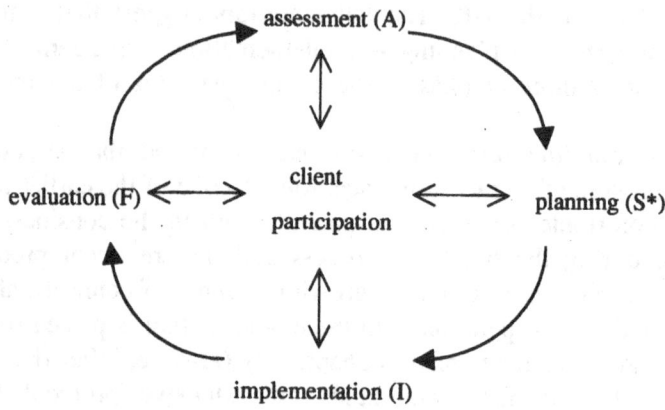

Figure 16.1 The process of professional thinking and treatment in relation to client participation

A Challenge for Practice and Research

Realizing a participatory approach to professionalization (cf. Chapter 1) will not happen by itself. On the contrary, it asks for a pro-active attitude from child and youth care workers: they face the *challenge* of actively helping to realize the conditions for a dialogue with clients, both in the direct interaction with children, youth and parents, but also in considering the organizational conditions that can facilitate client participation. Also, it is desirable that working models supporting such client participation that have already been developed or will be developed, are evaluated with the help of scientific research. Some examples of such 'practices' on the level of interaction with clients are: a negotiation approach of assessment with parents (Van Audenhoven & Vertommen, 2000); working with goal attainment scaling and contracting (Hermanns, 1995); to use a preparatory guide for youth for review meetings (Wheal & Sinclair, 1995); and the model of feedback-interviewing, as conducted by Singer et al. (Chapter 14) and Price (Chapter 15).

A type of research that is very appropriate for this combination of innovation and evaluation is known as *programme evaluation* (Harinck, Smit & Knorth, 1997). Programme evaluation is usually associated with the question of whether a programme – for instance a behavioural approach to the anxieties of a specific target group – produces the intended results (in the example: reduction of fear for the participating clients). This type of programme evaluation is also called *product evaluation*.

A second, and for practice, very instructive version of programme evaluation is known as *process evaluation*. As already suggested by the name, this type of research is pre-eminently suitable for answering all kinds of questions with regard to the process of child and youth care (Harinck & Smit, 1995; Pietrzak et al., 1990). Examples of questions are: What activities are involved in the programme? Which clients participate and what is their role? How do they perceive their role? Which clients drop out, and why? Which parts of the programme need adjustments? Et cetera. Characteristic for this type of research is also that, between the researcher and representatives of the practice (cyc-staff, clients), emphatic consultation takes place about the design (which questions do we want to be answered?) and about the results (what are the implications for practice?). The collected data are quickly fed back with a view to optimizing the quality of the programme concerned.

Interesting in this context is a research-agenda used to improve the prospects for children in out-of-home placement, that Courtney (2000) recently formulated. In the first instance he makes a plea for extensive programme evaluation research (see also Rutter, 2000). According to Courtney the purpose of this research is not only to find results in the long term ('ultimate outcomes'), but also to give more attention to 'intermediate outcomes' (for instance, an increase in parental involvement in treatment, a progression in the social skills of young people, a growth in self confidence, changes in the motivation of clients); these intermediate results offer a better starting point for feedback on the care process. Furthermore he requests attention for research on the quality of decision processes in child and youth care (and, we would add, the role of clients in these processes), and the impact of organizational variables. Finally, Courtney proposes to do more research on the course of the treatment process with clients from ethnic minorities; since active participation for these clients is under extra pressure because of the sometimes hard to bridge cultural differences.

With Courtney's agenda which in a general sense complements the line of thought described above, we give one short comment: that listening to what clients have to say about the care they received deserves extra attention in research. The results often are remarkably simple and committing. For example: When youth are asked what is the best that they have experienced in care – and this concerns residential care – then the answer is, according to Fletcher, that they '... were getting "treated well" and there was always "someone to talk to or someone to listen"...' (Fletcher, 1993, p. 84). Youth can describe what 'getting treated well' means in a detailed manner. There is a lot to learn from children and young persons in care and their parents.

Notes

1. For instance the voluminous publication by Alan Carr (1999) offers a good overview. Also very informative is the publication from the Department of Health (1998).
2. Van Strien (1986) distinguishes the phases: Formulation of Problem – Diagnosis – Plan – Intervention – Evaluation. Knorth & Smit (1999) distinguish the phases: Diagnosis – Decision-making – Planning – Implementation – Evaluation. Verheij (1998) distinguishes the phases: Examination – Diagnosis – Treatment Planning – Treatment/Support.
3. However, in the figure, the phase-designations of the AS*IF model are added between brackets (Garfat & Newcomen, 1992).

References

Courtney, M.E. (2000). Research needed to improve prospects for children in out-of-home placement. *Children and Youth Services Review, 22*, 743-761.

Carr, A. (1999). *The handbook of child and adolescent clinical psychology: A contextual approach*. London/New York: Routledge.

Department of Health (1998). *Caring for children away from home: Messages from research*. Chichester: John Wiley & Sons.

Fletcher, B. (1993). *Not just a name. The views of young people in foster and residential care*. London: National Consumer Council (in cooperation with the Who Cares? Trust).

Garfat, Th., & Newcomen, T. (1992). AS*IF: A model for thinking about child and youth care interventions. *Child and Youth Care Forum, 21*, (4), 277-285.

Harinck, F.J.H., & Smit, M. (1995). Process evaluation in residential care. In M.J. Colton, W. Hellinckx, P. Ghesquière, & M. Williams (Eds.), *The art and science of child care* (pp. 153-170). Aldershot: Arena.

Harinck, F.J.H., Smit, M., & Knorth, E.J. (1997). Evaluating child and youth care programs. *Child and Youth Care Forum, 26*, (5), 369-383.

Hermanns, J.M.A. (1995). Besluitvorming in de jeugdzorg; het hulpverleningscontract als alternatief. In J.M.A. Hermanns, E.J. Knorth, H.M. Pijnenburg, & I.A. Sleeboom (Eds.), *Besluitvorming in de jeugdzorg: Praktijk en perspectief* (pp. 111-127). Houten: Bohn Stafleu Van Loghum.

Knorth, E.J., & Smit, M. (1995). A systematic approach to residential care. In M.J. Colton, W. Hellinckx, P. Ghesquière, & M. Williams (Eds.), *The art and science of child care* (pp. 171-188). Aldershot: Arena.

Knorth, E.J., & Smit, M. (1999). Planmatig handelen in de jeugdhulpverlening: Theorie en praktijk. In E.J. Knorth, & M. Smit (Eds.), *Planmatig handelen in de jeugdhulpverlening* (pp. 25-54). Leuven/Apeldoorn: Garant.

Pietrzak, J., Ramler, M., Renner, T., Ford, L., & Gilbert, N. (1990). *Practical program evaluation*. London: Sage.

Rutter, M. (2000). Children in substitute care: Some conceptual considerations and research implications. *Children and Youth Services Review, 22*, 685-703.

Taylor, B.J., & Devine, T. (1995). *Assessing needs and planning care in social work*. Aldershot: Arena.

Van Audenhoven, C., & Vertommen, H. (2000). A negotiation approach to intake and treatment choice. *Journal of Psychotherapy Integration, 10*, 287-300.

Van den Bergh, P.M., & Klomp, M. (1998). Erziehungspläne als Steuerungsinstrumente der Jugendhilfe. *Praxis der Kinderpsychologie und Kinderpsychiatrie, 47*, 767-772.

Van Strien, P.J. (1986). *Praktijk als wetenschap: Methodologie van het sociaal-wetenschappelijk handelen*. Assen/Maastricht: Van Gorcum.

Verheij, F. (1998). *Behandelingsplanning in de jeugdzorg en het speciaal onderwijs*. Utrecht: SWP Publishers.

Verheij, F. (2001). Behandelingsplanning: Een misbare of onmisbare schakel? In H. Pelzer, & P. Steerneman (Eds.), *Diagnose van de diagnostiek* (pp. 47-67). Leuven/Apeldoorn: Garant.

Wheal, A., & Sinclair, R. (1995). *It's your meeting. A guide to help young people get the most from their review meetings*. London: National Children's Bureau.

Index

Active listening 243
Affective development 215
Antagonism (between parents and professional) 203
AS*IF model 242
Assessment 193, 243

Behaviour
    anti-social 180
    observable 225
    oppositional 225
    unacceptable 242
Being School 88
Blaming the parents 181
Body of knowledge 242
Breakdown of placement 180
Burnout 135, 149, 242

Care plan(ning) 107, 191, 196, 199, 243
Caseload 3
Century of the Child 27-31, 241
Century of the Participating Child 49-55, 241
Child abuse 125, 230-234
Child and youth care worker 3, 85
    characteristics 95
Child as Co-researcher 56
Child Behaviour Checklist (CBCL) 214
Child protection case conference 196
Children Act 39, 192
Circles of influence 83
Citizenship 54, 55
Client feedback 6, 245
Co-education 206
Coercive assistance 164
Cognitive-affective scheme 215
Collaboration strategy (of parents) 205
Collectivism 136
Communal living 121
Competence of parents 179
Connectedness 57
Constructionist Theory 215
Consultation 193, 195
Co-operation with parents 202, 206

Coping 138, 155
    process 138
    strategy training 155
Costs of Care 67
Cross-cultural difference 144
Cultural work value 136
CYCNet 83

Decision-making 193
Deductive 172, 217
Deficiency principle 186
Delegation strategy (of parents) 205
Delinquency 180
Depersonalization 150
Developmental perspective 213
Diagnosis 225
Dialogical character of care process 244
Dialogue 55, 57
Disciplinary situation 217
Disenchantment 31-33, 42
Dissociation 233
Dodging bullets 233
Doing School 88

Ecological model 71
Economic consideration 65
Educational level 3, 78
Educator 85
Effect, effectiveness 6, 54
Emotion culture 222
Emotional exhaustion 146
Empowerment 6, 179
Entzauberung 31-33, 42
Epistemology 179
Ethical standard 4
Ethics 66, 80
Eugenics 30-31
EUSARF xii
Evaluation 243
Expert model 111

Family Group Conference 196
Feedback interviewing 245
Femininity 136

FICE 66
Foster child 216-223
Foster family care 121
Foster home breakdown 179
Funding 72

Goal Attainment Scaling 244
Guard 85

Hofstede's Cultural Work Value Scale (CWV) 141
Holistic perspective 71
Homeless youth 56
Human rights 129

Ideographic theory 5
Images of childhood 34
    Original Sin 34
    romantic 34
    tabula rasa 34
Implementation 243
Individualism 136
Inductive 172
Inner logic 214
Input 2, 160, 167
Inquiry 193
In-service training 116
Institutional abuse 121
Involvement model 111
Involving children 185
Involving parents 179, 185, 207

Knowledges, Skills and Abilities (KSAs) 96, 97

Lack of placement stability 180
Learning environment 55
Legitimations of parents 204
    competency based 204
    formal 204
    normative 204
    presence based 204
Length of stay 109

Masculinity 136
Maslach Burnout Inventory (MBI) 135, 141
Model 71, 87, 91, 111
    AS*IF 242
    ecological 71
    expert 111
    involvement 111
    participation 111
    therapeutic home parent 87, 91

N=1 theory 5
Nederlandsch Mettray 36
Negotiation approach (of assessment) 244
New coalition 69
Normalization 53
Number of children in (residential) care 1, 18, 69
Nurse 85

Objective working condition 175
Observable behaviour 225
Opposition strategy (of parents) 205
Output 2, 160

Parental correlates of offspring psychopathology 94
Parental Strategy 205
Parenthood 202
Parents as co-ordinator 182
Parents as partners 179
Participation 193, 243
    of children 5-9, 49, 52-55, 193
    of parents 179, 201
    level of 8-9
    nature of 8
    reasons for 5-6
Participation ladder 9, 19
Participation model 111
Participatory 52, 58
    approach 11
    culture 199
    curriculum 58
    meeting 192
    pedagogy 52, 58-60
    planning 199
    school 58
Pedagogical
    pathology 38-39
    perspective 213
    province 50
    utopia 30
Peer-research 56
Personal accomplishment 152
Perspective
    constructivist 184
    developmental 213

Index

Philanthropists 35
Ping pong relationship 232
Positivist method 184
Power distance 136
Predetermined Standard 160
Preparatory guide (for review meeting) 244
Prevention (of burnout) 149, 171-175
Problem solving 236
Process
   of care 2
   linking 167
   primary 2, 160
Process evaluation 245
Product evaluation 245
Production system 149
Profession 123
Professional
   attitude 79
   identity 75
   organization 161
Professionalism 18, 76, 173
   as continuum 71
   degree of 69
   key aspects of 76-77
   level of 71
Professionalization 2-5, 122, 173
   bureaucratic approach of 10
   clinical approach of 10
   expert approach of 10
   market-like 70
   participatory approach of 11
   problems related to 67-69
   sources of 4
   values-based approach of 11
Programme evaluation 245
Protective factor 184
Public image of child care 82
Pyramid of learning 79-80

Quality 161
   care 2, 108, 126
   criteria 7
   indicator 108

Recognition of CYC profession 3, 82
Re-education 35-36
Re-enactment of trauma 234
Referral policy 172
Reform Pädagogik 30
Research-agenda 245

Residential care 35, 67-69, 122
Resilience 236
Respite foster care 201
Revictimization 229
Review-meeting 192-195
Rights (of parents and children) 6
Risk factor 184
Romanticism 30, 42

Self-government by children 51
Sitting Duck syndrome 234
Social
   education gap 49
   educator 85, 124
   participation 59
   pedagogue 124
   support 236
   work 164
Special Education 181
Staff shortage 84
Status of profession 66, 77, 81
Structure of habits 138
Subjective perception 175
Substance abuse 233
Supervision 154
Supervision order 202
Survival technique 229, 233-234

Team supervision 116
Teamwork training 154
Theoretical analysis 213
Theoretical framework 214
Therapeutic Home Parent Model 87, 91
Therapist efficacy 93
Therapist factors 92
Time registration 165
Tokenism 61
Total institution 129
Transparency 243
Trauma (theory) 229
Treatment plan 107

Ugly Duck Syndrome 234
UN Convention on the Rights of the Child 40, 52
Utopia 30

Vignette situation 226
Violence 236
Voluntary assistance 164

Work Behaviours (WBs) 96
Work Environment Scale (WES) 142
Workload 159, 168-169

Youthland 50